SUCCESS WITH
UNUSUAL PLANTS
James Compton

SUCCESS WITH
UNUSUAL PLANTS
James Compton

Photographs by David Russell

COLLINS
8 Grafton Street
London W1X 3LA

To my children, Philip, Clephane and Lara, and
to Rebecca

First published 1987 by
William Collins Sons & Co Ltd
London · Glasgow · Sydney
Auckland · Toronto · Johannesburg

British Library Cataloguing in Publication Data

Compton, James
Success with unusual plants.
1. Gardening—Great Britain
I. Title
635'.0941   SB453.3.G7

ISBN 0 00 410441 2

Photoset by Ace Filmsetting Limited, Frome, Somerset
Colour origination by Bright Arts, Hong Kong
Printed and bound in Italy by New Interlitho SpA, Milan

CONTENTS

Acknowledgements

I wish to thank all those whose love of plants has inspired me over the years. Special thanks go to David Russell who buoyed me up when doubt crept in. Much credit for the piecing together of this book goes to Yvonne Rees and David Palliser, whose editing and typing were essential.

Susan Conder enabled me to feel more creative and brought in a professional touch to the book, and on the same note so did Caroline White, my editor at Collins.

My appreciation and gratitude extend formally to The Trustees of the Chelsea Physic Garden, especially to Duncan Donald, the Curator, who often turned a blind eye to certain elements of research. Also to the Director of The Royal Botanic Gardens, Kew; The University of London's Botanic Garden at Egham; The Royal Horticultural Society's garden at Wisley and many other gardens too numerous to mention.

I hope above all that there will be enough space on one of Harriot's bookshelves for this book.

Note for North American Readers

North America has been divided into seven zones based on the annual minimum temperatures. These zones run nearly parallel to the southern boundary of the area, but their boundaries are modified by elevation, mountains, river valleys and other features. A map showing these zones can be found on p. 185 to help ascertain to which zones different regions belong and which plants included in this book may be expected to grow there. Under each plant entry the relevant climatic zone is listed.

Under favourable conditions and with proper protection plants will survive in localities further north than the zone to which they have been referred.

INTRODUCTION

The idea for this book came to me many years ago and has been lying dormant waiting for the right moment to germinate. In that time I have been slowly amassing information and increasing my personal knowledge of plants in the belief that one day, the seeds of my idea would take the shape you see here.

The book is principally a collection of beautiful, interesting and surprisingly easy-to-cultivate plants which I feel should be better known and more widely grown in our gardens. They are not botanical weirdos with little or no garden value: plants which grow massively tall and produce microscopically small flowers once every twenty years. Most are hardy and prolific, and all have been chosen for both their practical and aesthetic qualities. I have also taken care to include only plants which can be obtained commercially and there is a list of specialist nurserymen and useful addresses at the back of the book. It has been encouraging every year to see an increase in the number of these charming plants available.

Strange as it may seem, the popularity of a certain species is as vulnerable to the quirks of fashion as a hemline or hairstyle. I can remember working in C. R. Rassell's garden centre in London's Earls Court Road as a lad of eighteen and selling the fascinating climber *Cobaea scandens* 'Alba' which you very rarely see today. A much earlier memory is of my parents proudly buying a *Jasminum polyanthum* which now appears on every street flower stall but which was very unusual then.

It was when I was a student at the Royal Botanic Gardens, Kew, that I began to realize the vast number of species which are relatively unknown, even to the keen or ambitious gardener. I assumed that they must be difficult to grow or were in some way unsuitable, but was constantly astounded to learn that this was not always true. It often happens that a hybrid or cultivar will become popular and flood the garden centres, leaving very few people familiar with the species parent. It may not be as showy as its modern hybridized offspring, but it often beats it hands down on subtlety and charm, while frequently a feature such as scent will be lost to the cultivar.

This book deals mainly with the original wild species and forms from it; cultivars and hybrids may be referred to but only in a very limited capacity. There seems to be some general confusion over the terms species, cultivar and hybrid, so to clarify: the word species applies to plants from all over the world as found in their wild setting. A species of dahlia from Mexico for example, *Dahlia coccinea*, refers only to this plant which has single, bright red flowers, and not to hundreds of gaudy pompoms which are commonly referred to under the all-embracing name of dahlia. These are cultivars and hybrids which have been bred and altered from the parent species.

I have selected approximately 140 plants for this book and arranged them into six sections, one for each major category such as shrubs and small trees, herbaceous perennials and so on. The plants are not divided equally among these sections but reflect their natural distribution in a typical garden. Hence, there are far more shrubs and herbaceous perennials than there are climbers and alpines, for example.

I have tried to convey the virtues and statistics of the selected plants, based on my own experience and appreciation of them. Each one is described and full information is provided about its hardiness; soil and aspect preferences; moisture requirements; particulars of growth, habit and propagation; and any historical or cultural points of interest.

My words are supported by David Russell's photographs, which portray more than words ever could. Illustrations of the overall shape and growth habit are included where space permits, as well as close-ups of flowers, fruits or distinguishing features.

This is not intended as a standard reference book but rather as an inspiration to discover more about the kind of plants which Graham Stuart Thomas, Roy Lancaster and Rosemary Verey have written about and grown with such obvious interest and affection.

I hope that by reading this book you will gain some insight into the fascinating world of plants and be encouraged to grow some of these lesser known species in your own garden. You will most certainly be well rewarded.

Naming of Plants

I thought I had better deal first with the eternal question of why we have to struggle with long unpronounceable Latin names for plants. On the whole there is a very good reason for it, or I would not have spent as many years as I can remember trying to learn the meanings of some of the names.

Latin is still recognized universally as the language base for scientific names and thus *Hamamelis* is *Hamamelis* in China, North America or anywhere else. If the charming local or vernacular names were to be adopted, there would be all kinds of confusion especially with such a plant as this which has twenty different Chinese names and in North America is known as wych or even witch hazel. The English use of the wild hazel for divining led the early settlers to try the same trick with the totally unrelated but superficially similar *Hamamelis* in North America; the word 'wych' comes from the German 'wik' or 'wic' which means to bend and refers to the bending qualities of hazel, elm and alder and has nothing to do with witches. Both spellings, wych and witch, are correct, and you can see the problems that might arise using common names whose meaning can change through misunderstanding or the erosion of time.

It was in approximately 1750 that Linnaeus revolutionized and standardized the naming of plants which at that time had long, drawn-out Latin names often running to several descriptive lines. He organized them according to their common characteristics into families then broke them down further into genera and thence individual species. A plant's genus might be equated with a surname and its species with a first name thus: Smith (genus) John (species). Unfortunately life is not quite that simple in the plant world and there are smaller groups or divisions of species called subspecies, variety or cultivar. Subspecies are concise variations of a species usually caused by geographic distance, as in *Lavandula stoechas* (French lavender) and its subspecies *pedunculata* which is only found in Spain. Variety is a much misused title but correctly used applies to varieties or variants of a wild species and not to plants or seedling variants which are found in cultivation. These are

really cultivars and occur either naturally (mutants or sports) or by selection of hybrid crosses. Today all new cultivars must be given non-Latin names to differentiate the original Latin species from the cultivated variety as in *Liriope muscari* 'Majestic'. Confusingly prior to 1935 some cultivars were given Latin names. These are easily distinguished from wild varieties by the capital letter and single quotes.

The genus is always given a capital letter and the species a small one; any cultivar or hybrid name also has a capital letter and is enclosed in single quotes. These are the rules and I am bound to abide by them although I have tried to keep the names as simple and as easily understood as I can throughout this book. There is the occasional mouthful: *Allium carinatum* subspecies *pulchellum* 'Album', for example, but there are thankfully few of these!

Hybrids between two species have a × between the genus and the hybrid name; this refers to the 'cross' between the two species both of which are named in the text.

BOTANICAL AUTHORITY

The botanical names in their introductory titles are each followed by a surname or abbreviations of a surname. This is called the botanical authority and simply means that the plant's name used in this book has been made valid by that particular botanist. The botanist may have been assisted by another and so one or more names may be found alongside the introductory plant title. The authorities are important because there is often great confusion over the naming of a plant. Names in this book are the most up-to-date ones, and out-of-date names (synonyms) are given where important, e.g. *Iris unguicularis* Poir 'Alba' (syn. *Iris stylosa* Desfont). The same applies where a particular botanist in more recent times has divided one species up into subspecies or varieties.

CHANGES OF NAME

Name changes have always been the gardener's nightmare and perpetually serve to widen the gap between gardener and botanist; botanic gardeners like myself must act as mediator. There are various reasons why a plant should change its Latin name, the most common being that it was put in the wrong genus to begin with, or that the species is now reverting to an earlier name. In some cases, a plant was named at an early date, then that name overlooked for hundreds of years. *Vibernum fragrans*, for example, was collected from China in 1920 by Reginald Farrer and had to become *V. farreri* as the name *V. fragrans* had already been given to another Japanese species.

SOIL AND SUN

The world below ground level is as important to a plant as that above it, and while I have little technical knowledge of what the scientists call *pedology*, I feel it is useful to outline a few facts. There are many, many different types of soil but three main categories.

Clay soils are made up of tiny, tightly packed soil particles, which make them heavy and difficult to dig. Clay soils are usually fertile with plenty of well distributed nutrients, and good for general cultivation, but badly drained or even waterlogged. A clay soil consequently takes a long time to dry out and when it finally does, shows the characteristic mosaic of cracks over the surface. It is the least easy soil type to deal with, for apart from the effect it has on the roots of plants, it reduces digging to a slow back-wrenching process. To improve clay soil, incorporate as much manure or compost as possible; the bacteria helps break up its clay consistency and reduces clods. Incorporating sand also helps drainage.

Sandy soils are made up of large sand particles and a few smaller particles which make them lighter and easier to work. Being freely drained, however, they quickly lose nutrients. This process, in which the free-draining water washes away the goodness, is called leaching and sandy soils tend to be referred to as hungry soils. They are also often highly acid with little organic matter. Incorporate plenty of organic matter such as manure, leaf mould or compost and their continual use will eventually result in a heavier soil and less likelihood of leaching. Another problem with sandy soils and their deficiency in organic matter is that of drying out during hot summer spells. The addition of organic matter, even peat, ensures higher moisture content, making the soil less prone to desiccation and saving plants from likely death. Sandy soil can be made less acid with the ongoing addition of adequate amounts of lime, the same way that an alkaline soil can be made less so with flowers of sulphur. However, as both lime, in its natural condition, and sulphur are highly poisonous to plant roots, they should only be added to the soil when the land is clear of plants, or applied in very small quantities.

Loam soils are ideal: rich, dark and nutritious, with equal proportions of sand, silt and clay, as well as organic matter and near-neutral pH (this means an equal balance between acidity and alkalinity in the soil; acid soil has a pH below neutral, which is shown as 7 on the pH scale, and alkaline soil a pH above 7). Few gardens are endowed with this marvellous deep soil – well drained but food and water retentive – but even loam is improved by adding well rotted organic matter and keeping it well watered in dry weather.

LIGHT REQUIREMENTS

Different plants need varying amounts of sunshine in order to thrive. Large leaved, shade-loving plants tend to shrivel up and burn if they are subjected to too much intense sunlight and those such as *Kirengeshoma palmata* are far less tolerant in this respect than, say, *Mitella breweri* whose smaller leaves can withstand more light. Large-leaved shade seekers also suffer if too dry and prefer shaded woodland areas to the more exposed rock garden or herbaceous border. However, some unfortunate plants are exiled under a canopy of evergreen trees whose permanent shelter allows very little rain to filter through to the plants beneath. A tolerance to both shade and drought is asking rather too much from most plants, although there are a few willing to survive it, namely *Sasa veitchii* and *Liriope muscari* 'Majestic'.

Smaller leaved and grey-leaved plants are only happy in the open where their wind-resistant, often hairy, foliage is designed to fend off the desiccating effect of a dry wind and midsummer sun. These plants usually produce deep tap roots which are capable of providing anchorage and of seeking water a long way below ground level – the survival tactics of many herbaceous perennials, alpines and bulbs.

PROPAGATION OF PLANTS

I have always found the practical side of growing plants tremendously enjoyable. There is something very pleasing about taking on the responsibility of increasing plant life on this earth and there is a real pleasure to be had in witnessing growth in its purest form, surviving against the odds. Plants only have one chance in terms of time and energy to make roots and grow and they need all the help we can give them at this stage.

Propagation means to increase plants by natural processes from the parent stock. There are two ways of doing this: by seed and vegetatively.

PROPAGATING BY SEED

Seed is the ultimate condensing of genes from one generation of plant to another into the smallest, most self-sufficient unit. Seeds are always endowed with a combination of their parents' genes. There is therefore a risk when growing plants from seed that it may be the result of a hybrid cross between two species; it may also produce a whole variation of genetic forms which are not the same as the parent, resulting in seedlings which are not 'true to type'. Many seeds, however, will be true to type and seedlings grown from seed tend to be stronger than those grown from corresponding cuttings.

Failure with seed propagation is largely due to dormancy of the seed which can be physical or chemical. Physical dormancy is often indicated by an extremely hard seed coat which may need to be cracked slightly to allow water to penetrate and start germination. This is the case with seeds of *Halesia tetraptera*; in their natural state, their hard coats are usually cracked by frost during winter, a process which is called vernalization. There are exceptions, though. Seeds of some Australian species, for example, only germinate after forest fires burn off the hard seed coats and also help break down their chemical dormancy. Chemical dormancy is more complicated but basically is an inbuilt facility to prevent the seed's germination at the wrong time of year; thus arid terrain plants won't germinate before drought nor alpines before winter. To break chemical dormancy, the seed needs to be either heated to above say, 30°C (85°F) or frozen to well under 0°C (32°F) depending on the region of the world from which the plants originate.

A good knowledge of the plant and the climate and conditions of its place of origin are essential to successful seed germination. That said, some seeds are particularly difficult to germinate, requiring a fluctuating temperature or very specific light and temperature requirements. All seeds need water to germinate and they should not be allowed to dry out once propagation has started.

VEGETATIVE METHODS

One advantage of vegetative propagation is that you can be sure of exactly reproducing the original plant (genetic clone). There are various means of vegetative propagation.

Softwood cuttings are taken while the plant is still actively growing and are therefore green and sappy, making them root very quickly. These are best taken in late spring as soon as plenty of sappy new growth is available. Cut a 10–15cm (4–6in) branch under a leaf or alternate pair of leaves, and remove the bottom two sets of leaves before inserting the cutting into moist compost, ideally 50 per cent peat and 50 per cent washed sharp sand. Keep in an enclosed glass or polythene covered wind-free area with plenty of moisture in the air and enough light for the cutting's leaves to continue taking in energy.

Propagation units can be home-made kits comprising pots of peat with plastic bags over, supported by a stick stuck in the pot; glass jars over pots; plastic tray and cover propagators; glass-covered frames with electric heating cables under a layer of peat and sand; or, at the top end of the scale, there is a sophisticated unit which mists the softwood cuttings whenever the leaves show signs of drying out.

Semi-ripe cuttings are really softwood cuttings with a section of woody growth at the base. These can be treated in exactly the same way as softwood cuttings and are best taken in late summer as the air begins to cool. Softwood cuttings can root in under a week, but semi-ripe cuttings could take over a month. This method is particularly good for evergreens, both broad-leafed and conifer.

Hardwood cuttings are self-descriptive, taken just after the leaves of a deciduous tree or shrub fall in early autumn. Take pencil-thick cuttings 25cm (10in) long, again from below the leaf bud. Trim the top of the cutting above a bud. A hardwood cutting often takes months to root as it depends solely upon its own reserves of energy, and those reserves are utilized slowly because the cutting has to be placed outside in cool conditions. Insert up to three quarters of its length in sandy loam in a large bucket or unused flower border. Its only requirement is occasional watering if it threatens to dry out.

Once rooted, pot up all cuttings into a rich compost as soon as possible, as the peat/sand or pure sand rooting medium contains no nutrition. Overestimate the number of cuttings needed since it is easier to give away any you don't want than to make and prepare new ones, and wait for them to root.

Layering can occur naturally, as in the case of *Ribes speciosum*, or it can be encouraged. Lower branches of some shrubs, as they grow heavier, begin to bend downwards until they touch the ground. Such branches continue to grow horizontally, occasionally rubbing their undersurface against the earth when the wind blows. This rubbing slightly exposes the inner tissues and the shrub produces roots at that point. This process can be synthesized with certain shrubs by scoring the branch with a knife and pegging it to the ground with a light covering of earth to encourage rooting; induced layering works well with plants such as *Viburnum farreri* and *Punica granatum*.

By far the quickest and most practical method of increasing a plant is by dividing part or all of it up into smaller pieces. Nearly all groups of plants, except annuals, biennials and single-stemmed trees, are divisible. Herbaceous perennials, whether evergreen or deciduous, have for centuries been propagated from division. The method varies according to the growth and size of the plant; for example, a large creeping clump of *Centaurea macrocephala* can be divided when dormant into chunks of whatever size is desired by placing two large garden forks back to back and pushing them deep into the main clump. The forks are then pulled apart in opposite directions causing the clump to divide along its weakest joins beneath the soil. The resulting pieces can then be dug up and transplanted. A very large clump can be split into half a dozen or so sizeable pieces; keep these divisions as large as possible because they will settle into their new site more securely and flower earlier.

Clump-forming shrubs can be divided in a similar manner. The whole shrub should be dug up first, in order to see how big the root system really is and, once out, divisions can be made from the clump either with fork, spade or even carefully with an axe.

Finally, the approximate height and spread of each plant has been indicated. 'Approximate' is the key word, as both height and spread vary enormously according to the available space, light and nutrients, as well as the strength of nearby competing plants. In the case of most annuals, perennials and bulbs, spread is doubly theoretical, as the plants are most effective grown in tight clumps, rather than as single specimens. (In the case of semi-hardy plants, close growing affords protection from winter weather as well as visual delight.) In the text, seemingly narrow spreads indicate the optimum space between several plants in a clump.

ALPINES

Alpine plants have a dedicated clique of followers who specialize in this fascinating group of plants. I have gleaned many useful points from the writings of the master, the late Reginald Farrer.

An alpine is a plant which grows usually on the high mountain ranges of the world; 'alp' means a high green pasture, originating from the Swiss Alps. The plants are more likely to come from a windswept or rocky summit than a pasture, and there are many further subdivisions of habitat: scree, which is almost entirely shattered rock; moraine, which is glacial debris, and many different rock types which affect soil fertility and pH. Alpines tend to be perennial, rarely growing taller than a few centimetres (inches), as in *Arenaria montana*. They may, however, spread several metres (yards) horizontally, as in the case of *Genista sagittalis*, or form perfectly rounded cushions, like *Azorella trifurcata*. They can be shrubby, bulbous or herbaceous; the bulbous species are included in the bulb section of this book.

An alpine plant need not necessarily originate from a mountain summit. Similar plants inhabit the more barren boglands of New Zealand or the rocky wastes of the Arctic; some are even found in hotter, drier countries but behave like alpines in cool, temperate climates provided they are given some protection.

SITING OF ALPINES
The nature of the beast suggests exposure above ground and very often shallow or poor soils beneath. Most alpines need not sit in an immaculate reconstruction of their wild habitat and they can look very attractive set into walls, on steep banks, in the cracks of paving stones on terraces and in trough gardens. These latter can be reconstructed or natural stone, or constructed from white enamel kitchen sinks, scored then covered with cement and filled with gritty soil and rocks. The secret of alpine plants is the combination of exposed open habitat and a well drained soil.

PROPAGATION
Most herbaceous alpines, such as *Eryngium bourgati*, can be divided when dormant. Shrubs, as many silver-foliaged alpines are, can be propagated from cuttings taken in autumn, when the weather is cooler, and put in a frame or pot in a sunny position, glasshouse or cloche. Clay pots provide better drainage than plastic ones. The compost should be on the gritty or sandy side in imitation of the well drained natural environment. Sterilized garden loam, with sharp sand or grit to improve drainage, is fine or a mixture of equal parts peat and sand.

Many alpines come true from seed, left outside in pots for at least a year if the seed fails to germinate straight away. Chemicals called inhibitors sometimes prevent the seeds germinating until cold winter frosts have broken them down.

SHAPE, HABIT AND PLANTING
The adjectives applied to alpines – dwarf, squat, low, prostrate and flat – often describe a relation of a familiar plant whose physical make-up is diminished in size. *Campanula rotundifolia*, for example, is the alpine harebell as opposed to *Campanula latifolia*, a large herbaceous perennial. Alpines tend to form impenetrable cushions and mats over which snow, gales and frost pass unperturbed, as does the terrific intensity of heat from high altitude sun in summer. Many alpine bulbs have a short growing season and flower as the snow melts, before summer comes.

Alpines need a well drained, often poor, rocky soil to thrive. Many live quite happily in full sun in a small crevice with very little soil, even seemingly on the surface of the rock itself; others need a more sheltered or shady position. *Mitella breweri* can be found seeding in less exposed places. Others, such as *Veronica cinerea*, prefer a sunnier situation.

Average garden soil can be made alpine worthy by incorporating some gravel, or better still, grit, when planting alpines, ideally in spring. These, and indeed any plants, must be watered immediately after planting; the popular assumption that alpine plants live in drought conditions is erroneous. I give the rock garden a good sprinkling during dry weather, with the exception of the few alpine bulbs or tuberous plants which need a good baking to flower properly.

AETHIONEMA PULCHELLUM

Boiss.

FAMILY
Cruciferae

ORIGIN
Armenia, Turkey

HEIGHT AND SPREAD
30cm (12in) × 30cm (12in)

FLOWERING TIME
Midsummer

SPECIAL FEATURES
Pink flowers and glaucous foliage

CLIMATIC ZONE
Zone 5

Aethionema pulchellum.

It is curious how such a lovely genus fits into *Cruciferae*, the family which provides us with cabbage, radish, mustard, cress and turnip. This family, named after the Latin 'crucis' meaning a cross, has cross-shaped flowers with four filaments set between each petal also in the shape of a cross. Other *Cruciferae* genera which are garden delights include *Lunaria* (honesty), *Hesperis* (sweet rocket) and *Cheiranthus* (wallflower). There are nearly seventy species in the *Aethionema* genus, the majority easy to grow and surprisingly hardy, as they tend to come from Southern Europe or from the Middle East. Here is a clear case of a barely discovered plant waiting, like so many, to be placed in the limelight. Its beautiful cousin *A. coridifolium*, particularly in the form of its cultivar, 'Warley Rose', is known across the world, and celebrated by the great lady gardener Ellen Willmott.

Aethionema pulchellum is a rock garden beauty, the flowers a rare shade of pale pink, above glaucous dome-shaped mounds of narrow foliage and glaucous, floppy branches. These carry many minor shoots, most of which send up flower spikes. These spikes can be nearly 30cm (12in) long, although individual flowers are tiny.

Aethionema pulchellum is a lime lover and enjoys full sun and well drained soil, however stony. It is particularly attractive if planted in large clumps which ramble over the edge of rocks or sit perched between boulders. The plants may be grown very close together, say spaced 15cm (6in) apart, for a quick effect. It is very tolerant of drought, its near-succulent foliage and young branches effectively preventing water loss from the plant in driest weather. Hardy but not long lived, *Aethionema* is easily propagated. Split up large clumps in early spring or take cuttings in spring, and insert in a gritty compost in a cold frame. They may also be raised from seed, although the species do hybridize, and the resultant seedlings may not represent the parent.

ARENARIA MONTANA

L.

FAMILY
Caryophyllaceae

ORIGIN
South-west Europe

HEIGHT AND SPREAD
5cm (2in) × 15cm (6in)

FLOWERING TIME
Early summer

SPECIAL FEATURES
Robust trailing alpine with large flowers

CLIMATIC ZONE
Zone 5

The sandworts are a botanist's dream and a gardener's nightmare: there are now 250 recognized species of *Arenaria*, many of them transferred from the old genus *Alsine* which sadly no longer exists, having been divided between *Arenaria*, *Minuartia* and *Moehringia*. These three genera contain many insignificant weeds but one or two absolute treasures, such as *Arenaria montana*, acclaimed by alpine king Reginald Farrer as a must for every rock garden. *Arenaria* refers to the sand on which many of the species dwell and *montana* indicates the mountainous regions that this species comes from: rocky habitats on the Spanish and French mountains.

Arenaria montana is a mat-forming and slightly hairy plant whose green foliage is covered in white saucers which are very large in relation to the overall squatness and compactness of the plant. The branches trail over the ground like creeping thymes and can extend for more than 30cm (12in). The leaves are narrow and long, usually 1.5–2.5cm ($\frac{1}{2}$–1in), and positioned opposite each other on the branch. The flowers are produced on the ends of the branches and also on the laterals, all facing upwards to make a shining white carpet above the green. Each flower measures 1.5–2cm ($\frac{1}{2}$–$\frac{3}{4}$in) across and consists of five white petals surrounding the bright yellow stamens in the centre. A long flower stalk (pedicel) supports each flower, so that the flowers sit a little above the foliage.

Arenaria montana loves the sun and is tolerant of very cold weather. It prefers an open alkaline soil, but is not particularly fussy. I have seen it used imaginatively at Jenkyn Place, Hampshire, where it grew at the foot of a climbing plant, in a narrow strip of soil less than 10cm (4in) wide, overlapping the surrounding stones and softening the appearance of the whole area.

A. montana sets seed sparsely and is best propagated by division of the clump in early spring; its long trailing stems never layer themselves.

Arenaria montana.

AZORELLA TRIFURCATA

Pers.

FAMILY
Umbelliferae (Hydrocotylaceae)

ORIGIN
Chile and Tierra del Fuego

HEIGHT AND SPREAD
7.5cm (3in) × 1.8m (6ft)

FLOWERING TIME
Midsummer

SPECIAL FEATURES
Slow spreading compact cushion

CLIMATIC ZONE
Zone 6

An undulating carpet of *Azorella trifurcata* at Chelsea Physic Garden, London.

Azorella trifurcata was once known as *Bolax glebaria* and although both names sound slightly strange, neither really convey any impression of this remarkable plant. For me it always conjures up memories of Robert Louis Stevenson's *The Land of Counterpane* for it is literally a living tapestry, either creeping along the ground in a series of gently undulating waves no more than a few centimetres (inches) in height, or growing upwards from one point to make a perfectly round living dome.

The name 'trifurcata' means three pronged and alludes to the deeply pronged evergreen foliage which resembles a dense mat, usually no more than 7.5cm (3in) high. The plant grows by means of many branching, horizontal stems, each stem terminating in a tightly packed rosette of foliage no more than 2.5cm (1in) across. The complete cushion is made up of hundreds of these rosettes packed tightly together. The rosettes help retain moisture in times of drought and during dry, windy weather, and also protect the slow-rooting stems beneath from the worst frost. The plant has developed this way as a defence against its barren, windswept natural habitat, which makes it ideal for exposed sites in gardens.

The flowers are fairly nondescript: small, tight yellow umbels only a few millimetres (under an inch) wide or high. They serve only to produce seed and add nothing to the plant's visual merit.

As is usually the case with creeping or spreading plants, the larger they are, the faster they spread and once *A. trifurcata* has established, the clump is capable of increasing its overall size by up to 15cm (6in) all round each year. It is easy to manage and can be kept to whatever shape or size is required. It should be used more imaginatively, perhaps as an ornamental cushion in a raised bed or in an enclosed formal area, although I have never seen it grown this way.

Azorella trifurcata can be grown anywhere which is not too alkaline, preferring neutral to acid conditions. The plant does not object to heavy rainfall, but needs well drained soil, such as a gritty or sandy one, or it will rot.

Propagate by removing some layered rosettes.

ERODIUM × VARIABILE

Leslie

FAMILY
Geraniaceae

ORIGIN
In cultivation early 20th century

HEIGHT AND SPREAD
To 20cm (8in) × 20cm (8in)

FLOWERING TIME
Early summer to autumn

SPECIAL FEATURE
Excellent cushion alpine

CLIMATIC ZONE
Zone 5

The name *Erodium* rarely conjures up instant recognition and the tributes which the plants truly earn are even more rarely given. Although a hybrid, *Erodium × variabile* nonetheless represents the genus very well and shows off the plants' terrific attributes.

The genus *Erodium* is linked to *Geranium* and *Pelargonium* and tends to exhibit some of the attributes of both genera. In the case of *E. × variabile* (a hybrid of *E. reichardii* and *E. corsicum*) only the flowers of *Geranium* would give any clues as to its origin. This hybrid has an abundance of pretty whitish or pinkish, saucer-shaped flowers with reddish purple veins running into the centre. The habit of growth is a cushion and made up of many short stems, springing from a rather woody tap root.

Apart from hardiness and vigour, *E. × variabile* has the merit of blooming from early summer onwards, sometimes continuing right through to autumn. It needs full sun and well drained soil, ideally a hot, dry sloping spot in a rock garden or stony bank. The plant is a lime lover although it will also grow in well-drained acid soil. I must emphasize its preference for good drainage, because there is nothing that this plant (and many other rock garden species) hates more than a frozen, wet soil.

E. × variabile germinates freely from seed. It doesn't like being moved, but you can do so successfully providing the clump is still small and you attempt it in early spring when the weather is wet.

Erodium × variabile.

The spiky inflorescences of *Eryngium bourgati*.

ERYNGIUM BOURGATI

Gourn.

FAMILY
Umbelliferae

ORIGIN
Spain

HEIGHT AND SPREAD
45cm (18in) × 30cm (12in)

FLOWERING TIME
Late summer

SPECIAL FEATURES
Deeply cut foliage and long lasting inflorescences

CLIMATIC ZONE
Zone 4

Eryngium bourgati is a dwarf species originating in the Pyrenees. It is like the native English sea holly, *E. maritimum*, but in miniature and is green rather than blue and less obviously prickly. (I recall a painful walk over alpine turf high in the Pyrenees after paddling my feet in a mountain stream.) Less obvious is this plant's close relationship with *Daucus*, the carrot, although in the unlikely event of pulling out the roots and smelling them, you will find that many species do have a carrot-like aroma.

In the wild Pyrenean meadows the species is seen everywhere. When I was there the rosettes had already bloomed and the stout flower heads were only 30cm (12in) high. This is much shorter than the plants can grow in the tamer cultivation of our gardens. I grew some from seed and was amazed at the difference a protected site and more fertile soil made.

Eryngium bourgati is not bothered by exposure. It is indifferent to soil type and merely grows better if more food and water are made available. It slowly makes a large clump – I have seen one over 1m (3ft) across and so tightly packed that the flowers were pressed together. These are carried up to 45cm (18in) high on silvery green rigid stems. The main attraction of the flowers is the stiffly spiny radiating bract which sits like a cup beneath each one. The bract is also silvery and 7.5cm (3in) or more across.

The relatively small, deeply cut leaves of *E. bourgati* are green with prominent white veining which accentuates the leaf shape.

Lift and divide established clumps in spring or raise from seed sown in spring. Like many *Eryngium* species it may also be grown from root cuttings taken in early spring.

GENISTA SAGITTALIS

L.

FAMILY
Leguminosae

ORIGIN
South-east Europe

HEIGHT AND SPREAD
7.5–15cm (3–6in) × 45cm (18in)

FLOWERING TIME
Early summer

SPECIAL FEATURE
Evergreen ground cover

CLIMATIC ZONE
Zone 4

Although I have put this plant in the genus *Genista* it might well be found under the name *Chamaespartium sagittale*, a popular name with botanists. *Genista* itself has been acclaimed since medieval times for the yellow dye which comes from the flowers of dyer's greenwood, *G. tinctoria*, and there are more than seventy-five species, nearly all of which have yellow flowers. *Genista* has royal connections – it gave the Plantagenet kings their sobriquet, from the sprig of the plant worn as cognizance – but to most people it is familiar as the large shrubby broom and a far cry from this particular species.

Genista sagittalis is an excellent alpine plant, hardy even in the coldest climates and rooting as it grows, so it easily covers several metres (yards) of ground. One of the most attractive features is the flattened stem-like structure produced by each branch, which creates the impression of a mass of evergreen foliage lying against the ground; in fact, a few hairy leaves are scattered along the branches. In summer, clustered heads of strong yellow flowers appear at the ends of the many branches to produce a large area of almost solid brilliant yellow.

Genista sagittalis is versatile and tolerates a wide range of conditions, but prefers stony soil in full sun. It is a good plant for various habitats in and near the rock garden: cascading over large boulders like a green waterfall or spreading up gulleys like lava. It can also be grown as edging along a path or border and can be persuaded to grow in partial shade as a ground cover plant, though it will not flower so readily.

Most of the *Leguminosae* or pea family to which *Genista* belongs are best grown from seed which is usually freely made. *Genista sagittalis* is no exception and plants of flowering size can be had in a year.

Genista sagittalis, aptly known as the creeping broom.

Cuttings can be taken of semi-ripened branches, inserted in two parts sand to one part loam or peat in late summer. The easiest way to propagate this plant however, is simply to lift the edges of a large plant and cut off some rooted branches.

LINUM FLAVUM

L.

FAMILY
Linaceae

ORIGIN
Germany to Russia

HEIGHT AND SPREAD
30cm (12in) × 25cm (10in)

FLOWERING TIME
Midsummer

SPECIAL FEATURE
Unusually large flowers

CLIMATIC ZONE
Zone 6

Linum flavum, a yellow flax.

For centuries the flax plant *Linum usitatissimum* has been used to make linen cloth and as a source of linseed oil for oil painters and for cricketers who rub it into their willow cricket bats to help preserve the wood. It is an attractive annual with clear blue flowers. However, the flax genus covers over 200 interesting species, most of which are sub-shrubby or herbaceous with blue flowers.

Linum flavum is one of the flaxes which does not have blue flowers; 'flavum' means yellow and refers to the marvellous clear golden yellow flowers, up to 2.5cm (1in) across, which can look almost radiant shimmering in the heat of a midsummer sun. Each flower is borne among a cluster of buds to create a terminal flower head. Five separate petals close together make a small cup of yellow, contrasting well with the attractive dark green leaves which in milder winters remain evergreen.

Some admirable shrubby yellow-flowered flaxes do exist: again these are seldom seen but they are just as lovely as *L. flavum*. The three that come to mind are *L. arboreum* from Crete, *L. campanulatum* and *L. capitatum*, both from Southern Europe. The last of these is very similar to *L. flavum* except that its yellow flowers are carried in globular heads at the end of each branch rather than the more elongated inflorescence of *L. flavum*.

Linum flavum is a useful alpine plant, not particularly fussy about soil providing it is well drained. It likes full sun and shelter, and looks very attractive grown in the gaps between paving stones on a sunny terrace or patio, or in the cracks of a wall.

The main drawback of this plant is that a severe winter may well kill off top growth, although it often sends up new shoots in spring. It is also generally short lived and should be replaced once it begins to look a bit worse for wear.

Linum flavum can easily be replaced either by splitting up older plants, growing new ones from seed which is readily set, or by taking cuttings of soft, new growth in early summer. These cuttings can be put into a cold frame or under a cloche and should root in about a week at that time of year provided they are shaded from direct sunlight.

LITHODORA ZAHNII

(Heldr. ex Halacsy)
I. M. Johnston

FAMILY
Boraginaceae

ORIGIN
Greece

HEIGHT AND SPREAD
40cm (16in) × 60cm (2ft)

FLOWERING TIME
Early summer

SPECIAL FEATURE
Celestial blue flowers

CLIMATIC ZONE
Zone 6

I remember noticing this plant for the first time one cold March morning at The Royal Botanic Gardens, Kew and remarking to myself that it was one of the darkest green leaved plants I had ever seen. There were three or four of them, which had grown together to form a 'hedgehog' covering nearly a square metre (yard).

'Lithodora' in this case probably means gift of rocks or stones. The genus is very close to *Lithospermum* which means stone seed and refers to the extremely hard seeds, in fact a feature of both genera. *Lithosper-*

mum includes only herbaceous plants whereas *Lithodora* has many alpine shrubs, and the plant once known in the trade as *Lithospermum diffusum* and its cultivar 'Heavenly Blue' are now more correctly known as *Lithodora diffusa*.

Lithodora zahnii makes a dome shaped cushion of evergreen rigid branchlets 40cm (16in) high by 1m (3ft) across. This cushion is made up of many rosettes of rough, linear and dark green leaves with slightly greyish undersides.

In common with many members of the borage family, the flowers are a rich blue fading to pinkish white. As well as flower colour its coarse, rough leaves are reminiscent of comfrey, borage and hound's tongue, or the lovely viper's bugloss (*Echium vulgare*). (Bugloss originates from the Greek 'bougloseos' or ox-tongue and refers to the rough tongue-textured leaves.) The flowers are like those of a forget-me-not and look upwards from among the tufts of leaves — quite a spectacle when in full bloom.

The plant is prone to damage from frost and driving winds, and can be disfigured by extremely cold weather. However, a large specimen is rarely killed and protecting it from wind by siting it near another plant or a rock should limit any damage. If the plant does get damaged, prune these parts in early spring to encourage replacement growth which should quickly fill any gaps. This plant loves lime and it prefers a rocky, well drained soil like its native habitat in Greece, on top of a high cliff near to the sea.

Propagate from ripe seed which is set in a hot year, to make flowering plants eighteen months later. Keep the young plants containerized for a year before planting them out to allow them to establish themselves. *Lithodora zahnii* can also be propagated from 5–10cm (2–4in) semi-ripe cuttings, taken in spring or autumn when the weather is fairly cool and the plant is actively growing, and inserted in a loam-based compost mixed with a bit of sharp sand. Once rooted, they will not need repotting for a year.

Lithodora zahnii.

MITELLA BREWERI

A. Gray

FAMILY
Saxifragaceae

ORIGIN
North America

HEIGHT AND SPREAD
20cm (8in) × 25cm (10in)

FLOWERING TIME
Early summer

SPECIAL FEATURE
Curious fringed flowers

CLIMATIC ZONE
Zone 4

I find this compact little plant irresistible, though it seeds itself far too freely and I have to remove half of those seedlings which come up. Long before its extraordinary flowers appear its miniature domes of dark green catch the imagination, giving an impression of Lilliputian *Gunnera*.

The twelve species of *Mitella* are charming, low growing plants ideal for cooler, shadier parts of the rock garden or woodland edge. Their American common name is bishop's cap, derived from the mitre-like seed capsules, and interestingly, 'mitella' is Latin for little mitre. The genus is particularly noted for its highly fringed or pinnately cut petals which are filigree thin.

Mitella breweri is one of the smallest species, covering an area 25cm (10in) across as a neat, dome-shaped hardy perennial. Its leafy, semi-succulent stems are roughly clad in coarse hairs; the heart-shaped, lobed, semi-evergreen leaves form compact rosettes at the ends of the branches.

The small flowers are carried on one side of spike-like racemes, often facing outwards so that their centres are visible. They are bright pale green and up to twenty per stem. The five petals are highly dissected, making a delightful veil through which the five central stamens can be seen. Due to their colour and

The curious green spikes of *Mitella breweri*.

diminutive appearance, the flowers are often over-looked, but on closer inspection are quite remarkable and beautiful. The fine seed is shed quickly from the miniature bishop's mitres.

Seed often germinates in the smallest fissures, so that the foliage appears to grow from the very rocks; I once saw it flourishing in a partially shaded woodland where the combination of rocks and neat domes of *M. breweri* made an attractive edge to a path.

Mitella breweri prefers cool, moist, neutral to acid soil, and grows best in sandstone or granite areas.

Propagate by seed or division.

PHYLA NODIFLORA

L. Greene

FAMILY
Verbenaceae

ORIGIN
North America and Mexico

HEIGHT AND SPREAD
7.5cm (3in) × 30cm (12in)

FLOWERING TIME
Late summer to autumn

SPECIAL FEATURE
Very vigorous trailing perennial

CLIMATIC ZONE
Zone 5

Phyla nodiflora.

There are ten, mostly tropical, species of *Phyla,* all known as frogfruit because frogs are partial to the fruits. *Phyla nodiflora* is affectionately known as turkey tangle or matgrass. It survives harsh weather, always growing afresh each spring. I have seen it clinging to the cracks of a rocky site 240m (800ft) up; every year this Mexican plant produces a fascinating green waterfall covered in little white balls, which have barely any scent but are decidedly edible in appearance (and in fact are not poisonous). It also can be safely trampled under foot, which encourages compact growth. *Phyla* is Greek for a group or order. The species in this genus have been incorporated from other closely related genera such as *Verbena* and *Lippia*. This explains why the older synonym for

P. nodiflora, *Lippia nodiflora*, can sometimes be seen.

Phyla is an apt name and hopefully a lasting one. *Nodiflora* means flowering at the nodes — the junctions of leaves and stem — where not only the flowers are produced, but also the creeping roots. The stems straggle for metres (yards), crossing, rooting and branching as they spread. It could become a creeping menace, given too small an area. The small, light green leaves are ovate with slightly serrated edges. The globe-shaped flower heads are carried on stalks which can be over 7.5cm (3in) long. The curious, tightly crowded flower heads are like miniature *Lantana*, the small lobed flowers clustered together and the bottom ones opening first, leaving lilac-coloured buds in the centre. The individual flowers are tinged with pink and the flowers eventually fade to brown, but the overall effect is white.

Phyla nodiflora is easy to grow, on any soil in full sun or part shade. It is spectacular as a creeping plant on a terrace or down a dry stone wall. It can compete with other vigorous covering plants, such as *Tolmeia menziesii* and *Sedum* species in the drier fringes of woodland or even on the rock garden. It is quite happy on alkaline soils. It is extremely vigorous, covering several square metres (yards) of ground in one year. Even if cut back hard by frost, it will make a quick and successful recovery. Propagate by detaching a rooted branch.

POLEMONIUM REPTANS

L.

FAMILY
Polemoniaceae

ORIGIN
North America

HEIGHT AND SPREAD
40cm (16in) × 15cm (6in)

FLOWERING TIME
Spring to late summer

SPECIAL FEATURES
Creeping habit, blue flowers

CLIMATIC ZONE
Zone 4

Of all the fifty or so species in this genus, *Polemonium caeruleum*, or Jacob's ladder, and its white form are the only ones widely known. Jacob's ladder is a popular plant, attractive but vigorously invasive. Less well known but a superb alpine plant is its close cousin, *P. reptans*. The name Jacob's ladder still applies to its ladder-like leaves and blue flowers above symbolizing heaven, but *P. reptans* is much slower growing, making it easier to control.

Polemonium reptans creeps along the ground, forming a low mat by means of thick, fleshy rhizomes. Fortunately, it spreads only a few centimetres (inches) every year so is not invasive, nor does it seed itself freely like its ubiquitous cousin *P. caeruleum*. The saucer-shaped flowers may have the faintest suggestion of mauve in them, but to all intents and purposes they are a clear mid-blue, carried on loose panicles no more than 30cm(12in) above the foliage. Each flower hangs down shyly and gives off a delicious scent reminiscent of violets, particularly in the evening. Everything comes in fives: five clear lobes for the calyx with five overlapping petals and five white shining anthers inside. Each branch of the inflorescence produces no more than five flowers (usually less).

Hardy even in cold districts, *P. reptans* is extremely easy to grow and is ideal for an exposed rock garden or front of a herbaceous bed. It thrives in full sun and tolerates alkalinity. Annual mulching with organic matter encourages the clump to rejuvenate any patchy

areas that may develop in time, and is very important on a dry soil, to help retain moisture. I have seen the plant growing happily at the foot of a rock garden, where it thrives on a combination of full sun and damp soil.

Polemonium reptans can be grown from seed which is sparsely set, or by division. There is a white form of *P. reptans* which is equally attractive and seed-sown plants may produce either white or blue flowers.

Polemonium reptans, a creeping Jacob's ladder.

VERONICA CINEREA

Boiss. and Bal.

FAMILY
Scrophulariaceae

ORIGIN
Turkey

HEIGHT AND SPREAD
To 10cm (4in) × 60cm (2ft)

FLOWERING TIME
Early to midsummer

SPECIAL FEATURES
Neat, silver foliage and clear azure flowers

CLIMATIC ZONE
Zone 5

The blue-flowered form of *Veronica cinerea*.

Although small, this plant, like certain people, attracts one instantly by its natural colouring. The combination of bright azure-blue flowers radiant above greyish-white branchlets is stunning. It is ideal for planting between the paving stones of hot terraces, where a single plant can run along the length of the crack, spilling over on to the stones on either side.

Nearer to speedwell than to the herbaceous-border species of *Veronica* is this alpine gem, *V. cinerea*. It sends up many stems of ash-grey foliage from a loose cushion. The narrow leaves are densely covered in very fine hairs and the leaf edges are rolled under. These are both features of plants growing in hot, dry places and help reduce water loss: the first by preventing the heat of the sun penetrating to the surface of the leaf, and the second by protecting the 'breathing' undersurface of the leaf. The grey spikes have smaller side branches and opposite leaves, similar at first sight to the foliage and growth of French lavender, *Lavandula stoechas*, although without the scent.

Veronica cinerea produces a month-long display in summer when its eye-catching azure-blue flowers appear on spikes 5cm (2in) high. There is also a pink form of the species which I don't find as spectacular as the blue. The small, starry, four petalled flowers are loosely arranged alternately opposite each other on the spike, with the blue stamens protruding noticeably from the petals.

Veronica cinerea tolerates very cold winters provided the drainage is good. Being an alpine plant, it really only succeeds when planted on an almost gravelly or gritty slope, and its grey foliage is prone to rot if wet. The branches of *V. cinerea* creep along the ground, rooting as they go and sending up vertical spikelets every so often. Cutting off a small rooted section is the safest way to propagate the species, as cuttings can be difficult to root, because the base must be kept moist but the grey-leaved tops dry. I have never seen seed set, but presume it does during a good, hot summer.

ZAUSCHNERIA CALIFORNICA

Presl. 'DUBLIN'

FAMILY
Onagraceae

ORIGIN
South-west USA

HEIGHT AND SPREAD
30cm (12in) × 30cm (12in)

FLOWERING TIME
Late summer, autumn

SPECIAL FEATURE
Fuchsia-like flowers

CLIMATIC ZONE
Zone 6

Zauschneria californica 'Dublin' overhanging a rock at the University of London Botanic Gardens, Egham, Surrey.

The Californian fuchsia or hummingbird's trumpet is widely known in North America and this is a fine coloured cultivar, 'Dublin', raised at the Glasnevin Botanic Garden in Dublin, Ireland. I first saw it growing on the sandstone rock garden of the University of London at Egham. There, in the botanic gardens, several plants grew in sprawling patches among large boulders and covered an area 3m (10ft) across. It seemed perfectly happy in the acid gritty soil and was covered with a mass of brilliant red flowers, tubular and fiery like so many of the plants which come from California and Mexico.

The family *Onagraceae* is chiefly known for the genus *Fuchsia* and perhaps also for willow herbs and evening primroses; the latter are now in the genus *Oenothera* but were in fact once called *Onagra* by Philip Miller of London's Chelsea Physic Garden. *Zauschneria* includes a handful of species, three or four of which are found in south-west USA and Mexico.

Z. californica 'Dublin' has intense orange-red, tubular, fuchsia-like flowers with darker red veining on the petals. The four petals curve gracefully backwards revealing the eight stamens and even longer single style with its club-shaped stigma on the end.

The plant is something of a half-way creature between shrub and herbaceous perennial, only growing a little over 30cm (12in) but with long arching branches which spread outwards in all directions. It is softly hairy all over, except the four petals, and the foliage is scanty and narrow, and evergreen in very mild climates. *Zauschneria californica* 'Dublin' is a late-flowering plant taking the early and middle part of the year to recover from the ravages of winter and spreading itself both along the surface and below the ground, in a herbaceous manner. This underground meandering is from white stoloniferous growth which can be very vigorous.

Zauschneria californica 'Dublin' enjoys full sun and a well drained soil. Happiest on acid soils, it survives a modicum of lime providing the soil is light and well drained; what it does not like is cold, heavy clay soil and under these conditions is best treated as a pot plant. It is ideally suited to the rock garden, where drainage is excellent, and given plenty of room to spread, will meander under and around rocks as well as through other, taller plants. Propagate by division in late spring; always plant a large clump as small clumps are more prone to damage from severe frosts. A little protection such as peat or sand over the top of the plant will help it survive the winter. In cold climates, it is sensible to take cuttings in late summer and overwinter them in a frost-free greenhouse. The rooted plants should flower the following summer.

ANNUALS, BIENNIALS
AND
TENDER PERENNIALS

Annuals are plants which germinate each year from seed. They often grow through the season, usually to flower in summer or autumn, producing abundant seed before dying. The complete life cycle of the plant is restricted to a period of twelve months, hence the name annual, and it is important to harvest that seed or risk losing the plant totally from the garden as many do not survive the winter.

Biennials have a two-year life cycle, with two separate stages of growth. They survive the winter, germinating successfully out of doors. The first year follows that of any other plant from seed and results in the production of a low, often broad, mass of foliage emanating from a developing tap root or swollen stem. This foliage is called a rosette and produces no flowers. The rosette sometimes withers at the end of the growing season, leaving a dormant swollen root tuber. In other cases, for example, *Verbascum*, the mulleins, and *Digitalis*, the foxgloves, the evergreen rosette survives the winter. The following spring or summer, the plant produces a flowering stem which can be extremely large, with hundreds of flowers. At the end of the season, the whole plant dies, producing thousands of seeds which start the whole process all over again. The growing requirements of biennials are the same as those of herbaceous perennials except that seed must be collected every second year.

Tender perennials are those of borderline hardiness in cool temperate climates, though larger specimens of a particular plant tend to be hardier than small ones. Obviously hardiness varies according to site, habitat, and the climate, particularly the severity of the winter. Protect tender plants in winter and wherever possible always propagate any plants of doubtful hardiness, either by collecting seed each year, or by taking cuttings. 'Ripen' tender plants by placing them outside in the sun, as soon as danger of frost is over. They can lignify, or harden, the soft green twigs then. The larger the specimen the better

its chance of surviving, but only if it is large and woody, not soft twigged. With some perennials, such as *Diascia rigescens*, buy new plants each year.

Annuals, biennials and tender perennials need a little extra care and attention and should be sited where they will not be overlooked or forgotten.

SOWING AND SITING

Hardier annuals often self sow but more tender species have to be coaxed along under warmth if they are to go out as early in the year as cold weather will permit. These are simply sown on a regular seed compost in a light airy place somewhere inside and kept watered. The other method is to sow them directly onto bare earth outside in early summer well after frosts have departed and once the soil has begun to warm up. Plants such as *Silene coeli-rosa* and *Linum grandiflorum* are best sown outside, because they are not good subjects for transplanting, and make a good thick patch if sown directly. Rake the soil level, remove stones and debris and tamp the soil with the end of the rake until it is firm. Sow the seed evenly and then cover it by raking the area sown over and firmly tamping it again. Encircle the sown area with a thick ring of sand, to show where the seeds are, and where you can weed up to from outside the patch in the weeks to come. At the Chelsea Physic Garden, this practice also encourages the stretching of visitors' imaginations, as to the purpose of such a curious ring of sand. Slug traps? Bird baths?

By and large most annuals must have sun, plenty of water while growing, an open situation and a well drained soil. Bear firmly in mind the colour scheme of a border or bed when siting annuals. I have seen the bright pink of *Malope trifida* next to the orange of African marigolds and the purple of *Clarkia unguiculata*. One wished for the softening effect of sunglasses at this spectacle. Height and size should also be considered. Sunflowers are annuals!

AGAPANTHUS AFRICANUS

(L) Hoffmann 'ALBUS'

FAMILY
Alliaceae (or Amaryllidaceae)

ORIGIN
South Africa

HEIGHT AND SPREAD
1m (3ft) × 30cm (12in)

FLOWERING TIME
Late summer

SPECIAL FEATURE
Large white flowers

CLIMATIC ZONE
Zone 6

The sun-loving *Agapanthus africanus* 'Albus'.

'Agape' in Greek means true love and 'anthos' means flower, which gives some indication of the loveliness of this group of clump-forming perennial plants, originally from South Africa. There are half a dozen species and they are all beautiful, but *A. a.* 'Albus' I would rank amongst the loveliest of flowering bulbs.

Agapanthus africanus 'Albus' is the white-flowered cultivar of the evergreen *A. africanus*, which has blue flowers of varying shades and sizes. *Agapanthus africanus* 'Albus' produces a spectacular inflorescence like a flattened sphere some 15cm (6in) across made up of as many as thirty flowers. Each flower is pure white, shaped like a large hyacinth flower and sometimes as large as 2.5cm (1in) across. There are few sights as majestic in late summer as these spires of white flowers standing proud above the glossy dark green foliage.

The foliage is also attractive. Linear leaves radiate from a nearly bulbous base typical of the lilies, irises and daffodils, to which *Agapanthus* is related. Each plant is made of several of these bulbous stems attached to a hard underground, plate-like stem with roots below. The plate increases in size each year sending up more stems and thereby growing bigger until the clump reaches several metres (yards) across if grown in a sheltered sunny protected space. The larger the clump, the hardier the plant is, as it is difficult for even the harshest winter to penetrate the centre thanks to the protective outer stems.

Agapanthus africanus 'Albus' is not the toughest or hardiest of the genus and needs to be positioned carefully with some protection in winter. In very cold weather the evergreen foliage may be killed off but this will not prove fatal. Mulch round the plant with leaf mould or compost in autumn before the first frosts and if the weather turns really cold, cover the whole crown with mulch for extra protection. *Agapanthus* respond well to being container grown. My mother has large terracotta tubs of both blue and white *Agapanthus africanus* cultivars. During winter they are stored in an airy cool greenhouse and kept dry. The more tightly packed the plants, the more flowers, as energy is diverted from growth to flower production, a principle which applies to very many pot plants as well.

Agapanthus africanus 'Albus' can be lifted and divided, using a spade and fork to get through the tough roots, in early spring. The plants then have time to re-establish themselves in the growing season ahead; they may even flower.

CESTRUM PARQUI

L'Herit.

FAMILY
Solanaceae

ORIGIN
Chile

HEIGHT AND SPREAD
1.8m (6ft) × 1.8m (6ft)

FLOWERING TIME
Late summer

SPECIAL FEATURE
Abundant, night-scented flowers

CLIMATIC ZONE
Zone 6

Cestrum parqui.

Cestrum includes 200 species of shrubs, all of which are native to South America, but *C. parqui* is the only one which is reliably tough enough to succeed in cool, temperate climates. Even then, it only thrives in sheltered sites, but where conditions are right it grows quite large and its flowers fill the night air with scent. In the quadrangle within the Fulham Palace, ancient home of the Bishops of London, a whole corner of the quad is devoted to *Cestrum parqui*. On a still summer's evening, the delicious scent is reminiscent of sub-tropical fragrances such as that of the trumpeted (and closely related) *Datura* genus. Unfortunately, the yellowish-green flowers of *C. parqui* are the least spectacular of all the species, those of the tender *C. 'Newellii'* and *C. aurantiacum* being respectively red and orange. *Cestrum diurnum* has whitish flowers, fragrant during the day, and *C. nocturnum* has similar flowers fragrant only at night, but both are too tender to survive winters outside.

Cestrum parqui is sometimes called the willow-leaved cestrum and its deciduous foliage definitely has a willow-like quality. The leaves are reputed to be poisonous and have a rank, foetid smell when bruised, like that of boiled milk, the odour of *Clerodendron bungei* or that of the foetid but beautiful *Salvia confertiflora*.

The elliptic leaves are dark, lustrous green on top and paler green below. They go a clear, pale yellow in late autumn. The flower panicles, produced on the tips of the branches, may be more than 15cm (6in) long and consist of shortly branched clusters. The tubular flowers are a curious colour: predominantly creamy white, fading to brownish yellow but with a hint of green. The flowers have no scent in the heat of the sun but emit a sweet fragrance in duller weather which can be intoxicating on still summer evenings; this implies that the species may be pollinated by moths or bats which emerge after the heat of the day is past.

Cestrum parqui is happiest with shelter, sun and protection from frost. If planted in too exposed a position, the plant can be cut back to ground level in a severe winter. While I have never seen a large plant killed as a result of frost, I have witnessed one planted in an unprotected border which was constantly hammered by the weather each year, only to fight back bravely, producing a handful of flowers before the onslaught of another winter.

Cestrum parqui produces jet black, shiny fruits which contain one seed and are highly poisonous, being in the same family as deadly nightshade and henbane. Softwood cuttings may be easily rooted in spring or early autumn.

DIASCIA RIGESCENS

E. Mey ex Benth.

FAMILY
Scrophulariaceae

ORIGIN
South Africa

HEIGHT AND SPREAD
40cm (16in) × 30cm (12in)

FLOWERING TIME
Mid to late summer

SPECIAL FEATURE
Abundance of flowers

CLIMATIC ZONE
Zone 6

Diascia, with its quick growth and long flowering season, is used more and more in large gardens and by the National Trust in Great Britain. The plant reveals its South African origins in its salmony pink flowers with their rust-brown stamens. Neither colour could be found easily in northern realms and I admire these welcome foreigners now settled and capable of giving much reward for a little nurturing. Variety is the spice of gardening life!

There are over forty species of *Diascia*, all native to South Africa. They are mostly tender perennials or annuals and there are several species in cultivation, their attractive pink flowers making a distinct display in a summer border. *Diascia rigescens* is among the hardiest; an extreme frost might kill the top growth, but new growth will appear in spring. The plants send out sprawling, arching branches up to 60cm (2ft) long. The four-angled stems and toothed leaves are bright green and soft.

'Diascia' means two spurs and these are evident on the back of the small, five-petalled flowers. The flowers are dark, flesh pink and it is easy to spot the resemblence to *Mimulus*, the monkey flower. Both belong to the *Scrophulariaceae* family and both have expressive, impish-faced flowers. The flowers of *D.*

Subtle pink flowers of *Diascia rigescens*.

rigescens are clustered tightly together on long spikes. The flowers open in succession and last for months.

Diascia rigescens spreads slowly by its creeping root system. Six plants spaced 30cm (12in) apart should join up in one season to make a large, single clump and a splendid display. Plant after all danger of frost is past, preferably in a bright sunny position in the front of a border, rock garden or terrace. Light soil is best.

Lift and divide older clumps in late summer, or insert cuttings of new growth in spring in a closed frame or, even better, under a mist unit. Always keep one plant indoors over winter to safeguard the stock, should the weather turn severe.

EUPHORBIA MARGINATA

Pursh

FAMILY
Euphorbiaceae

ORIGIN
North America

HEIGHT AND SPREAD
60cm–1m (2–3ft) × 15cm (6in)

FLOWERING TIME
Late summer

SPECIAL FEATURES
White variegated foliage and bracts, good for flower arranging

CLIMATIC ZONE
Zone 6

Euphorbia marginata, the snow on the mountain.

Snow on the mountain is the attractive common name of this North American annual, a fine species of *Euphorbia* which is by and large a race of perennials. *Euphorbia* is an extremely large genus of some 2000 species, some of which are succulents or grey-leaved shrubs and trees. The best known are *E. characias* with its form *wulfenii*, and *E. pulcherrima*, the ubiquitous 'poinsettia' house plant.

Euphorbia marginata is unique for an annual in that it is green and white for the whole of its life; this may sound dull, but it is in fact one of the showiest and most invigorating plants I know. It remains bright yet never clashes with nearby plants. My grand-mother always used to grow *Euphorbia marginata* between her staked outdoor tomato plants in Scotland, and it really stood out against the nearly black soil. She always maintained (as with French marigolds) that this plant kept away the pests wishing to commit malpractices against her tomatoes. Possibly the unwary aphid may have been conned by the colour scheme. Its upright stem is clothed in green leaves but the uppermost leaves are white margined. The small flower cluster at the top of the stem is surrounded by several large white bracts, creating the dazzling effect which gives the plant its vernacular name. The flowers, like those of most *Euphorbia* species, are not particularly stunning, but the cumulative effect of a clump of plants in flower together is quite an eye catcher. The picked flowers last an exceedingly long time, provided the cut stems are scalded first to stop the flow of milky sap. The flowers are followed by fairly large fruits which are contained in round, hairy shells.

Euphorbia marginata is a hardy annual which sets plenty of fertile seed and perpetuates itself year after year at no expense! It thrives in a number of different habitats but produces the most striking variegation in full sunlight; the variegated foliage tends to revert to green if grown in a shady area. The species tolerates both alkaline and acidic soils, a rich soil producing taller plants and a poor, dry soil simply limiting growth and flower production. I find it easiest to sow the seeds where it is to grow in mid-spring.

HELIPTERUM MANGLESII

(Lindl.) F. J. Muell ex Benth.

FAMILY
Compositae

ORIGIN
Southern Australia

HEIGHT AND SPREAD
45cm (18in) × 5cm (2in)

FLOWERING TIME
Midsummer

SPECIAL FEATURE
Everlasting flowers

CLIMATIC ZONE
Zone 6

The Swan River everlasting has been with us for 150 years and was once much more popular than it is today. In recent years there has been a move away from annuals, and towards 'self-help' plants. It would be such a pity to lose the spectacular display of colour put on by many annuals, to say nothing of their usefulness in infilling for a single year. The genus *Helipterum* literally means sun-wings, in reference to the sun-loving nature of the plants and the papery wing-like pappus under the flower heads. There are some ninety species which all come from Australia and South Africa. (The sun-baked stretches of Australia have given us some of our most exciting annuals, and the Nullabor Plain in bloom after the first rain in months is truly wondrous to see.) The term everlasting refers to the dried flower heads which retain their shape and colour for months and are often seen on sale as decoration. All the *Helipterum* species produce everlasting flower heads; each 'flower' is, in

The everlasting flowers of *Helipterum manglesii*.

fact, an inflorescence made up of many small individual flowers.

Helipterum manglesii was once called *Rhodanthe manglesii* and some still call it by its older name; 'rhodos' means pink and 'anthea' flower, in reference to the colour of its blooms, while *manglesii* commemorates Captain Mangles, a naval sea captain who brought the seeds back from Australia. *Helipterum manglesii* is an erect annual with glaucous green and stalkless leaves surrounding the stem. The plant has three or four branches which terminate in the flower buds, made up of many small greyish, scale-like bracts. The flower consists of many rosy purple or pinkish scales with numerous tubular florets in the centre. These eventually fade leaving the scaly bracts to persist for months as the seeds ripen. There are various colour forms of the species: 'Alba' has white scales, 'Sanguinea', dark red scales, and 'Maculata', flowers with a conspicuous ring of dark purple around the central tubular florets, sometimes more than 5cm (2in) across. This plant was a wild collected form and is sadly now very scarce in cultivation.

Helipterum manglesii is easily grown as a half-hardy annual, sown directly in situ, either in the rock garden or a sunny border after the danger of late spring frosts is past. It produces abundant seed which should be gathered each year and stored in an envelope in a dry place during winter.

L A G U R U S   O V A T U S

L.

FAMILY
Gramineae

ORIGIN
South-west Europe

HEIGHT AND SPREAD
30–60cm (12–24in) × 15cm (6in)

FLOWERING TIME
Mid to late summer and autumn

SPECIAL FEATURES
Ornamental grass, fluffy heads useful for dried flower arrangements

CLIMATIC ZONE
Zone 6

Lagurus ovatus, hare's-tail grass.

Once seen, the hare's-tail grass is instantly recognizable, and its Linnaean name perfectly describes its appearance: 'lagos' is Greek for hare; 'ourus' means a tail, and 'ovatus' means oval and tapering, which is the shape of the inflorescence. It is a fine example of an annual ornamental grass: easy to grow, useful and intriguing, and deserves to be as popular as the better known *Coix lacryma-jobi*, Job's tears, and *Briza maxima*, the quaking grass.

Lagurus ovatus is a hardy annual, and young plants can overwinter in mild localities outdoors. It is usually treated as a half-hardy annual, sown each year in spring, though less substantial plants result, because seedlings may be killed in severe winters. Its leaves are softly downy and clasp the stems. The main stem grows straight upwards and carries the attractive inflorescence, composed of many styles and anthers clustered closely together, to produce the hairy, woolly effect. When ripe, the male anthers are a cream colour and the whole inflorescence can be more than 2.5cm (1in) long.

The other great glory of *Lagurus ovatus* is that it lasts for several months when cut. If you want them for dried flower arrangements, cut them before fully mature, in late summer. Grown annually from seed produced in great quantities, it self seeds in situ and usually remains self-perpetuating for several years until either disease or weather eventually weakens it. (I always keep some seed, which remains viable for up to three years, as a precaution.) Ordinary, well-drained soil and sun suit it best. As is the case with most annuals, a single plant in flower looks lonely, but a mass of several plants is tremendous.

LAVANDULA STOECHAS

L. subspecies PEDUNCULATA

FAMILY
Labiatae

ORIGIN
Central Spain

HEIGHT AND SPREAD
1m (3ft) × 1m (3ft)

FLOWERING TIME
Mid to late summer

SPECIAL FEATURE
Huge magenta flower bracts

CLIMATIC ZONE
Zone 6

Spanish lavender, *Lavandula stoechas* subsp. *pedunculata*.

This Spanish lavender is rather more tender than other lavenders but it is so beautiful I think it is worth the extra care to protect it over the winter. I first came across the subspecies while passing through Sierra Nevada in Spain. The grey clumps were dotted through the monotonous grey rocky hillsides, with the magenta bracts hovering above the plants like flames above the sea. On closer investigation, we were immediately aware of a strong and spicy but pleasant fragrance, like camphor and lavender, from the bruised foliage.

Lavandula stoechas, French lavender, is now fairly well known and this Spanish relation is so close that it is sometimes classified as a species, *pedunculata* meaning flowering stem or stalk: very tall in the Spanish lavender but short in the French. They are more or less equally hardy and in fairness I would say that neither is as hardy as the old-fashioned lavender, *L. angustifolia*.

The generic name comes from the Latin 'lavo': I wash, and alludes to the use of lavender water for cleansing and refreshing. Lavender water is made from the leaves of *L. angustifolia* (also known as *L. spica*, *L. vera* and *L. officinalis*) and *L. latifolia*. There has long been confusion between these two species, mainly due to their capacity for hybridizing. *L. pedunculata* with its narrow, loose foliage and strong camphor scent is entirely distinct.

It makes a fine plant of tightly packed grey branches from which the flower stems arise, sometimes over 30cm (12in) tall. These are stiff and narrow, four angled stems with the typical lavender inflorescence of tightly knit, tiny flowers. The most spectacular feature is the tuft of bright magenta bracts on top of the spike. Each bract is more than 2.5cm (1in) long, the longest sometimes twice the length of the whole inflorescence. The flowers themselves when fully out are no more than indigo funnels which produce an intoxicating scent when gently pressed.

This plant is best treated as tender and can be lifted (if small enough) and potted up to overwinter under glass. All silver foliage plants need maximum light in the winter months, so position accordingly. For new plants, take semi-ripe cuttings and put them into a cold frame in late summer, or soft tip cuttings put into the same frame prior to flowering. Nearly all lavenders prefer hot, open situations where wind and sun can reach them in summer. Protect both Spanish and French lavender by growing them near the base of a wall or large shrub and, if too large to lift in autumn, pack the plants with peat, sacking or straw.

LINUM GRANDIFLORUM

Desf.

FAMILY
Linaceae

ORIGIN
Algeria

HEIGHT AND SPREAD
60cm (2ft) × 10cm (4in)

FLOWERING TIME
Midsummer

SPECIAL FEATURE
Brilliant red flowers

CLIMATIC ZONE
Zone 6

There are well over 200 species of flax, most of them perennials and almost exclusively with blue, white or yellow flowers. *Linum grandiflorum* is a red-flowered exception. This robust but lanky hardy annual tolerates a wide range of soil and climate conditions and rewards the gardener with one of the brightest displays of summer colour I know. It was once more widely grown as a hardy annual than it is now and illustrates the fashion changes which occur in gardening. It is certainly time for *Linum grandiflorum* to make a come-back. (Among the few plants whose flowers can rival it in brightness are *Verbena peruviana* which is red, and rock purslane, or *Calandrinia umbellata*, a dark magenta. *Linum grandiflorum* should be planted en masse for best effect; few annual plants look good planted singly unless, like the sunflower, they are unusually large.

The erect, bright green stems have a few lateral branches and light green oval leaves thinly distributed up the stems. Growth from seed to flowering usually takes two or three months and the flowering period can be prolonged by making a first sowing in late spring then, as soon as that batch has germinated and is a few centimetres (inches) tall, sowing a second batch among the new seedlings. Flowering may continue right through the summer if the weather is good.

Linum grandiflorum has slightly funnel-shaped flowers whose petals open wide in full sun, their edges curling gently backwards to reveal a smooth texture that seems to shine. Each flower can be more than 2.5cm (1in) across, large for a flax and justifying its name *grandiflorum*. They stand upright and each plant may support several flowers with a score or more plants to a decent clump.

Linum grandiflorum prefers full sun and is ideal for the front of a border or in a rock garden, where it will flower and seed itself freely. It may even self sow in very poor soil in rocks or walls where it will be limited to a height of a few centimetres (inches). It is a useful plant for hot, dry places since it can survive scant watering, although it prefers regular supplies of water. Flower colour may vary slightly but the best red forms come true from seed.

Collecting seed only takes a few minutes each year and is well worth it for the rich rewards of the flowers next season. I have never understood why so many people are prepared to go to the trouble of lifting begonia and dahlia tubers yet are reluctant to collect seed. The seed is lozenge shaped and sits inside the

Linum grandiflorum, red flax.

three or four compartments of a spherical capsule. It is ready to collect as soon as the capsules turn from green to pale brown. Always use paper envelopes for storing seed, because plastic encourages rotting.

MAURANDYA BARCLAIANA

Lindl.

FAMILY
Scrophulariaceae

ORIGIN
Mexico

HEIGHT AND SPREAD
To 3m (10ft) × 1.8m (6ft)

FLOWERING TIME
Spring, summer and autumn

SPECIAL FEATURES
Long flowering period, free flowering

CLIMATIC ZONE
Zone 6

Varying shades of pink flowers on the tender climber *Maurandya barclaiana*.

Few climbing plants bloom as long and prolifically as those from the strong but tender *Maurandya* genus. These desirable plants can be forgiven for their obscurity as they are too tender for winter cultivation in cool temperate climates. They should be grown as annuals, for as such they are so easy and so very rewarding. After all, *Tropaeolum* (garden nasturtium), morning glory and several other tender climbers are widely grown. Apart from anything else, *Maurandya* produce far more seed annually than any gardener could cope with.

Maurandya barclaiana is one of the gems of the genus, which includes several species. It is a vigorous climber which clings by means of its petioles which slowly coil around the support. The leaves of *M. barclaiana* are almost triangular, and the petioles are wire-like and smooth, as are the leaves themselves.

The flowers are trumpet shaped and vary in colour, but there are three distinct colour forms. The type is dark violet and there is also a rose pink form: *M. b.* var. *rosea* and a white form: *M. b.* var. *alba*. The flower is enclosed in a rough, hairy, pale green calyx. The tube of the flower has two channel-like grooves underneath on a flat sort of base, and two corresponding ridges on its flattened top. The tube terminates in five petal-like rounded lobes and the inner throat of the tube is white.

Maurandya barclaiana is easy to grow from seed each year, though it is technically a perennial. It will live outside only if given a very sheltered position. New plants may be raised from cuttings taken during the growing season and rooted in a closed frame.

MENTZELIA LINDLEYI

Torr. & Gray

FAMILY
Loasaceae

ORIGIN
California

HEIGHT AND SPREAD
To 30cm (12in) × 50cm (20in)

FLOWERING TIME
Mid to late summer

SPECIAL FEATURE
Showy, long-lasting yellow flowers

CLIMATIC ZONE
Zone 6

Mentzelia lindleyi, the annual blazing star.

The annual Californian blazing star is aptly named for its yellow and gold blooms and long flowering season. It is ideal for sowing over bare patches of dormant spring bulbs and its sprawling habit quickly covers the earth with interesting foliage followed by eye-catching flowers. The genus *Mentzelia* was named after a 17th century botanist and covers at least seventy species of usually annual plants, many with showy flowers. Surprisingly, *M. lindleyi* is the only species ever seen in Britain and is often called by a much older name, *Bartonia aurea*.

It is an excellent plant, with the capacity to produce more flower than foliage or branch. A single plant, under ideal conditions, makes shrubby growth which sprawls over an area about 50cm (20in) across. The individual flowers are carried on loose racemes and open in ones and twos; each flower has five pale yellow, pointed petals. The base of each petal has a golden brown blotch or stain giving the centre of the flower a ring of gold and from this centre emerges a mass of stamens. Superficially the flower resembles that of *Hypericum calycinum* and is nearly the same size – more than 5cm (2in) across. The flowers of *M. lindleyi* have a habit of opening in the early evening and emitting a gentle fragrance, then lasting until morning and well into the next day.

The seed capsule is rather curious: it can be over 5cm (2in) long and is distinctly ribbed and the remains of the calyx give it a star-like effect. The foliage is sparse and the leaves are very dark green and deeply incised. They are quite hairy and resemble the texture of certain members of the cucumber family – *Cucurbitaceae* – which some people regard as a distant relative of this plant.

Mentzelia lindleyi loves a hot sunny spot and is tolerant of exposure to wind. Sow in situ once the weather warms up, or sow in trays indoors, then harden off and plant out when the seedlings are large enough. The golden rule with annuals is to remember to collect the seed, an excellent and free source of future plants.

MODIOLASTRUM LATERITIUM

Nicholls

FAMILY
Malvaceae

ORIGIN
Uruguay

HEIGHT AND SPREAD
10cm (4in) × 15cm (6in)

FLOWERING TIME
Midsummer

SPECIAL FEATURE
Free-flowering ground cover

CLIMATIC ZONE
Zone 6

Modiolastrum lateritium, a creeping relation of the hibiscus.

This attractive creeping plant is hardy in very mild, sheltered areas but is susceptible to frost during bad winters. However, it is worth taking the trouble to protect the plant as it more than compensates for its slight tenderness by producing a wonderful profusion of flowers. *Modiolastrum lateritium* has been known as *Malva* or even *Malvastrum lateritium* in the past but now, hopefully, it has come to rest in the genus *Modiolastrum* which has only six species, all South American. 'Modios' is Greek for the circular nave of a wheel; the flowers have a nave-like centre out of which the petals emanate.

The green creeping branches of *M. lateritium* emerge in spring from a slightly tuberous rootstock. They grow several metres (yards) long in a season. The sparsely hairy branches root where they touch the soil and a large clump can form in a single season. The small, palmate leaves are carried sparsely along the stems and are a shiny dark green on their upper surfaces. The first flowers appear at the end of the stems and later in the leaf axils. They are vaguely mallow shaped – not surprising as this is the family to which *Modiolastrum* belongs – and a rich reddish orange like weathered brick. Each flower can be more than 2.5cm (1in) across with a mass of central stamens. The flowers are an arresting sight and appear in succession from midsummer onwards.

Modiolastrum lateritium grows in any type of soil but thrives in a slightly acid, sandy one. I have seen it growing in a chalky clay soil and noticed that the foliage was slightly yellow, although the plant itself was vigorous. It prefers full sun and shelter, with maximum protection against frost. The rapid and vigorous growth habit means it can be treated in several different ways. I have seen it trained up a trellis at Sissinghurst Castle in Kent, where it looked spectacular. It can also be grown along the ground, on a terrace or over the rocks in a rock garden. In the coldest areas treat it as an annual, saving the seed which it sets and germinates freely. Alternatively, propagate by removing rooted layers or from soft tip cuttings taken in late spring before the flower buds start to develop.

NICOTIANA SYLVESTRIS

Speg. and Comes.

FAMILY
Solanaceae

ORIGIN
Argentina

HEIGHT AND SPREAD
1.8m (6ft) × 1.2m (4ft)

FLOWERING TIME
Late summer and autumn

SPECIAL FEATURE
Large stately plant with very fragrant flowers

CLIMATIC ZONE
Zone 5

Before I had encountered many of the forty-seven species of *Nicotiana*, the name conjured up the inevitable tobacco plant, *N. tabacum*, whose stimulative drug nicotine is more than familiar to most. I was aware of the decorative tobacco plant, *N. alata,* and its various coloured forms, but *N. sylvestris* came as a glorious surprise, with many of the merits of the garden-worthy *N. alata*, and much more besides. It is another plant whose virtues were once better appreciated and it lingers on from year to year only in the great gardens of those who know it. John Codrington grows it near Oakham in Leicestershire and there is a fine patch of it bordering woodland at Hidcote Manor, Gloucestershire. It also grows in the Chelsea Physic Garden and we are inundated with requests for it.

Nicotiana sylvestris is best grown as an annual, which may seem an impossible brief, given that a mature six-month-old plant in flower can have leaves over 30cm (12in) across, sometimes 60cm (2ft) long. This is, however, the average growth which a healthy plant of this species can make in a season. It is, in fact, a perennial, dying back to a tuberous rootstock, but is best treated as an annual because bigger, healthier plants are formed from seed sown fresh each year.

Clammy and sticky with oils, *N. sylvestris* produces large basal leaves which are rich dark green. Several racemes of flowers are produced, the largest being 30cm (12in) long. The tubular white flowers are

7.5cm (3in) long and 2.5cm (1in) across. The flower is deliciously scented and remains open longer than the evanescent flowers of *N. alata* which are only properly open in the evening to attract moths.

Nicotiana sylvestris grows well in any rich soil and benefits from a good application of leaf mould or manure. It also needs plenty of space and can be grown in half shade (*sylvestris* meaning of the woods), although this is not essential provided it is not exposed to strong winds. *Nicotiana sylvestris* is happy in strong sun. Its small brown seeds can be sown early in the year under cover in a propagator and then the young plants planted in situ well after any risk of frost is past. In sheltered areas, *N. sylvestris* seeds itself freely producing healthy plants which may need thinning out or removing altogether before they take over. It is marginally frost tolerant, succumbing to very hard frosts.

The giant tobacco plant with its white scented flowers.

OLEARIA × SCILLONIENSIS

Dorrien-Smith

FAMILY
Compositae

ORIGIN
Hybrid

HEIGHT AND SPREAD
1.5m (5ft) × 1.8m (6ft)

FLOWERING TIME
Early summer

SPECIAL FEATURE
Free-flowering daisy bush

CLIMATIC ZONE
Zone 5

The daisy bush laden with flowers.

Olearia × scilloniensis is a hybrid daisy bush which came into being spontaneously, that is unpremeditated, on the island of Tresco, one of the Scilly Isles off the south-west tip of Cornwall. The island is a garden haven created by the Dorrien-Smith family, mostly during the early part of this century. Because it is in the sweep of the Gulf Stream, Tresco enjoys a particularly mild and favoured climate which, thanks to the imagination of Major A. A. Dorrien-Smith, has fostered many wonderful plants. This genus is a prime candidate for cultivation on Tresco because many of its hundred species are rather tender and will succumb to a hard frost. There are four reliably hardy plants which would suit cultivation in colder regions: *O. × haastii* from New Zealand which is the toughest of the lot; *O. nummularifolia* and *O. macrodonta* also from New Zealand; and *O. × scilloniensis* which is not quite as hardy as the others, but is way and above the best for flowers. It can be damaged but is very seldom killed by very cold weather.

O. × scilloniensis is a hybrid between *O. lirata* and *O. phlogopappa*, both from Australia and Tasmania. When growing happily, the hybrid is so smothered in flowers that the dark evergreen foliage is completely covered by white daisy blossoms for several weeks in early to midsummer. *O. × scilloniensis* has a faint scent about the foliage, no doubt a legacy from *O.*

phlogopappa whose foliage is strongly aromatic. The narrow, oblong leaves are dark green above with white, felt-like down beneath and conspicuously wavy edges. The shrub is much branched and densely clad with foliage. The flowers are typically *Compositae*, and both the inner and outer ray florets are white, forming a tight white daisy over 1.5cm ($\frac{1}{2}$in) across. The seed-heads which follow are also atttractive, like miniature dandelion heads with papery bracts and feathery parachutes, and maintain the shrub's fine display into late summer.

Given the necessary protection for a front tender plant, *O. × scilloniensis* will reward the gardener by flourishing for many years. The plant is indifferent to acidity and alkalinity and, an excellent bonus for maritime gardens, is salt tolerant. It forms a compact bush which needs little attention except the removal of damaged or dead branches periodically and an annual tidy up, removing the oldest wood. It strikes easily from cuttings taken of semi-ripe wood in late summer, which root quickly in a heated frame or more slowly in an unheated one. Plants should reach flowering size within two years.

OSTEOSPERMUM JOCUNDUM

(E. P. Phill.) T. Norl.

FAMILY
Compositae

ORIGIN
South Africa

HEIGHT AND SPREAD
45cm (18in) × 1m (3ft)

FLOWERING TIME
Mid to late summer

SPECIAL FEATURE
Pink, daisy-like flowers

CLIMATIC ZONE
Zone 6

Osteospermum literally means bone seed and refers to the smooth, spineless seeds of this group of seventy species of tender, very beautiful half-shrubby plants. There are several species which were once included in the closely related *Dimorphotheca* genus, and *O. jocundum* is sometimes still called *D. jocunda* or *D. barberae*.

Osteospermum jocundum is a good name for this plant as it is certainly a jolly sight when in flower. The two-tone daisy-like flowers are very striking: purple on the upper side and mauve beneath each 'petal': I use this term loosely, as each petal is a complete flower equipped with ovary, a feature of the daisy family. There are also several hybrids and cultivars, with colours ranging through purples and pinks to white, some, such as 'Tresco Purple', with attractive dark 'eyes'.

The foliage is luscious and dark green, with some of the long, narrow leaves lobed and others not. Branches sprout in all directions and layer themselves wherever they touch the ground, particularly if the weather is damp and the soil is rich.

Osteospermum jocundum is easily cultivated; it prefers a rich, well-fed soil but will simply be less vigorous on a dry, poor one. It thrives in full sun and demurely closes its flowers at the onset of cool, wet weather to reveal the more subdued mauve hues of the 'petal'

Osteospermum jocundum, one of South Africa's bright tender perennials.

undersides. Sunshine again soon brings out the marvellous bright purple of the upper 'petal' surfaces.

Osteospermum jocundum is used effectively in some National Trust gardens, particularly at Crathes Castle in north-east Scotland, where it creeps along the ground, only stopping when the paving stones of a path prevent further rooting. At Powys Castle in Wales it cascades over the edge of a wall.

This tender perennial survives mild winters but succumbs to hard frosts. Propagate by division or from cuttings of new growth taken in late summer. These should be kept in a frost free but well ventilated spot over winter; a protected frame or cloche is ideal but an airy, well lit kitchen window sill would do. *Osteospermum jocundum* can also be raised in early spring from seed, though it doesn't often set seed.

RHODOCHITON ATROSANGUINEUS

(Z u c c .)   R o t h m .
FAMILY
Scrophulariaceae
ORIGIN
Mexico
HEIGHT AND SPREAD
3m (10ft) × 1.5m (5ft)
FLOWERING TIME
Late summer to autumn
SPECIAL FEATURES
Vigorous annual climber with unique flowers
CLIMATIC ZONE
Zone 6

Although tender and best grown as an annual, the purple bell vine, as *R. atrosanguineus* is known, is an excellent flowering climber. It can certainly hold its own among other plants, such as *Thunbergia alata* (black-eyed Susan), *Maurandya barclaiana* and the charming, fragrant sweet pea, already popular as annual climbers.

Rhodochiton means rosy cloak, a reference to the enclosing cloak-like calyx. *Rhodochiton atrosanguineus* is the only species in the genus and is a true climber, clinging to its support by means of leaves whose stems

The extraordinary hanging parachutes of *Rhodochiton atrosanguineus*.

are sensitive to contact and which twist around anything they find. The flowers are highly distinctive and hang from the branches like small chocolate fingers protruding from the plum-red umbrella or cloak of the calyx. *Atrosanguineus* literally means dark, blood red and refers to the colour of the tube-like flower. The prominent balloon-like calyx can reach 3.5cm (1½in) across. The whole flower, calyx and all, hangs, parachute-fashion, from the branches.

The foliage is vaguely heart-shaped but with pointed lobes at the extreme angles of the heart and a long, thin point at the apex. An overall plum red hue is evident on the branches, leaf stalk and the undersurface of the leaves.

When ripe, the spherical seed capsules break open to release many flat papery seeds. Sow in early spring under cover or late spring outside when the weather is

SALVIA GUARANITICA

St. Hil. 'BLUE ENIGMA'

FAMILY
Labiatae

ORIGIN
South America

HEIGHT AND SPREAD
2.1m (7ft) × 1.8m (6ft)

FLOWERING TIME
Late summer through autumn

SPECIAL FEATURE
Intensely blue flowers

CLIMATIC ZONE
Zone 5

Mention the genus *Salvia* and most people think of a bright flame-red plant associated with municipal gardens, or of the culinary herb sage. *Salvia guaranitica* is nothing like either of these and serves to illustrate the diversity of this vast and fascinating genus, which contains nearly 500 species in South America alone, many of them beautiful garden plants.

Salvia guaranitica is the correct name for a plant which has been grown incorrectly as *S. caerulea* and *S. ambigens*. There are at least two different clones within the species. The taller, *S. guaranitica* 'Black and Blue', has rough, heart-shaped leaves and is very robust, growing against a wall to over 3m (10ft) or as a free-standing plant to 1.8m (6ft) or more. The flowers are an intense sky blue, tightly packed on a spiky inflorescence some 15cm (6in) long. A striking feature of this lovely plant is the appearance before flowering of nearly black calyces which contain the 2.5cm (1in) long flowers.

The other form, *S. guaranitica* 'Blue Enigma', has bright green, smooth leaves and paler blue flowers on a shorter spike, with green rather than black calyces. It is no less beautiful, however, and makes a clump 1m (3ft) across, producing over a dozen flower heads in late summer and early autumn. This clone is slightly shorter at full maturity and has been in cultivation for a longer time.

Salvia guaranitica is semi-woody at the base but is

warmer. It needs fertile soil and plenty of moisture in the early stages of growth. Raise young plants in partial shade, then plant in full sun against a wall or up a tripod. Soft tip cuttings can also be taken in spring or autumn and overwintered in a cold frame.

Habit of *Salvia guaranitica* 'Blue Enigma'.

Close-up of flowers.

classed as a herbaceous perennial because it tends to suffer frost damage to the non-woody top growth. It has been known to survive almost unscathed when planted against a west-facing wall and given further protection in the form of yew branches and sacking at its base. Propagate from soft cuttings in spring or late summer and these should root within a week in a propagating frame. Cut the young plants back to prevent them getting tall too quickly after they have rooted. Alternatively, divide established clumps when dormant. *Salvia guaranitica* grows in a variety of soils and tolerates lime. It prefers a hot sunny position protected from cold winds and may need staking. It also makes a superb pot plant for winter flowering.

SALVIA INVOLUCRATA

Cav. 'BETHELII'

FAMILY
Labiatae

ORIGIN
Mexico

HEIGHT AND SPREAD
1.5m (5ft) × 1m (3ft)

FLOWERING TIME
Late summer, autumn

SPECIAL FEATURES
Handsome foliage, striking flowers

CLIMATIC ZONE
Zone 5

The opening cerise-pink flowers of *Salvia involucrata*.

I hardly dare mention the genus *Salvia* again, but the plants are so diverse, and so lovely, that I could find one for almost every section of the book. This plant, with its dark cerise-pink flowers, breaks the unspoken rule of Mexican species, which all have red or blue flowers. It is a superb plant for late summer displays in a herbaceous border. At Powys Castle gardens in mid-Wales *Salvia involucrata* 'Bethelii' was planted in large blocks, 3m (10ft) across, on one of the wider terraces. The flowers stood out against the grey stone terrace wall above, and yellow chrysanthemums grew at the base of the large clump.

Salvia involucrata 'Bethelii' has splendid, square, four-angled reddish flushed stems as well as the symmetry of alternating opposite leaves on each alternate face of the square. (It is always enjoyable looking down the length of a *Salvia* stem from the knob of the flowers through the highly symmetrical foliage.) The spear-shaped leaves have prominent pink-flushed midveins and serrated edges. The inflorescences, carried at the apex of the branches, consist at first of dark pinkish magenta bracts. The tight globe of pink bracts resembles the outer tunic of an onion through which the flower spike thrusts itself. The flowers are narrowly tubular with velvety hairy mouths and sit in a long-lasting green calyx which remains after the bracts fall off. A large plant of *S. involucrata* 'Bethelii' may have two dozen inflorescences at once in an erect mass of stems.

The plant is not hardy and is a short-lived perennial in most places. It will survive mild winters as a dormant rootstock, producing new growth by the following summer. It loves sun and heavy, moisture-retentive soil. Tip cuttings can be taken any time and will root in less than a week in a closed frame. All parts of the plant have a faint but pleasant aroma.

Close-up of flowers of *Salvia sclarea*.

SALVIA SCLAREA

L.

FAMILY
Labiatae

ORIGIN
Southern Europe

HEIGHT AND SPREAD
1.8m (6ft) × 1.2m (4ft)

FLOWERING TIME
Midsummer

SPECIAL FEATURE
Long-lasting bracts

CLIMATIC ZONE
Zone 5

The soft pink mass of flower spikes of *Salvia sclarea*, showing the many coloured bracts.

Clary is one of the earliest plants to be cultivated yet is still little known. It is a sage of great distinction and one of several members of the *Salvia* genus included in this book, simply because they are so diverse and so many have excellent points of interest. *Salvia sclarea* gets its name from 'clarus' meaning clear; in ancient times the seeds and foliage were ground up to produce potions which were said to encourage good sight. In fact, the entire plant has a pungent odour which some like and some don't; I like it in small doses.

Clary is really a hardy perennial but makes poor growth after the second year and is much better treated as a biennial. In the first year it produces a large rosette of sizeable, wavy-edged leaves, some more than 30cm (12in) long. These leaves are dark green above and coarsely covered in pimples on their upper surface; the pimples often have hairs protruding from their tips. The following year the flowering shoot is produced in spring. The inflorescence can be over 1m (3ft) tall by half as much wide and the total mature plant as tall as 1.8m (6ft). The flowers are in clustered whorls around the stem in the typical manner of the *Labiatae* family, with normally four or five flowers at each whorl. One of the loveliest aspects of *S. sclarea* is the abundance of ornamental bracts. These are like floral leaves under the flowers, borne in pairs around the four-angled stem. They are white flushed with pink when the inflorescence first opens, fading to dark pink when the seeds ripen, thus maintaining the colour of the inflorescence long after the flowers have faded. The two-lipped flowers are not very large and vary from white to lilac in colour.

Salvia sclarea var. *turkestanica*, the Vatican sage, differs only slightly from the species in its larger, paler bracts and white flowers flushed pink rather than lilac; the name is frequently applied to *S. sclarea*. There are several species in the Middle East which are extremely similar to *S. sclarea*, one of the best being *S. macrosiphon*, with white flowers and whitish green bracts which take on a faint pink tinge when the seeds are fully ripe.

Salvia sclarea is easy to grow and likes full sun or partial shade. Plant 45cm (18in) apart so that the large basal leaves completely cover the ground, and the huge inflorescences produce a misty soft lilac effect. In my own garden I planted a tight clump in an enclosed area between a hedge and fence. The inflorescences entirely filled the space and self seeded in situ for year after year.

It self seeds prolifically; the seedlings overwinter as small rosettes and flower the following year. Seed may be sown in summer or under cover in spring.

SCABIOSA ATROPURPUREA

L.

FAMILY
Dipsacaceae

ORIGIN
Southern Europe

HEIGHT AND SPREAD
75cm (2ft 6in) × 15cm (6in)

FLOWERING TIME
Midsummer to late autumn

SPECIAL FEATURE
Dark maroon flowers

CLIMATIC ZONE
Zone 6

The dark red flowers of scented sweet scabious.

This plant has been held in high esteem for centuries and has a range of common names, from the sombre mournful widow, so-called because of its very dark flowers, which in its native Spain and Portugal were woven into funeral wreaths; to the more cheerful sweet scabious or pincushion flower. Normally grown as an annual, it is actually a perennial and is one of a hundred species of *Scabious* which superficially resemble the cornflower, but are in fact part of the teasle family. Its generic name comes from its alleged use in treating scabs or the itchy disease, scabies; no medical evidence supports this and the belief probably grew out of the Doctrine of Signatures theory of medicine that a plant's appearance symbolized the ailment it cured: in this case, the scab-like protrusions on the whorl of bracts surrounding the inflorescence. Whether or not the plant has medicinal value, its dark, scented flowers draw one to it aesthetically. This wild species was once the only colour available but in this century blue, purple, red, pink and white forms have been raised which although highly ornamental I feel are not an improvement on the species.

Scabiosa atropurpurea has deep maroon-red flowers clustered together in a rounded flower head with protruding pale pink stamens. Each small flower decreases in size from the outside of the head towards the centre, and the whole inflorescence is about 2.5cm (1in) across. In common with many species of *Scabiosa*, it has interesting seed heads. The foliage is finely divided; a particular feature of *Scabiosa* is that the foliage begins life more or less entire with little or no dissection and becomes more dissected and pinnate as the leaves grow older.

Scabiosa atropurpurea can be treated as a hardy annual or raised under glass and planted out once any danger of frost is past. It has a long flowering season and will grow on any soil in full sun.

SILENE COELI-ROSA

(L.) Godron

FAMILY
Caryophyllaceae

ORIGIN
Canary Isles and south-west Mediterranean

HEIGHT AND SPREAD
50cm (20in) × 1m (3ft)

FLOWERING TIME
Mid to late summer

SPECIAL FEATURE
Flowers change colour as they age

CLIMATIC ZONE
Zone 6

The prettily named annual, rose of heaven, is seldom seen these days although it was once quite widely grown. Though correctly *Silene coeli-rosa* it is often sold as *Viscaria elegans*; in old gardening books it is sometimes called *Lychnis*. Whatever its name, it has a special charm which warrants its inclusion here. *Silene* is a large cosmopolitan genus best known for campions or catch-flies – so called because many are sticky.

Silene coeli-rosa has sparsely-leaved slender stems and, like all small annuals, is only effective if grown in a clump, as individual plants look straggly. Its flat, disc-like flowers change colour as they age, which creates an interesting effect seen en masse. The white stamens and sterile stamen-like parts are flushed rose pink. The base of the five, overlapping petals is also white and becomes increasingly pink until it reaches the outer edge where it is rimmed with dark pink. The pale pink and white eventually deepen to a kind of salmon pink before turning fawn brown, at which stage the colour is uniform throughout the flower. There is a subtlety about the combination in one clump of pink and pale salmony brown, and all the hues in between, which is very unusual in nature.

Silene coeli-rosa is a sun-loving plant, happy on all soils except water-logged heavy clay. Sow in situ in late spring or early summer. Collect the ripe seeds before they fall to the ground as they will not survive the winter.

None of the cultivated forms of this species, ranging from red to blue, is as attractive as the wild species itself.

Silene coeli-rosa, whose flower colour changes with age.

SMYRNIUM PERFOLIATUM

L.

FAMILY
Umbelliferae

ORIGIN
Southern Europe

HEIGHT AND SPREAD
1m (3ft) × 60cm (2ft)

FLOWERING TIME
Early summer

SPECIAL FEATURES
Yellow young leaves and shoots

CLIMATIC ZONE
Zone 5

If there ever was a more delightful weed than *Smyrnium perfoliatum*, I have yet to meet it. This biennial plant is as easily established in a woodland as it is eradicated, and captivates the hearts of all who see it.

Smyrnium perfoliatum is a purely ornamental relation of the old-fashioned vegetable alexanders or alisanders, once popular but superceded by the introduction of celery. As its name indicates, *S. perfoliatum* has perfoliate leaves — that is, leaves which do not have a petiole or leaf stalk. Instead, the two leaf bases clasp the stem, creating a small flat platform. The edges of these fascinating perfoliate leaves are toothed; the large basal leaves are bright green but the plant's undisputed beauty lies in the top growth and uppermost foliage. This is bright lime green, verging on greeny yellow and at first glance gives the impression of being a late-flowering form of *Euphorbia polychroma* (*E. epithymoides*).

The plant is extremely effective en masse, as a ground cover for shady areas, especially in an otherwise dismal part of the garden; because it grows so thickly and luxuriantly during the earliest part of the year, it is effective in preventing the spread of other self-sown plants such as honesty. Sadly, the bright colour does not last all summer, but tends to fade once the umbels of clear yellow flowers start producing their black seeds.

S. perfoliatum is tolerant of most soils, and will live in bright sun or deep shade. It provides the best growth and truest colour in partial shade. Propagate from seed.

Smyrnium perfoliatum's lime green flowers and foliage.

SPHAERALCEA MUNROANA

(Dougl.) Spach.

FAMILY
Malvaceae

ORIGIN
North America

HEIGHT AND SPREAD
1m (3ft) × 2.1m (7ft)

FLOWERING TIME
Early summer to autumn

SPECIAL FEATURE
Trailing shrublet with brick-coloured flowers

CLIMATIC ZONE
Zone 6

Sphaeralcea species are commonly known as globe mallows in North America. 'Sphaeros' is Greek for globe, from which we get the word sphere; and *alcea* is Latin for the genus *Alcea*, or *Althea*, the true mallows or hollyhocks.

Sphaeralcea munroana is one of the hardier of the sixty species, making a thick woody trunk at and below ground level, and surviving reasonably mild winters in sheltered gardens. It is a mounded plant, with many trailing branches that will cascade gracefully over a wall or large rock. The plant grows in an unusual way, first vertically and then, when unable to sustain itself, falling over to let the lateral branches take up the upwards drive. I once grew this plant successfully as a low climber up a support where its flowers were seen to good effect.

The flowers are cup shaped and typical of the mallow family with pinkish petals and a faint hint of orange. They are borne in the leaf axils sometimes singly or in a loose raceme consisting of two or three flowers. I learnt very much by mistake that siting this plant in a small protected area was unsuitable; the shrub rampaged over the nearby path and its neighbours, covering all and sundry in a beautiful but choking mass of leaves and flowers. It was then tried on the top of the rock garden, where it grew very well, smothering only the bare rock beneath it. Like other members of the mallow family, it can be regarded as a shrub with herbaceous tendencies (or vice versa). Because of its invariable die back during winter I treat this plant as an annual. Stronger, tidier plants result, rather than the limpid growth which may or may not gather momentum after the ravages of a hard winter on a perennial plant.

Propagate from seed which quickly germinates or from softwood cuttings in late summer or spring. Keep stock plants dry in winter to avoid rotting.

Sphaeralcea munroana.

BULBS, CORMS, TUBERS AND RHIZOMES

To all but the botanist, a bulb or corm is more or less the same thing. There are other botanical differences, but suffice it to say that bulbs are essentially made up of water and food-filled swollen leaf bases, enclosed one over the other in layers like an onion (which is indeed a bulb). Corms are short, squat, swollen stems which flower and leaf from the top. Rhizomes and tubers are both storage organs, the former growing horizontally and the latter vertically in the soil.

Bulbs (and other underground storage organs) are highly adapted to their environment, most originating from regions with inhospitable climates. There are many ways in which plants can survive severe weather conditions, whether drought or extreme cold when water is frozen solid, creating its own type of drought. One way is to reserve all their hard-earned energy and water in these storage organs. Luckily many bulbous plants are highly adaptable and survive very different conditions from those in the wild.

Bulbous and bulbous-type plants vary as much as any other group of plants in size, height and rate of growth. Most, like *Amaryllis belladonna*, are clump-forming plants and others, like *Ornithogalum nutans*, are natural carpeters. Some, such as *Iris unguicularis*, colonize slowly, while others, such as *Allium moly*, spread rapidly.

DRAINAGE

One of the most important factors when growing bulbous plants is good drainage. A few, such as *Camassia* and *Leucojum aestivum*, actually thrive in very damp conditions and waterlogged soils, but these are the minority. The majority prefer a light sandy or gritty, free-draining soil. When the bulb is dormant, it is essential that it is not waterlogged; dormancy is usually during winter, when a combination of cold and wet may easily prove fatal, either by rupturing and damaging the bulb or by encouraging rot and diseases. A dry, well drained sloping site suits most bulbous plants.

SITING

Erythronium tuolumnense thrives in shade. Others, such as *Scilla messeniaca*, tolerate both sun and shade equally well, but most bulbs enjoy sunshine. Many, such as *Amaryllis belladonna*, only flower properly if grown in a hot dry sunny spot. Bulbous plants with variegated foliage also look their best in sunshine.

PROPAGATION

Bulbs, corms and rhizomes often produce a few very small offset bulbils below ground, like babies rising from the circular base of the bulb, top of the corm or sides of the rhizome. These are affectionately known as daughter bulbs. They are identical to the plant or mother bulb and are a good source of new plants. As with all flowering plants, bulbous and bulbous-type plants make seed which usually germinates well in spring and sometimes germinates as soon as it is ripe, as in the case of *Narcissus*.

PLANTING

Bulbs are generally most effective if grown in a clump, although there are a few, such as *Camassia* species, which are large enough to be planted singly and, as a single plant, they can be very effective. Bulbs which come from warmer regions of the world do grow best if planted deeply. They then can escape the worst of penetrating frosts. These bulbs also thrive if planted in a protected site, such as against a wall or beneath a shrub. The depth of planting varies from species to species, and some bulbous plants even have their own contractile roots which act like springs to pull the plant to the required depth. A general rule might be to plant bulbs twice as deep as the height of the bulb itself, and as close together as possible. This is, of course, more costly but the clump tends to flower better because there is more competition and, as a result of this, flowering is encouraged at the expense of foliage growth. It is a fact of nature that if there is a difficulty imposed on a plant, particularly on its root system, it rewards us with flowers, as survival of the species takes precedence over normal luxuriant growth. Bulbs can withstand constraint on their root systems much better than most plants; indeed, the only time I have ever seen a really happy clump of the Scarborough Lily, *Vallota speciosa*, was when about thirty bulbs grew one on top of another in a small pan on the window sill of a cottage on the Hebridean Island of Mull. It is important to clear away debris and dead foliage from around the necks of the bulbs, otherwise infection can set in.

ALLIUM CARINATUM

L. subspecies PULCHELLUM

FAMILY
Liliaceae (or *Alliaceae)*

ORIGIN
Mediterranean

HEIGHT AND SPREAD
30cm (12in) × 10cm (4in)

FLOWERING TIME
Late summer

SPECIAL FEATURES
Showy pink flowers on a slowly spreading plant

CLIMATIC ZONE
Zone 5

Allium carinatum subsp. *pulchellum.*

It is the *Allium* genus we have to thank for leeks, onions, garlic, shallots and chives – but there are also many species worthy of the herbaceous border, meadow or rock garden. *Allium carinatum pulchellum*, obligingly, suits any of these positions.

The species plant produces few flowers but a head full of bulbils which ripen and drop off as a means of rapidly spreading. This subspecies is much less invasive; *pulchellum* is Latin for beautiful, and an apt description of this plant.

Allium carinatum pulchellum produces greyish green, narrow leaves about 15cm (6in) long from which emerge the flower stems. These are much stiffer than the rather loose leaves and each inflorescence is enclosed by a pair of green bracts, which remain prominent as they age, drying out to become papery

and brown. The flowers resemble small pink cups, and each one has its own short flower stalk. The inflorescence can be more than 7.5cm (3in) across and looks like a flowery fountain as the blooms age and fall. There is a white form, *A. c. p.* 'Album', which emerged as a spontaneous seedling at the famous bulb firm of Van Tubergens and, surprisingly, comes true from seed.

Allium carinatum pulchellum is reliably hardy and never fails to produce a six-week-long display of flowers every year. It is most at home in a rock garden or raised bed in full sun, but can also be grown under creeping or trailing plants, including the creeping thymes, and *Campanula garganica* and *Campanula poscharskyana*. The young leaves and flowers will push through the ground cover, for a two-tier display. The subspecies increases slowly from bulbils and from seed which is sparingly set. Self-sown seedlings can be weeded out at will or transplanted.

ALLIUM KARATAVIENSE

Regel.

FAMILY
Liliaceae (or Alliaceae)

ORIGIN
Central Asia

HEIGHT AND SPREAD
15cm (6in) × 10cm (4in)

FLOWERING TIME
Early summer

SPECIAL FEATURES
Large inflorescence and good foliage

CLIMATIC ZONE
Zone 5

This plant is a classic example of how diverse the remarkable onion tribe – a genus composed of some 450 species – can be. The garden of Walpole House in Chiswick Mall, West London, is full of different *Allium* species and after many years the architect owner is still looking for more. This garden is sometimes open and is well worth a visit.

Allium karataviense could never be called a delicate plant but certainly it is very handsome; its name refers to the Karatan mountains in Turkestan where it was first found. The thick, smooth leaves are sufficiently striking to draw attention to the plant even before the flowers appear. The 15cm (6in) leaves are particularly broad, often 10cm (4in) wide, glaucous above and maroon red below. This maroon sometimes attractively edges the leaves.

The plant usually produces two leaves, growing opposite each other and bending back until their rounded tips touch the ground. The erect, central flower stem bears a globular sphere of pink stars. Although each starry flower is tiny, many make up a single umbel of which the diameter can be 7.5cm–10cm (3–4in) across.

The large globular flowerheads of *Allium karataviense*.

This plant always displays something of interest, from emergence of foliage in spring to when it dies back in late summer. After flowering, *A. karataviense* produces a striking display of large seed pods which are first glaucous, eventually dying in the heat of the sun to a straw brown colour. They remain erect on their stalks like brown globes after the leaves have withered.

A. karataviense is ideal for hot, dry spots, either in a sunny rock garden or at the edge of a border. Like all species of *Allium* it prefers well drained soil.

The clump increases slowly by the production of offsets, but it is easier to propagate this plant from the seeds it produces so freely. The plants should flower three years after sowing.

A L L I U M   M O L Y

L.

FAMILY
Liliaceae (or Alliaceae)

ORIGIN
South-west France and Spain

HEIGHT AND SPREAD
20cm (8in) × 10cm (4in)

FLOWERING TIME
Midsummer

SPECIAL FEATURE
Bright yellow flowers

CLIMATIC ZONE
Zone 5

The lily leek has been in cultivation for hundreds of years and is also known as the yellow onion, or golden garlic. It is one of the best of many ornamental onions. Much has already been said about the *Allium* genus, so suffice it to say that the yellow ones are somewhat scarcer than other colours and that *A. moly* is still not as well known as it should be.

Allium moly produces one or two greyish green lance-shaped leaves which appear in early spring and are gone by late summer. These leaves, 15cm (6in) long, make a fine contrast to the clear yellow flowers but will shrivel and die in exposed places even before the flowers have a chance to come out. The leaves may

Golden garlic, *Allium moly*.

persist longer in shadier places, and are more usually seen as a clump, as the species freely produces offsets and makes a massed effect of grey-green leaves. The inflorescence, typical of *Allium*, is an umbel of loose, starry radiating flowers which together can measure nearly 7.5cm (3in) across. Each flower is a quite distinct, deep lemon yellow and fades to a much paler colour as it gets older. The whole plant completely disappears from sight by late summer, showing no signs of its existence save a few withered leaves, and can be profitably positioned under a loose ground cover plant such as *Geranium* species.

Allium moly is extremely easy to grow and where conditions are right becomes invasive, so the site needs to be chosen carefully. In the wild, it grows in poor, dry soil so will be quite happy in the same and is useful for tucking in partially shady banks or the cracks in a paved terrace. I once saw it used as under-planting in a formal rose bed. Its place was later taken by grey-foliaged pinks which complemented the *Allium moly* in early summer and took over after the bulbs had died back.

Raise *Allium moly* from seed or from offsets which are produced in great profusion.

AMARYLLIS BELLADONNA

L. 'RUBRA'

FAMILY
Amaryllidaceae

ORIGIN
South Africa

HEIGHT AND SPREAD
60cm (2ft) × 30cm (12in)

FLOWERING TIME
Autumn

SPECIAL FEATURE
Large scented flowers

CLIMATIC ZONE
Zone 6

Amaryllis belladonna 'Rubra'.

Bulbous plants include many fragrant species and a high proportion of the best are those in the *Amaryllidaceae* family: *Narcissus*, *Crinum*, *Hymenocallis*, *Eucharis* and *Amaryllis*. This pink beauty is the true *Amaryllis*, unlike the large bulbous South American species belonging to the genus *Hippeastrum*, which is often sold as *Amaryllis*. *Hippeastrum* is equally fine and does bear a resemblance to *Amaryllis* in that both flower without producing visible foliage and both have large trumpet-shaped flowers. The true *Amaryllis*, though, is a more delicate plant with a deliciously sweetly scented flower and hails from South Africa. 'Amaryllis' is the name attributed to a beautiful Greek shepherdess and 'belladonna' means beautiful lady, indicating the great feminine qualities which the plants possess. As it flowers without any visible foliage, it is sometimes referred to as 'naked ladies'.

Amaryllis belladonna 'Rubra' is a superbly coloured dark red-flowered form, unusual and as appealing as the pink-flowered species, which actually smells of 'pink'. The flowers on all forms are borne on tall erect stems which have two enclosing bracts (spathes) under which are seven or more flower buds. The tightly packed umbel opens out in a similar manner to the not-too-distantly related *Nerine*, also hailing from South Africa. Each trumpet-shaped flower is 10cm (4in) long and composed of six curved, petal-like tepals, each with a dark central line. The whole umbel exudes a delicious and subtle fragrance. A mature clump of *A. belladonna* 'Rubra' can produce a dozen or so umbels of flowers.

A. belladonna needs a hot summer to flower; the bulb remains totally inactive until late summer, resting underground while its internal structure prepares for the cooler weather, when it flowers and seeds, just as in its native South Africa. It flowers best grown in a large clump against a south-west facing wall, or even better next to glass or heat-reflecting surface. A narrow bed between a wall and paving stones is a possibility, or even a sunny, gravelled corner. Plant 15cm (6in) deep in gritty or sandy well drained soil, acid or alkaline, enriched with food. A cover of yew branches or bracken helps protect against frost.

To propagate, very carefully remove bulbs from the main clump in early spring, while still dormant.

Close-up of *Camassia quamash*.

CAMASSIA QUAMASH

Greene

FAMILY
Liliaceae

ORIGIN
North America

HEIGHT AND SPREAD
1m (3ft) × 15cm (6in)

FLOWERING TIME
Early summer

SPECIAL FEATURE
Highly adaptable plant good for naturalizing

CLIMATIC ZONE
Zone 5

There are five species of *Camassia*, all native to the Americas. 'Camass' is the Red Indian word for the bulbs of all the species which can be eaten, and from this word we get both *Camassia* as well as the more transmuted 'quamash'. The *Camassia* genus could be regarded as the American equivalent of *Scilla* as there are no species of *Scilla* native to North America.

Camassia quamash is a variable species, in the size and shape of its foliage, and the flower colour, which ranges from deep violet blue, through pale blue to white. The deep-blue form is the most common in cultivation.

The fairly loose leaves are bright green below and slightly greyish green above. They are 30cm (12in) long and thrust upwards vertically in spring to make a shuttlecock, from the centre of which the spike-like inflorescence emerges. It is very similar to a giant elongated *Scilla* inflorescence and carries its attractive star-shaped, usually dark-blue flowers. Although bulbils are not freely produced, *C. quamash* eventually makes a neat clump with several inflorescences, and it seeds itself freely.

Like all *Camassia* species, *C. quamash* flowers early in the summer and then the whole top growth dies back in late summer, leaving no sign of life on the surface. This enables the diligent gardener to use the plant carefully in a wide range of locations. *Camassia quamash* is found in varying habitats in the wild from dry hillsides to wet meadows. I have seen it growing in a swathe across a traditional buttercup meadow and remember clearly the wonderful contrast of the dark blue spikes mingled with the yellow buttercups. The great advantage is that after the plant has flowered, the meadow can be mown without any damage being done. *Camassia quamash* can be grown on the edge of the woodland and also to fill in gaps in the herbaceous border before late-flowering perennials such as *Scabiosa*, *Liatris* or *Salvia* species appear. Plant the bulbs 7.5cm (3in) deep and 15cm (6in) apart in the herbaceous border in a clump. They may be planted at the same depth but randomly spaced apart in a meadow where, if they establish well, they will seed themselves.

Other species worth growing include *C. cusickii*, a taller plant, with pale blue flowers, and *C. leichtlinii*, which is taller still and comes in a range of colours, and has double as well as single flowered forms. This species although more spectacular is not so versatile and lacks the charm of *C. quamash*.

Camassia quamash.

D I E R A M A
P U L C H E R R I M U M

Baker.

FAMILY
Iridaceae

ORIGIN
South Africa

HEIGHT AND SPREAD
1.8m (6ft) × 15cm (6in)

FLOWERING TIME
Late summer

SPECIAL FEATURE
Unique long flowering stems

CLIMATIC ZONE
Zone 5

The *Iridaceae* family contains many delightful and diverse plants such as crocus, freesia, gladiolus – and the lovely *Dierama*. Of the twenty-five species of *Dierama* none excels this one, known affectionately as the wand flower, or, to my mind even more appropriately, as the angel's fishing rod. There is an impressive clump growing in the Chelsea Physic Garden and an even bigger clump in my father's garden at Newby Hall in North Yorkshire.

Dierama pulcherrimum (*pulcherrimum* means most beautiful) isn't strictly speaking a bulb but in fact a corm, common to many of its iris relations. This storage organ – a swollen stem base – has evolved so that the plant can withstand unfavourable weather conditions; in South Africa, where the plant originated, it has to endure a hot, dry period every year. It is fortunate for those in colder regions of the world that this evolution enables an otherwise tender sub-tropical plant to survive unfavourable weather conditions during winter too.

Dierama pulcherrimum produces narrow 1.5cm ($\frac{1}{2}$in) wide leaves which are stiff and slightly glaucous. They may reach over 1m (3ft) in length and are produced slowly throughout the summer, gradually accumulating energy for the grand finale at the end of

Pendulous flowers of *Dierama pulcherrimum*.

summer when the plant flowers.

The flowers are enclosed in a silvery, papery calyx and resemble miniature gladiolus hanging down from the bowing stems. The colour of the flowers can vary even within a single clump, from purple or pale pink to a dark reddish pink with purple stripes on the petals, and there is a white form. These flowers are loosely scattered in little chains along the flowering stems, which may reach over 1.8m (6ft) in length and are supremely graceful.

Dierama pulcherrimum, for the best effect, should only be planted as a clump of several corms, never as a single specimen. This not only produces an abundance of flowers, but the more corms there are, the better protection the clump will have from frost.

The corms increase annually by the production of cormlets of the same generic stock as the parent. *Dierama pulcherrimum* may also be propagated from seed which is fairly freely produced. The resulting seedlings will take three to four years to produce a flowering-sized plant.

This plant flowers best in a hot dry position with the corms planted 15cm (6in) deep. A sandy soil is ideal and I recommend a position at the foot of a wall in cold clay soil regions. The foot of the wall is always drier than an open herbaceous border and this protects the corm from sitting in a quagmire where it could succumb to rot.

ERYTHRONIUM TUOLUMNENSE

Appleg.
FAMILY
Liliaceae
ORIGIN
California
HEIGHT AND SPREAD
25cm (10in) × 30cm (12in)
FLOWERING TIME
Spring
SPECIAL FEATURES
Miniature, lily-like flowers and attractive foliage
CLIMATIC ZONE
Zone 5

Generally speaking, plants of the *Erythronium* genus aren't very easy to cultivate, but there are a few exceptions. *Erythronium tuolumnense* is one of these; the

Erythronium tuolumnense, a yellow-flowered dog's tooth violet.

European *E. dens-canis*, the dog's tooth violet, is another. Both have been included in the lists of specialist nurseries for years, but have only really been grown by keen gardeners.

I first became fascinated by this genus at Kew; the flowers reminded me instantly of miniature martagon lilies, a few centimetres (inches) above the ground. *Erythronium tuolumnense* struck me in particular because of its bright green, unmarked leaves. These leaves are usually borne in pairs through which the flowering shoot emerges. Each ovate leaf is 20–25cm (8–10in) long, brilliant green and quite leathery looking. Like many *Erythronium* leaves, it undulates along the edge. The flower shoot carries up to three but more often only one, bright yellow flower with six petals curved gracefully back, perhaps not quite as obviously as those of other species. Six prominent stamens protrude and give these yellow flowers a distinct similarity to the martagon lily. A clump of *E. tuolumnense* in full flower in a shady woodland is a really lovely sight.

The elongated corm of *E. tuolumnense* is equally distinctive, with its ability to reach exactly its optimum planting depth. This is not unique among corms, as members of the *Iris* family such as *Crocosmia* and *Gladiolus* will do the same. It is however unusual for the lily family to produce a corm, let alone one which is self-adjusting.

Erythronium tuolumnense prefers a semi-shaded spot and is quite hardy, slowly increasing itself from cormlets and also from seed. (Sow the seed fresh as soon as it is ripe in a damp, peaty compost.) These are by nature acid-loving plants, growing in open woodland; *Erythronium tuolumnense*, however, will tolerate a good deal of sunlight. 'Pagoda' is a beautiful hybrid with soft lime and light yellow flowers, which tolerates an open position. Both these plants as well as the European wild dog's tooth violet, *E. dens-canis*, grow in exposed positions at Chelsea Physic Garden. Here, under the deciduous cover of a *Ceratostigma willmottianum*, *E. tuolumnense* grows on the rock garden! The soil is very stony and the plants thrive, dying back to the corms by early summer before the shrub has started its growth.

EUCOMIS COMOSA

(Houtt.) Wehrh.

FAMILY
Liliaceae

ORIGIN
South Africa

HEIGHT AND SPREAD
60cm (2ft) × 5cm (2in)

FLOWERING TIME
Late summer and early autumn

SPECIAL FEATURE
Unusual flower spikes

CLIMATIC ZONE
Zone 5

By far the majority of bulbous or tuberous-rooted plants originating in South Africa are too tender to grow outside in cool temperate climates. But *Eucomis*, with fourteen species, is fortunately an exception. They are best grown in a tight clump so that each bulb serves to protect the other during the worst of the winter and in particular against severe frosts. *Eucomis* can be grown to great effect near a wall, which serves as a backdrop and protection, and there is a wonderful ribbon of *E. comosa* planted against the whitewashed walls of the fern glasshouses at Royal Botanic Gardens, Kew.

Eucomis comosa, also known as *E. punctata*, is particularly appealing, *comosa* referring to the extraordinary shuttlecock effect of the leafy bracts formed above the flowering spike. These leaves look remarkably like the leaves on top of a pineapple. Masses of flowers cling tightly to the single stem, each flower about 2.5cm (1in) across with pale cream petals and dark mauve centres. They look rather like dark-centred stars.

The flowers appear in late summer, well before any danger of frost, and the flowering shoots remain erect for two or three months after the flowers have faded, developing green, star-shaped seed capsules which are equally attractive.

Eucomis comosa prefers a sunny position, ideally a wall or hedge, but can be equally effective bordering a path or the front of a bed providing it is not too exposed to frost. They tolerate all types of well drained soil. Clumps are easily divided once the

Eucomis comosa.

Curious flower spikes of *Eucomis comosa*.

foliage has died down and been cleared away. Plants can be raised from seed quite easily and, although the foliage is not really outstanding, seed-raised plants may produce yellow- or red-tinged leaf forms. Keep the seedlings together, rather than thinning or pricking them out and keep them under cover for the first year. This speeds up their flowering by a whole season and you can plant the larger bulbs out in clumps a year later. Three years from seed to flower is quick for a bulb, especially if it will go on flowering successfully from then on, as this one certainly will.

GLADIOLUS COMMUNIS

L. subsp. BYZANTINUS

FAMILY
Iridaceae

ORIGIN
South Europe, North-west Africa

HEIGHT AND SPREAD
1m (3ft) × 7.5cm (3in)

FLOWERING TIME
Early to midsummer

SPECIAL FEATURE
Striking plant for naturalizing

CLIMATIC ZONE
Zone 4

Gladiolus communis byzantinus.

The European species of the sword lily – 'gladus' means sword in Latin – are less often seen than the familiar garish hybrids which are raised from the hundred or so wild South African species. Their parentage is highly complex and much of their origin is now obscure, although I do find some to be glorious plants. Of the few wild *Gladiolus* species in Southern Europe, the commonest is probably *G. communis* and the closely related subspecies *byzantinus*. This subspecies was previously regarded as a separate species but has recently been re-categorized under *G. communis* as the two are so close in structure. Philip Miller of the Chelsea Physic Garden originally thought the species came from Turkey, hence the name: *Gladiolus byzantinus*. It may well have got its vernacular name, Turkish corn flag, from boat cargoes carrying the corms from North Africa to Istanbul, or from the earlier use of Byzantine in reference to North Africa as well.

The first signs of growth are in late winter, when the clump of sword-shaped leaves protrudes at ground level, enclosed in reddish-tinged sheaths. The leaves are stiff, very dark green with slightly grey overtones. As spring progresses the leaves grow to a height of 60cm (2ft), their protruding parallel veins showing. The two-sided flower spike pushes through the leaves and stands erect, bearing more than ten flowers in two rows facing in slightly different directions. The colour is variable, but is usually magenta-crimson.

Gladiolus communis byzantinus is best grown where it is baked dry in late summer and well drained in winter. I have seen it beautifully naturalized on a dry, sunny, grass-covered bank in chalky soil. (The grass was not cut until after the foliage had begun to die back in midsummer.) I have also seen it grow well in an exposed but hot position in a rock garden where the corms must have been 12.5cm (5in) deep and the soil almost gravel. Lastly, I shall never forget seeing it growing in open meadow with blue *Camassia quamash* and yellow *Lilium monadelphum*, at the wonderful garden of the late Vicomte de Noailles, a noble French plantsman. His garden was at Grasse in south-east France.

Gladiolus communis byzantinus increases by cormlets but seed is seldom set.

IPHEION UNIFLORUM

(Graham) Rafinesque

FAMILY
Liliaceae

ORIGIN
Uruguay, Argentina

HEIGHT AND SPREAD
15cm (6in) × 7.5cm (3in)

FLOWERING TIME
Late spring

SPECIAL FEATURES
Prolific colonizer with starry lilac flowers

CLIMATIC ZONE
Zone 5

Here is a glorious plant which is at last becoming better known. *Ipheion uniflorum* is the sole representative in cultivation of a genus comprising some twenty-five species, all natives of South America. This plant may be forgiven its botanical obscurity, having been pushed by botanists from one genus to another in the past: *Ipheion* is closely related to both *Brodiaea* and *Triteleia*. However, there is no excuse for its obscurity in the garden, as it is easy to grow, sweetly fragrant and extremely desirable. Even on a balcony in a quiet back street of London, *Ipheion uniflorum*, interplanted with daffodils, was most effective as a ground cover in pots containing deciduous shrubs.

Ipheion uniflorum produces one flower per stem hence the specific name 'uniflorum' meaning one-flowered. The plant's leaves smell strongly of onion or garlic; there are one or two other groups of plants, including the South African *Tulbaghia*, which must contain similar sulphur-based chemicals. The bulbs of *I. uniflorum* are often matted together by their fleshy roots, and produce a carpet of stems and loose, grassy pale-green leaves. These often curl back gently from tip to base. The star-shaped flowers, well over 2.5cm (1in) across, are borne face upwards from the

Star-shaped flowers of *Ipheion uniflorum*.

top of each stem. There is a wide range of flower colour in the species, from white to blue violet, but the most common colour is lilac, with a central black line on the underside of each petal-like tepal, which heightens the star-like effect.

Ipheion uniflorum is a sun lover and grows happily on the poorest, stoniest soil, but hates water-logged clay soils. It is useful for growing under deciduous shrubs which allow it full sun for the vital first four or five months of the year. The plant begins to grow as the snows are melting and the frosts are still hard. I have seen it thriving in the gaps of a wall, where bulbs had spread themselves into nooks and crannies, and flowered at head height.

Divide the offsets at any time of year but the best time is after the foliage has died in summer. 'Froyle Mill' is a very good reddish purple cultivar and *I. u. album*, a white form which retains the black streak. 'Wisley Blue' is a very nice dark blue.

Latin, although it should perhaps be called the late spring snowflake. *Leucojum aestivum* is widely distributed even in Ireland and Southern England, and I suspect there may be some naturalization which probably occurred many years ago. It grows beautifully wild on the damp meadow banks of the river Loddon in Berkshire and is sometimes known as the Loddon Lily. The buds of the summer snowflake are like stiff grey-green daffodil buds, those friendly heralds of spring, and can sometimes be found in as much profusion. There is a neglected apple orchard, never mown and full of ancient anthills, in the Hertfordshire Chilterns. There, in late spring, grow pheasant's eye narcissus and summer snowflakes, with cowslips and ladies' smocks as a bonus.

Leucojum aestivum, pretty and charming though it is, is not the most beautiful species. It is not as spectacular as *L. vernum*, the spring snowflake, or the pocket Venus, *L. autumnale*, but it is far more durable. It forms dense clumps of bulbs which start into growth as early in the year as the closely related

LEUCOJUM AESTIVUM

L.

FAMILY
Amaryllidaceae

ORIGIN
Central and Western Europe

HEIGHT AND SPREAD
60cm (2ft) × 15cm (6in)

FLOWERING TIME
Late spring to early summer

SPECIAL FEATURE
Green and white flowers

CLIMATIC ZONE
Zone 4

The *Leucojum* genus contains twelve species, including the autumn, spring and summer snowflakes. *Galanthus*, a closely related genus, contains the more popular snowdrops. *Leucojum* probably originates from the Greek 'leucos' meaning white and 'eios' an eye, pinpointing the clear beauty of the nodding green and white flower. *Leucojum aestivum* is the summer snowflake, its specific name meaning summer in

Leucojum aestivum 'Gravetye Giant', growing in the stream at the RHS Garden, Wisley, Surrey.

Narcissus, and the lustrous, dark green foliage is like that of many *Narcissus*. The species is very variable, and the worst forms can have flaccid, excessively large foliage and flowers which are far too small in relation to the height of the stems and leaves: sometimes as much as 1m (3ft). A good form, such as 'Gravetye Giant', grows 60cm (2ft) high and should have three to five pendulous flowers per stem.

The stem has a conspicuous green bract at the top from which the bell-shaped flowers emerge, each about 2.5cm (1in) across. The flower consists of six green-tipped petal-like tepals, surrounding six golden yellow stamens.

L. aestivum thrives in any moist soil. I have seen it flourish 10cm (4in) deep in clay, submerged as an aquatic in running water, and it adores stream sides in full sun or shade. That said, the plant is so adaptable that it can grow if planted fairly deep in dry shade under an evergreen canopy. It makes a good herbaceous border plant for a difficult area and will survive cold boggy conditions. *L. aestivum* can be easily raised from seed or by division of the bulbous clumps.

Wild jonquil.

NARCISSUS JONQUILLA

L.

FAMILY
Amaryllidaceae

ORIGIN
South-west Europe and North Africa

HEIGHT AND SPREAD
40cm (16in) × 45cm (18in)

FLOWERING TIME
Late spring

SPECIAL FEATURE
Fragrant jonquil flowers

CLIMATIC ZONE
Zone 4

I would love to coax this beautiful plant out of the pages of the catalogues and literature that have been extolling its virtues over the centuries and into widespread cultivation. It has been hovering on the fringes for hundreds of years and in fact, two hundred years ago, was a great deal more popular than it is today. Unlike *Narcissus poeticus*, whose fragrant flowers are seen to flourish in many a garden, *Narcissus jonquilla* remains something of an unknown quantity.

Its name comes from the Latin word for rush which is 'juncus', because of its rush-like leaves. The Spanish, in whose country this plant can be found, called it 'la juncuilla', the little rush, and the French 'la jonquille'. The name survives in the charming, double-flowered 'Queen Ann's jonquil'. The large *Narcissus* genus consists of some fifty to sixty species, and half a dozen or so resemble the jonquil: the closest are the much smaller *N. requienii* and the similar *N. wilkommii* and *N. pusillus*, which have very small flowers.

The inner and outer parts of the 2–3cm ($\frac{3}{4}$–$1\frac{1}{4}$in) wide flower of *N. jonquilla* are deep yellow. The leaves are a rich, smooth dark green and can be as tall as the flowering shoot. There are usually two or three flowers per shoot but there can be as many as five or six. *N. jonquilla* adapts itself well to a wide variety of growing conditions and, because of its delectable fragrance, is often grown as a pot plant. It seems to prefer a dry location in the garden, and is therefore a good candidate for the rock garden or sunny border where it enjoys being baked in summer. It also thrives in rough grass providing the foliage is not cut until the middle of summer. I have seen it growing dotted throughout an old apple orchard, where it looked charming. It responds to a mulch of manure in the autumn by making extra growth the next year, followed by even more flowers.

Narcissus jonquilla can be grown from seed but it can take several years to flower. It is more easily propagated from bulbils removed immediately after the plants have flowered or in the following autumn.

Flower spikes of *Ornithogalum nutans*.

ORNITHOGALUM NUTANS

L.

FAMILY
Liliaceae

ORIGIN
South-east Europe, Turkey

HEIGHT AND SPREAD
30cm (12in) × 5cm (2in)

FLOWERING TIME
Late spring, early summer

SPECIAL FEATURES
Excellent for naturalizing, unusual green flowers

CLIMATIC ZONE
Zone 4

Ornithogalum nutans is a marvellous plant with greenish flowers, completely different in colour from the other 150 species in this genus, and very attractive — not always the case with green flowers. The specific name *nutans* simply means nodding which its lovely, almost translucent, flowers certainly do.

The genus *Ornithogalum*, derived from 'ornis', the Greek word for bird, and 'galos' which is Greek for milk, also contains the South African 'Chincherinchee', whose panicles of white flowers last for a month when cut. However, for the most part, the species are southern European, starry, white-flowered, low-growing bulbs.

Ornithogalum nutans is naturalized in several parts of northern Europe, including Britain. It thrives in light woodland and will grow in dryish meadows where I have seen large colonies in flower. Perhaps it is not very well known because it blends so well with its surroundings. There is a two-acre beech woodland near the holly walk at Kew Gardens, with swathes of *Ornithogalum nutans* in its loosely covered grassy floor as dense as bluebells in the average bluebell wood.

Its dark-green leaves emerge early in the year, producing growth well before the competing grasses nearby. By late spring and early summer, the 30cm (12in) flower stems have emerged, carrying one-sided inflorescences of pale, whitish green flowers. The six, petal-like tepals of each flower spread themselves widely, and have the characteristic green stripe on their outer edge. The flowers continue to nod from the bud stage, through opening, and then during old age and are excellent for cutting.

Ornithogalum nutans is remarkably easy to grow, given partial shade and a dry, well-drained soil. It seeds itself prolifically and freely produces bulbils.

PUSCHKINIA SCILLOIDES

Adams var. ALBA

FAMILY
Liliaceae

ORIGIN
Caucasus, Turkey

HEIGHT AND SPREAD
15cm (6in) × 15cm (6in)

FLOWERING TIME
Spring

SPECIAL FEATURE
White squill-like flowers

CLIMATIC ZONE
Zone 4

Pushkinia scilloides var. *alba* at Kew Gardens, Richmond, Surrey.

The genus *Puschkinia* is named after Count Apollo Apollosevich Mussim-Puschkin, a Russian chemist with a penchant for the Caucasus region, because he so admired the beauty of their flowers. There are two species but only one, *scilloides*, and its forms are in cultivation. These are sometimes called striped squills, and the specific name means scilla-like. The plants are surprisingly unknown, probably neglected in favour of the better known true squills, of the *Scilla* genus.

The flowers of *Puschkinia* differ from those of closely related *Scilla* and *Chionodoxa* in that they have a corona, a cup-like structure similar to that of a daffodil. The other prominent feature, found in the species, is a pronounced dark blue stripe down the middle of each of the six petal-like tepals. *Puschkinia* forms a spike-like inflorescence with ten to fifteen flowers and the effect of a large clump in bloom is very striking.

Puschkinia scilloides alba is a naturally occurring white form, often found among populations of the pale blue species and every bit as attractive. The pure white form is all the more lovely for the pale yellow anthers in the centre of each flower. The plant illustrated is a particularly large-flowered form.

Puschkinia scilloides alba is found high on the snow line in the Middle East and extends to Lebanon where it inhabits the woodland fringes. Here it is reliably hardy and slowly increases itself by means of bulbils

and seed. It flowers in early spring, the flowers often lasting as long as a month or more. It prefers to grow near larger plants which provide shelter from freezing winds likely to damage the flowers, but does not really like dense shade. There is a marvellous display of this plant at the foot of a tall yew hedge along the boundary of the Fulham Palace garden in West London, where it receives full sun and some protection. The soil there is well drained and slightly alkaline.

SCILLA MESSENIACA

Boiss.

FAMILY
Liliaceae

ORIGIN
Greece

HEIGHT AND SPREAD
15cm (6in) × 7.5cm (3in)

FLOWERING TIME
Late spring

SPECIAL FEATURE
Large number of flowers per inflorescence

CLIMATIC ZONE
Zone 4

What sets *Scilla messeniaca* apart from other spring-flowering squills is its tendency to produce as many as thirty flowers in an inflorescence, while its close relatives are humble, sparsely flowered creatures. The name squill comes from the Greek name for a massive bulbous plant once used extensively both medicinally and metaphysically. This ancient plant, *Urginea maritima*, can be found growing to over 1m (3ft) tall from Greece all the way round the Mediterranean.

Scilla messeniaca is not as massive, but retains the beauty of the ancient squill and is one of the prettiest and easiest to grow of the spring-flowering bulbs.

Scilla messeniaca starts to poke its head above the ground as soon as the frosts begin to subside and produces ten or more fairly large, glossy green leaves. The inflorescence is pyramid shaped and made up of many star-like, pale blue flowers opening from the bottom upwards. Each flower is quite small, but there are so many per inflorescence that the clump provides a mass of colour.

Like most *Scilla* species, *S. messeniaca* is impartial to soil type. I have seen it growing equally well in quite a dry situation in slight shade, and also in very open positions where it received the full brunt of wet and cold weather. There were more flowers on the drier site; in common with many spring-flowering bulbs, the plant probably requires a dry rest period at the end of summer to encourage the development of next year's flowers.

Propagate established clumps from offsets, dug up when the leaves are dying back in late summer or as soon as they appear in spring. This species also sets seed readily and will self sow.

Scilla bythinica is a close relation worth growing. It has larger flowers but there are less of them, nodding over at the apex of the inflorescence, like a small bluebell.

Scilla messeniaca.

CLIMBERS AND WALL SHRUBS

Climbers are plants which naturally twine themselves up supports or over obstacles, whereas wall shrubs merely grow against supports and need artificial aid to keep them trained in. Climbers have different ways of attaching themselves to their supports: their leaves may be modified into small circular sucking pads or discs which resemble the feet of tree frogs, or they may have sensitive tendrils, such as those of *Cobaea scandens*. Sometimes the leaf stalks (petioles) wrap themselves round the support, as in *Rhodochiton* and *Maurandya*. In some plants, the entire stem twines; in others, such as *Hydrangea petiolaris*, the stems produce roots which attach themselves to tree trunks or walls. Climbers may be annuals, as in the case of *Ipomoea* (morning glory), herbaceous perennials like *Cobaea scandens*, or shrubs, such as *Vitis coignetiae*.

Wall shrubs need support and usually have to be pruned into shape. Many vigorous shrubs, excluded from this chapter for lack of space, would make very attractive specimens grown against a wall. *Ribes speciosum*, for example, with its red flowers, would be spectacular against grey limestone or blue-grey flint. Nearly all climbers flower best in a sunny position, though some like shaded roots.

METHODS OF SUPPORT

Trellises are predominantly square or diamond-shaped lattice in wood, plastic or galvanized metal. Trellis fixed to battens prevents the plant coming in contact with wall surfaces, which the plant may damage. Trellis can also be used to create a partition or screen, making a kind of living fence. *Holboellia coriacea* makes a fine green barrier grown in this way. Trellis is available in large, detachable sections, so that a whole piece can be removed with the plant intact, should the wall or fence need repairs or alterations. Arbours, often of sections of trellis, make a kind of outside room, delightful if covered with plants.

Pergolas are a series of arches, either squared or curved, over and around which plants twine, creating a walkway or covered area. *Wisteria sinensis* is a superb plant for a pergola as the flowers hang tantalizingly close to the eye and nose.

Tripods can support climbing plants to make a living, three-dimensional display. Three stout stakes tied like a wigwam at the top with string wound around the stakes from bottom to top make a light, all-round support.

Wire is the easiest method of training climbers and wall shrubs; use adjustable self-tightening screws with an eye at the end through which the wire can be passed. The gauge of the wire depends on the type of wall, size of plant and distance between the wires. Some believe the wires should run up and down the wall; others, myself included, prefer to fix them horizontally, parallel to the ground. Always tie the main branches in front of the wires, rather than between them and the wall, where the branches may be chafed and damaged.

PLANTING

Always leave 60cm (2ft) between the stem of a climber and the wall or support, because the roots must have ample room to spread, initially. I prefer to plant shrubby climbers in spring so that the plants have a whole growing season to establish themselves. A mulch of well rotted manure around the newly planted climber undoubtedly gives it a boost. Annual and tender perennial climbers, such as *Cobaea scandens* and *Maurandya barclaiana*, can be grown in small pots under cover until frosts are over, and staked with a single cane up which to grow, until planted out in the garden. Even if the soil is damp I always water them in, to help the small root hairs to absorb water.

PRUNING

Climbers and wall shrubs are required to grow laterally against the wall and not out from it. Healthy new growth which could have been tied on to wires or trellis is all too often ruthlessly removed. When this happens, the older spent growth is left, and the plant naturally suffers, having to expend even more energy to make more new vigorous growth. It is much better to follow the basic rules for shrub pruning: prune out any dead or very weak branches, remove any obviously unwanted growth, then stand back and take a long look.

It is usually best to tie back as much vigorous growth as possible on to the support. Some plants are more difficult to prune. *Wisteria*, for example, makes most of its flowering growth from short spurs at the basal end of long straggling branches. Never prune right back to the trunk or the flowering spurs are lost. Pruning is best done in late summer, leaving 30cm (12in) long spurs, and a light prune of any newly produced straggly growths immediately after flowering encourages better flowering the following season.

SHAPE AND HABIT

Vigorous twining climbers such as *Cobaea scandens* might need curtailing in their rapid scramble through and over the obstacles; if left untended the tendrils can damage other plants. I once saw a large and vigorous *Buddleia* completely covered with *Cobaea scandens* and several of the branches eventually broke from the combined weight. Other climbers, such as *Solanum jasminoides*, perform best if allowed to roam freely and let their flowers hang gracefully from the ends of their branches.

Although only a few are included in this section, there are a great many shrubs which could grow successfully against a wall. A wall shrub needs tying back to some form of support, and it often needs hard pruning to keep it from growing too far from the wall and becoming an impediment. Wall shrubs can be trained as single-stemmed or multi-stemmed plants. The latter method is safer: if one stem dies another can quickly replace it. Evergreen wall shrubs and climbers are best pruned in early spring before the main thrust of growth occurs.

ABUTILON MEGAPOTAMICUM

St. Hil. & Naud.
FAMILY
Malvaceae
ORIGIN
Brazil
HEIGHT AND SPREAD
1.8m (6ft) × 1.8m (6ft)
FLOWERING TIME
Early summer to autumn
SPECIAL FEATURES
Unusual, lantern-like flowers, long flowering time
CLIMATIC ZONE
Zone 5

This genus is part of the mallow family which also gives us cotton, okra and the delectable *Hibiscus*. *Abutilon* contains mainly tropical and subtropical species but a few of its progeny, including *A. megapotamicum*, are reasonably hardy, providing they are grown against a wall. Thus protected, they can be relied upon to be as hardy as rosemary or lavender.

In its natural homeland of Brazil, *A. megapotamicum* is an untidy sprawling shrub which grows into a large mound or spreads itself over other plants. Its lax, slender stems make it very responsive to training.

The attractive but scentless flowers are produced in

The hanging flowers of *Abutilon megapotamicum*.

Abutilon × milleri.

COBAEA SCANDENS

Cav. var. ALBA

FAMILY
Polemoniaceae

ORIGIN
South America

HEIGHT AND SPREAD
To 8m (25ft) × 8m (25ft)

FLOWERING TIME
Midsummer to autumn

SPECIAL FEATURE
Large, cup-and-saucer shaped flowers

CLIMATIC ZONE
Zone 6

succession for as long as six months. Each unusual flower blooms for several days and looks like a narrow Chinese lantern, hanging from the leaf axils. The calyx is over 2.5cm (1in) long and a bright rich red, acting as a sort of cup for the trumpet of brilliant yellow petals, from which the male and female organs hang like a sort of club to attract insects. (This club-like structure is a feature of the mallow family and is particularly striking in the flowers of the popular genus *Hibiscus.*) The ovate, evergreen leaves are pointed and coarsely toothed.

Abutilon megapotamicum prefers a light dry soil and full sun. It can be pruned and tidied in early spring when growth is rapid. Propagate either from 7.5cm (3in) long softwood or semi-ripe cuttings put in a mixture of peat and sand in a frame.

There is a good group of hybrids, *A. × milleri*, crosses between this species and *A. pictum*. *Abutilon × milleri* has splendid golden-orange flowers, similar in shape to those of *A. megapotamicum*, but much larger, and capable, when winters are mild, of flowering non-stop all year round. In most winters, however, the plant is defoliated along with the flower buds. This hybrid has flowered profusely for two uninterrupted seasons in the Chelsea Physic Garden.

The *Polemoniaceae* family is a diverse and interesting collection of plants and the best known perhaps are the Jacob's ladders (*Polemonium*), and phloxes. An interesting feature is the fascinating range of pollinating creatures this family attracts, from bats and hummingbirds to hawk moths, flies, beetles and bees.

There are eighteen species of *Cobaea*. *Cobaea scandens* has single flowers which fade after a day to deep violet purple. The opening flower is foul smelling and attracts bats and flies while the purple stage is sweetly scented to attract bees. The bell-shaped flowers are 3.5cm (1½in) wide by 5cm (2in) long, and have a curled outer edge which furls back to reveal the greenish-tinged centre. *Cobaea scandens alba* is, as its name implies, the white-flowered form, and the one I prefer.

Scandens means climbing and this remarkable plant can cover 3.5–5m (12–16ft) of wall in one season provided it receives enough water. Allen Patterson, when he was curator of the Chelsea Physic Garden, planted several *Cobaea scandens alba* against a wall beneath a large yew tree and then allowed the climbers to scramble through and over the yew. In late summer and autumn, the *Cobaea* in flower atop the yew was a fabulous sight, and was shortly followed by large pods which continued to be attractive.

Cobaea scandens alba climbs by means of its leaf tendrils which curl around an object on contact. The tendrils are unusually sensitive to contact and you can almost see them curl; they are technically the modified leaflets of a pinnate leaf, and not all the leaves produce them. *Cobaea scandens alba*, in common with other white-flowered forms of non-white flowering plants, produces a clear fresh green-foliage which is not found in the type. This fresh green enhances the albino flowers.

Cobaea scandens alba may be treated as an annual climber in harsh climates; this involves collecting seed annually or taking cuttings. Seed is set spasmodically and when it does set, a large green fruit 7.5cm (3in) long develops and eventually ripens to split open and reveal many large flat papery seeds. These will geminate readily in spring. Cuttings may be taken at any time from soft tip growth inserted in a frame and they should root in less than three weeks. Keep them in a frost free but light airy place during the winter months.

Cobaea scandens alba prefers a sunny wall or tripod

and can also sprawl over shrubs. If the base is given adequate protection by surrounding plants or cloth sacking, straw or bracken, *C. scandens alba* can be grown as a perennial plant and may over a period of a few years become very large. It will tolerate a wide range of well drained soils.

JASMINUM MESNYI

Hance.
FAMILY
Oleaceae
ORIGIN
China
HEIGHT AND SPREAD
To 3m (10ft) × 3m (10ft)
FLOWERING TIME
Late spring
SPECIAL FEATURE
Bright yellow flowers
CLIMATIC ZONE
Zone 5

The primrose jasmine is a good name for this fine plant and in fact it was once called *Jasminum primulinum* after its pale yellow flowers that bloom at around the same time as the primrose.

Jasminum mesnyi resembles to some extent its winter flowering cousin *J. nudiflorum*, although the former is semi-evergreen, losing its leaves only in severe winters. The flowers of the primrose jasmine are frequently semi-double, enhancing the primrose effect.

The foliage of *J. mesnyi* is a bright glossy dark green with three leaflets about 5cm (2in) long making up a trifoliate leaf. Like many of the yellow-flowered jasmines, its flowers have no scent. (Some species, such as *J. odoratissimum*, are exceptions to this rule.)

J. mesnyi is hardier than was first suspected, but it needs to be well protected and supported with wires or trellis, as it is not a self climber. I have seen it survive several severe winters with temperatures well below −5°C (24°F) on a west-facing wall in London and have had similar reports of success in the country.

Cobaea scandens var. *alba*, the white form of the cup and saucer plant.

Sunny flowers of the primrose jasmine.

LATHYRUS GRANDIFLORUS

Sibth. & Smith

FAMILY
Leguminosae

ORIGIN
Southern Europe

HEIGHT AND SPREAD
3.5m (12ft) × 1m (3ft)

FLOWERING TIME
Early summer

SPECIAL FEATURE
Versatility

CLIMATIC ZONE
Zone 4

A west or south-facing wall protects the plant from the ravages of an east wind and provides maximum summer sunlight.

It is by nature a rambling plant and in its native China I would imagine it tumbles over itself, growing as it does at a rate of well over 1m (3ft) per year. It looks at its best trained against a wall where its arching four-angled stems show off the bright yellow flowers. Prune annually after the plant has flowered in early summer to remove any dead or weak growth, and tie back the most vigorous branches. It should continue to grow throughout the summer, producing new growth on which next year's flowers are made.

Propagate from cuttings of soft or semi-ripened wood taken in early or late summer. These take about a month to root but normally afford a high success rate. This plant never sets seed.

This 'everlasting' pea is rightly named because it is perennial and will live for many years. Though it has been around in our gardens for a long time, it is still unknown to most people and rarely grown today. The everlasting pea is easy to grow in a wide range of situations and when it flowers is a real beauty.

Having climbed rapidly by means of its gripping tendrils, *Lathyrus grandiflorus* slows down to produce flowers in early summer. It is aptly called *grandiflorus* as the flowers are large for a pea – up to 3.5 cm (1½in) across – and resemble those of the much loved and better known sweet pea. Although they have no fragrance, the flowers are attractively two toned with rich pink upper petals and the lower ones, or keels, plum red. The plant also produces appealing bluey pea-like leaves.

The everlasting pea can be grown up a wall, a trellis or over a pergola or arbour. Because it dies back completely in autumn, it leaves a noticeable gap for a large part of the year and is best sited where other plants will infill or indeed, where it may grow into or over other plants. I have seen it in a large London garden trained up either side of a painted white arbour surrounding a seat. When in flower the plants meet at the top creating an arch festooned with blossom. In late summer, when the plant begins to look untidy, it is simply cut to the ground and removed from the support.

It also grows well in a herbaceous border, up stakes

Lathyrus grandiflorus, the largest flowered everlasting pea.

PUNICA GRANATUM

L.

FAMILY
Punicaceae

ORIGIN
South-east Europe, West Asia

HEIGHT AND SPREAD
3.5m (12ft) × 3m (10ft)

FLOWERING TIME
Late summer to autumn

SPECIAL FEATURE
Unusual, showy flowers

CLIMATIC ZONE
Zone 5

or metal tripod; the support can be removed each autumn and the area filled with winter- or spring-flowering plants. *Lathyrus grandiflorus* is not particularly fussy about soil, although heavier soils will restrict its creeping root system to some extent and could be considered an advantage. It flowers best in full sun but tolerates light shade, such as the edge of woodland where it can ramble freely and makes a fine sight.

The plant is rather shy of setting seed but produces new plants willingly from its creeping root system. These should be lifted and divided in winter. *Lathyrus grandiflorus* is not the only species of perennial pea, although it does have the largest flowers. Others which I would recommend are: *L. latifolius*, *L. tuberosus*, *L. rotundifolius* and *L. nervosus*. The first three produce pink flowers, although *L. latifolius* also has a beautiful white-flowered form, *L. latifolius* 'White Pearl'. The last has blue-lilac flowers.

The pomegranate has been cultivated in Southern Europe for as long as people can remember and its name comes straight from the Latin 'pomum' meaning apple, and 'granatum' meaning of seeds. It was after this fruit that the Spanish city of Granada was named and also from this word originated the projectile grenades for which the grenadier regiment was famed. The French syrup grenadine is made from fermented pomegranate fruits.

The deep-green oval leaves of *P. granatum* are shiny on both surfaces and in autumn they fade a rich golden yellow, highlighting the dark red fruits. The 5cm (2in) long flowers are orange to scarlet and are borne in clusters at the ends of the branches. The flowers are uniquely structured, comprising a persistent fleshy calyx from the base of which the fruit develops, forming a tube with five to eight pointed lobes. Inside this orange calyx emerge the five to eight delicate orange crinkly petals which soon fall, revealing a mass of stamens. Although in cool temperate climates the pomegranates are often formed during warm summers, the fruit never ripen to full size, remaining miniatures of their Mediterranean counterparts. They do colour properly, though, and can remain attractive on the plant for several weeks. In hotter climates the fruit develops slowly, maintaining a hardened exterior which turns yellowish brown with dark maroon-red patches. The seeds develop inside, surrounded by a delectable-tasting fleshy pulp.

Opening flowers of the pomegranate.

ROSA BANKSIAE

R. BR. 'LUTEA'

FAMILY
Rosaceae

ORIGIN
China

HEIGHT AND SPREAD
12m (40ft) × 8m (25ft)

FLOWERING TIME
Early summer

SPECIAL FEATURES
Vigorous, free flowering, thornless

CLIMATIC ZONE
Zone 5

The pomegranate is grown successfully as a free-standing tree in the Southern Mediterranean, but not in a cool temperate climate. However, it will thrive against a sunny wall, and may need severe pruning to rejuvenate it after several years. It likes abundant manure or compost and prefers an alkaline soil.

Punica granatum nana is a superb dwarf form with miniature foliage and flowers only half the size of the larger plant. This can be attractively grown in a pot or as a free-standing shrub where it may reach 1.5m (5ft). I have heard of, but never seen, rich dark red-flowered forms, white-flowered, streaked-flowered and double-flowered forms of both the large and dwarf plants.

Propagate from softwood cuttings taken early in the year; or from fertile seed.

No book on unusual plants would be complete without a mention of the delightful Banksian rose which is quite distinct from all other types of rose. My father grows the double Banksian rose outside in Yorkshire but the plant that stands out most firmly in my mind is the ancient specimen against the south wall of Pixton Park, near Dulverton in Devon. It covers the whole of the corner end of the three storey house and looks lovely against the white stone walls.

Rosa banksiae 'Lutea' is the yellow double-flowered cultivar of the wild *R. banksiae* and is its only form which can be recommended as reliably hardy in cool temperate climates. The first form of *R. banksiae* to be cultivated was the single white flowered wild form, *R. b.* 'Alba', now rarely seen, and this was followed by the double white *R. b.* 'Alba Plena'. Next was the single yellow *R. b.* 'Lutescens' and finally, the reliable *R. b.* 'Lutea' or double yellow. All flower early in the year and are rarely killed by frost, but only the double yellow rose flowers well, if at all, after a hard winter. The flowers of *R. b.* 'Lutea' are an unusual pale apricot yellow, 2.5cm (1in) across and carried in abundant clusters on side branches two to three years old, never on current season's growth. The effect of these deliciously coloured double flowers is further heightened by the smooth thornless stems and shining pale-green foliage. The foliage will remain evergreen in mild winters, only becoming deciduous when subjected to continual freezing winds.

The double yellow Banksian rose growing
up the author's house.

The plant prefers full sun and plenty of rain early in the year to encourage regrowth, and is tolerant of both alkaline and acid soils. Well drained lightish soil that allows the roots to spread and seek water is ideal. The rose is thornless, so is not self supporting and needs training against a wall on wires, trellis or over a suitable support.

Rosa banksiae 'Lutea' is easily struck from semi-ripe cuttings in late summer and rooted directly into the ground in a favourable position or in a cold frame if available. It is always worth putting in ten times the number of cuttings you think you need to reap the reward of a few rooted plants at the end of the day. I have grown this vigorous rose from a cutting to produce a plant 4m (12ft) high by 1.8m (6ft) across in only three years from planting.

SOLANUM JASMINOIDES

Paxt. 'ALBUM'

FAMILY
Solanaceae

ORIGIN
South America

HEIGHT AND SPREAD
To 7m (21ft) × 4m (13ft)

FLOWERING TIME
Late summer through autumn

SPECIAL FEATURE
White, star-shaped flowers over many weeks

CLIMATIC ZONE
Zone 5

I have long been fascinated by the potato family which, as in the case of *Datura*, often combines beauty with a deadly poisonous nature. Woody nightshade, aubergines, and of course the potato, are all species of *Solanum*, proving what a diverse genus it is, with over 1500 species. *Solanum jasminoides* couldn't be more different from its cousin the potato, yet their family ties are obvious from their similar, star-shaped flowers.

Solanum jasminoides 'Album' is a white-flowered cultivar of the species, which normally has lilac-blue flowers. The cultivar, like the species, is a vigorous climbing plant which, when fully mature, and providing frost does not stunt its growth, can cover the side of a house. It grows literally metres (yards) in a single year and often sends up more than one stem from ground level. The young branches and semi-evergreen foliage are bright green, the foliage scattered freely but not thickly along the length of the branches, each leaf producing a twining petiole or leaf stalk to enable the plant to climb. The white flowers, 2.5cm (1in) across, have a tube of dark yellow stamens at the centre, and cluster loosely together rather like the flowers of some *Jasminum* species – hence the name *jasminoides* or jasmine like. These flowers are produced continuously on the new growth and look very striking against the bright green of the foliage. Flowering can last several months until the first frosts, reaching a glorious peak during autumn.

A large plant of *Solanum jasminoides* 'Album' at the
Chelsea Physic Garden, London.

SOPHORA MICROPHYLLA

Aiton.

FAMILY
Leguminosae (Papilionaceae)

ORIGIN
New Zealand

HEIGHT AND SPREAD
To 10m (30ft) × 4.5m (15ft)

FLOWERING TIME
Early summer

SPECIAL FEATURE
Free-flowing wall shrub

CLIMATIC ZONE
Zone 5

Solanum jasminoides 'Album' is excellent for growing in association with other climbing plants or wall
shrubs and looks good trained over larger plants.
Grown among evergreen climbers it produces the
effect of a second, completely different flowering.
Another advantage is that, should frost kill most of
the top growth (it rarely kills the whole plant), you
are not left with an unsightly wall or fence until the
plant re-grows in spring. New growth is quite
phenomenal, capable of covering metres (yards) in as
many months and often requiring serious pruning.
Propagate *S. jasminoides* 'Album' from soft cuttings,
which root quickly when placed in peat and sand in a
frame. It tolerates a variety of soils but thrives on
chalk and produces most flowers in full sun.

In New Zealand, where this marvellous plant originates, it is a large shrub but more often a sizeable tree
with a trunk as big as 60cm (2ft) in diameter.
Everyone knows it by its Maori name 'Kowhai' and
the New Zealanders regard it as their national flower.
I remember vividly standing underneath a fully
grown Kowhai tree in Lowry Bay on Wellington
harbour. It had a 45cm (18in) diameter trunk and a
large open crown covered in bunches of bright yellow
flowers which were out just as the pale green pinnate
leaves emerged. It is a first class spring tree there and I
have never seen one perform like this anywhere else,
although as a wall shrub it is still a show stopper.

Sophora is a unique genus in the pea family because
some of its eighty or so species have flowers with

Close-up of the flowers of *Sophora microphylla*.

corollas made up of standard, wings and keel, characteristics of that family, yet are unrecognizable as such. The petals of the corolla are almost all the same shape and differ only slightly in length, which makes the flowers look unlike those of a *Leguminosae* and gave Linnaeus the excuse to make an academic pun. *Sophera* with an 'e' was originally applied to any Middle Eastern pea-like plant, the name coming from the arabic word for a pea-like plant. He was apparently so bemused by the introduction of a *Sophera* from East Asia that he changed the 'e' to an 'o' making a pun on the word for wisdom and implying that a wise person would not be fooled by this group of plants.

Although *S. microphylla* will grow in the open as a free-standing plant in sheltered positions, it is sensible to give it wall protection if you want it to flower freely. The flowers are carried in short racemes along the branches, each flower comprising a green calyx from which emerge the five golden yellow petals (standard, two wings and two keels).

Sophora microphylla is a forest fringe tree in the wild, growing in open woodlands, in grassland or near water. It does not mind alkaline soils but will not grow well in either very heavy soils or extremely dry conditions. It is one of several plants from New Zealand which show neoteny, a juvenile stage often seen as a mature plant. In this the adult foliage varies in leaflet number and shape from the juvenile—clearly seen in the genera *Eucalyptus* and *Acacia* but also evident to some extent in *Sophora microphylla*.

The plant is deciduous, the foliage breaking into growth as the flowers begin to drop, and it looks particularly magnificent against a dark background wall which contrasts with the yellow flowers and bright green pinnate leaves. The species *S. microphylla* has twenty or so pairs of leaflets, many more than the other New Zealand species, *S. tetraptera*, although the plants are similar in all other respects. Both species exhibit the marvellous four-angled seed pods which give *S. tetraptera* its name — 'tetra' means four and 'ptera' means wing. The pods can be 10cm (4in) long and they contain hard, dull coloured, yellowish seeds which freely germinate if soaked.

Sophora microphylla growing against a house wall.

VITIS COIGNETIAE

Pulliat. ex Planch.

FAMILY
Vitaceae

ORIGIN
Japan

HEIGHT AND SPREAD
To 20m (65ft) × 10m (30ft)

FLOWERING TIME
Insignificant flowers

SPECIAL FEATURE
Autumn colour

CLIMATIC ZONE
Zone 4

The true grape vines have been well known to mankind for a very long time, with *Vitis vinifera* supplying wines, vinegar and raisins in Europe; and allied species providing similar benefits of food and fibres in other parts of the world. There are some seventy species of *Vitis*, most of which are climbers. Half a dozen species, *V. coignetiae* among them, originate mainly in East Asia and North America and are completely hardy, making them good garden plants.

The sheer size of this plant is enough to impress even before its leaves turn colour in autumn and prove its sobriquet of crimson glory vine. I have grown it for many years at Chelsea and find it controllable in a smaller area than it would otherwise occupy. Its real nature is undoubtedly sprawling over trees and shrubs. At Brockenhurst in Hampshire it covers the dark green foliage of several holly trees with crimson heart-shaped foliage. Trained up a wall or grown on a 3m (10ft) high tripod, it can be hard pruned in late winter and again in summer to curtail its growth.

Although popular, *V. coignetiae* is less widely available than it merits for one very good reason: it is difficult to propagate, particularly from cuttings. Yet it is such a phenomenal plant that it warrants inclusion here for the benefit of the nurserymen who still

bravely layer the vine or grow it from seed. The name of the species recognizes Madame Coignet who collected seeds of the plant in Japan in 1875.

Vitis coignetiae is a massive plant with rounded to heart-shaped and rather indistinctly five-lobed leaves. The larger leaves are 30cm (12in) long by almost as much across. The leaves are green and smooth on top but both the young shoots and leaf undersides are covered in a felt-like, almost russet brown mat of hairs. The undersides of the leaves also show the intricate veining which protrudes prominently from the leaf surface. The greatest glory of this plant is not its cluster of insignificant greenish flower pedicles, nor the small black grapes which follow, but the wonderful autumn hues and tints of the foliage. Every large, heart-shaped leaf colours the whole plant a rich plum red while the green beneath the plum red turns bright orange. The leaves finally turn a rich crimson.

Vitis coignetiae has another 'small' drawback: it must have enough space in which to grow. I have seen it cover an entire wall of a three storey house, and climb most successfully over the top of a group of large English oaks; this made a particularly good partnership because the oaks did not turn their drabber brown autumn colour until the vine leaves had fallen. *Vitis coignetiae* can be controlled in smaller areas by planting it in hot, dry sites, where it will not grow so vigorously; and also by hard pruning before the growth really gets going in late spring.

Leaves of *Vitis coignetiae* beginning to show autumn colour.

WISTERIA FLORIBUNDA

(Willd.)
D.C. forma MACROBOTRYS

FAMILY
Leguminosae

ORIGIN
Japan

HEIGHT AND SPREAD
Up to 10m (30ft) × 4.5m (15ft)

FLOWERING TIME
Midsummer

SPECIAL FEATURES
Variation of flower colour and length of flowering shoots

CLIMATIC ZONE
Zone 4

The long flower trusses of *Wisteria floribunda macrobotrys*.

Wisteria floribunda and other long-cultivated forms which come under the umbrella *macrobotrys*, meaning large truss, must be among the world's loveliest climbing plants.

I first saw *W. floribunda macrobotrys* as a student at the Royal Botanic Gardens, Kew, and remember being transfixed by the immense length of the racemes: some were over 1m (3ft) long. The plant's general growth and foliage are very similar to the more familiar *W. sinensis*, which has scented lilac trusses reminiscent of Oriental watercolours and English summers. When *W. floribunda macrobotrys* flowers, the difference is strikingly apparent. Its individual florets are not as tightly compacted, so that the inflorescence looks looser and less stiff than those of *W. sinensis* and the colour varies from a clear lavender blue to a pale purple blue with yellow centres. This latter colouring, sometimes referred to as 'Multijuga', is more common and is the one to be seen at Kew. There is also a beautiful white form.

The flowers are typically pea-like and quite large, usually 2cm (¾in) across, clustered on the inflorescence. Although the individual flowers are only faintly scented, collectively their fragrance is delectable. As an additional bonus, it is comparatively fertile. *Wisteria sinensis* very rarely sets seed but *W. floribunda macrobotrys* produces a number of brown, velvety covered seed pods.

The two ancient specimens at Kew are trained around and over a wooden circular support 1.8m (6ft) high with a diameter of around 3m (10ft) and supported by several large wooden posts. The plants are pruned in early spring, to remove any straggly new growth, leaving short flowering spurs.

The species can also be grown to great effect on a wall or up a large tree, in which case pruning is not so essential although you can encourage flowering by pruning much of the whippy new growth back to flowering spurs in late summer.

Wisteria floribunda is not easy to propagate. Seed does not germinate freely. New growths pegged on to the ground, with the bark underneath scraped off first, may produce roots, given time.

WISTERIA SINENSIS

(Sims) Sw. 'ALBA'

FAMILY
Leguminosae

ORIGIN
China

HEIGHT AND SPREAD
To 7m (21ft) × 4.5m (15ft)

FLOWERING TIME
Early summer

SPECIAL FEATURES
Vigorous, with fragrant white flowers

CLIMATIC ZONE
Zone 4

Scented white flowers of *Wisteria sinensis* 'Alba'.

The Chinese Wisteria is a wonderful plant, its lilac-coloured flowers well loved and familiar throughout the world. According to that master of trees and shrubs W. J. Bean 'No climber ever brought to this country has added more to the beauty of gardens.' The white form of this lovely species, however, is rarely seen in gardens. It was introduced by Robert Fortune and produces just as fine a display of blooms as the species, though with smaller scale flowers and foliage than the white cultivar of the Japanese Wisteria, *W. floribunda* 'Alba'.

The scented flower trusses of *W. sinensis* 'Alba' are 15cm (6in) long, composed of clear white 'pea' flowers with yellow-tinged basal petals. Its leaves are typically pinnate, and made up of eleven rounded leaflets.

In the wild, *W. sinensis* is a woodland twiner and in Savill Garden there is an old oak with this plant growing through it, which at first sight, from a distance, looks like some tropical leguminous tree in full flower. Arbours, pergolas, walls and trellis are suitable supports, but it is nicest to be able to stand beneath the drooping trusses. It is ideal for covering the gate entrance to a house, so that one walks under an arch of those pure white flowers.

Wisteria sinensis and its white-flowered cultivars grow fast and flower freely when still quite young. The more sunlight the plant gets the better its flowering capacity is bound to be. It loves acid, well drained soils but will grow fairly well on alkaline soils provided leaf mould, manure and peat are incorporated. Pruning back the lengthy current season's growth to about 30cm (12in) from the older branches in late summer encourages flowering.

Wisteria sinensis 'Alba' is not easy to propagate. Seed is unreliable and scarcely sets. Cuttings are equally difficult – a job best left to the professionals.

HERBACEOUS PERENNIALS

Herbaceous perennials are non-woody or barely woody plants, capable of living for many years. A fairly flexible approach, however, is needed when classifying plants as herbaceous perennials. They are generally clump forming and emerge from a collective rootstock each year, the top growth dying back every autumn. This rootstock can be a matted mass of short rhizomes or tubers, as in *Veratrum*, or fleshy stems which are almost bulbs, as in *Agapanthus*. Strictly speaking, bulbs, corms and tubers are herbaceous perennials, as they function in the same way. Because of their very individual nature, though, they are a separate category.

SHAPE AND HABIT
Herbaceous perennials may be multi-stemmed and erect like *Centaurea macrocephala*, or creeping like *Caltha polypetala*. They tend to be upright plants that grow rapidly from the moment their buds break through the soil's surface in spring until the flowers have faded and seed is made. Such plants trap and store energy from the sun throughout the long days of summer to be kept in the rootstock over winter. Most herbaceous plants originate from continental plains and meadows, although some come from hotter, drier regions with winter rainfall. Many of this group are evergreen, such as *Helleborus corsicus*, *Iris japonica* and *Phormium tenax*. Meadow plants such as *Uniola latifolia* and *Hemerocallis dumortieri* are used to the coldest winters and are among the hardiest plants known. Other species, such as *Agapanthus*, come from more Mediterranean-type climates and are only hardy if planted deeply and in a more sheltered position.

PROPAGATION
By far the best method of propagating herbaceous perennials is by division of the plant clumps. The newly divided sections should be large, as re-establishment and further growth can be almost impossible if a tiny piece is planted straight into the border where it is prone to disease, frost and competition from other plants. A small piece may also take many years to flower.

Growing herbaceous perennials from seed is also generally successful with the reservation that some species tend to hybridize and others, such as *Veratrum*, can take up to six or seven years to flower.

SITING
Blending shapes and colours is a matter of personal preference, but there are also practical considerations. *Veronica cinerea*, for example, won't be happy too close to *Hosta plantaginea* as the large leaves of the latter will shade the former from the light causing severe deterioration and, eventually, death. Likewise, a shade-loving herbaceous perennial would scorch and dry out in full sun.

Most herbaceous plants are content in a wide range of soil types, irrespective of structure, texture and pH value. They do not like to completely dry out and an eye should be kept on their watering requirements.

STAKING
Sprawling and top-heavy species need staking to prevent them falling over their neighbours. Sometimes, plants may help support each other, but as a general rule, any supports should be as unobtrusive as possible, such as interwoven hazel branches, or wire and branches. Insert stakes alongside clumps long before they need support, so the supports are better hidden and it won't need doing later in the season, when there is plenty to do already.

CUTTING BACK
Herbaceous plants need cutting down in late summer or autumn, so they don't use up all their energy in producing masses of unwanted seed. Cut down stems between the end of the plant's flowering and the beginning of seed ripening. One must also consider the beauty of many seeds before cutting the plants back; compromise is sometimes best.

MANURING AND COMPOSTING
Most herbaceous plants benefit from a good layer of mulch put on the bed and dug well in beside the

rootstock during the dormant season, in late autumn or late winter. Take care not to damage the rootstock.

PLANTING AND TRANSPLANTING

Although a herbaceous plant can be moved or planted while it is in active growth, it is not a good time to do it and the plant, unless it is bought established in its container, will generally tell you so, by aborting its flowers and prematurely dying back to the roots. Early spring or late autumn, that is, the beginning or end of dormancy, is the best time to plant and transplant, especially during or immediately after plenty of rain when the ground is soft and moist. If you are planting several creeping, fleshy or rhizomatous rooted plants, to form an 'instant' clump, dig a shallow crater in the required area and place the roots over the base, then replace the earth. This is much easier than trying, as I once did, to plant all the roots individually.

ACANTHUS HIRSUTUS

Boiss.

FAMILY
Acanthaceae

ORIGIN
Turkey

HEIGHT AND SPREAD
1m (3ft) × 1m (3ft)

FLOWERING TIME
Midsummer

SPECIAL FEATURE
Tall spikes of green flowers

CLIMATIC ZONE
Zone 4

The genus *Acanthus* is usually associated with the classical motif of leaves decorating Corinthian pillars;

A clump of the green flowered hairy acanthus.

which species was represented, can only be guessed at, though I think it is probably *Acanthus mollis*. Most *Acanthus* are grown as much for their architectural leaf forms as for their flowers. In this species, the flowers excel in beauty the smaller-scale but still attractive foliage.

The genus is diverse, including species which make fair-sized shrubs in tropical parts of the world, and perennials with large tuberous roots. *Acanthus hirsutus* is a showy, hardy and useful herbaceous perennial with narrower, shorter leaves than those of *A. mollis*. *Hirsutus* means covered in stiff hairs and refers to almost all the growing parts of the plant which are indeed clothed with hairs. Most of the leaves have prominent lobes characteristic of the genus but the youngest leaves are often without lobes, which gives the clump a rather strange appearance. The leaves are only about 20cm (8in) long, much smaller than those of other species.

The flowers of *A. hirsutus* are particularly large for the genus, especially when seen in relation to the smaller foliage. The flower spikes can be up to 1m (3ft) long. Each flower has conspicuous lips and is an unusual pale green with streaks of white. The flowers are enclosed in stiff, spiny darker green calyces; the combination of colours always reminds me of gooseberry fool and cream. In a clump 1m (3ft) across there may be half a dozen or more of these stiff inflorescences, bristling with hairs. You may be lucky enough to get some ripe seeds.

Acanthus hirsutus is happiest on heavier, alkaline soils. It will grow on lighter soils, but more slowly. It likes full sun and will tolerate the coldest weather.

One of the great attractions of this plant for me is its slow, steady increase in clump size, in contrast to the two better known species, *A. mollis* and *A. spinosus*. *Acanthus mollis* is an impossible-to-eradicate weed once the seedlings get a hold, and it seeds freely; *A. spinosus* spreads everywhere by means of long fat rhizomatous roots and can be difficult to control. *Acanthus hirsutus* can be easily divided once the clump is large enough and is easy to grow from seed.

ACONITUM VULPARIA

Reichenb.

FAMILY
Ranunculaceae

ORIGIN
Europe and Asia

HEIGHT AND SPREAD
1m (3ft) × 1m (3ft)

FLOWERING TIME
Midsummer

SPECIAL FEATURE
Yellow flowers

CLIMATIC ZONE
Zone 4

Aconitum vulparia and other *Aconitum* species have been known as 'wolf's bane' since the Dark Ages, and sometimes 'badger's bane'. These names derived from the belief that the black tuberous roots left by the window or door, particularly in winter, would discourage packs of wolves from entering; hence the meaning of 'vulparia' — 'of the wolf'. It is a beautiful but highly poisonous plant and the reasoning was that the wolves would be tempted to eat the 'food' put out for them and suffer an agonizing death. All parts of the plant are poisonous and shepherds used to muzzle their sheep in fields where *Aconitum* grew to prevent them grazing it.

However, as a garden plant, *Aconitum vulparia* is a highly desirable herbaceous perennial, joining a long list of lovely but deadly plants: *Laburnum*, lily-of-the-valley, foxglove and many more. The blue-flowered species are the more usual, and I was surprised to discover the beautiful soft yellow flowers of *A. vulparia*.

The foliage is typical of the *Ranunculaceae*, or buttercup family: broad, deeply divided flat leaves which are bright green and shiny. The strong, much branched flowering stems often bend over under the weight of the flower buds and staking is necessary. Each 'helmet' is pale yellow and can be up to 2.5cm (1in) long by half as much broad, with several flowers per stem. The flowers are cowl, helmet or hooded in shape, hence the vernacular monkshood.

Aconitum vulparia, a yellow-flowering monkshood.

Aconitum vulparia, like all allied species, is completely frost hardy. It grows in any soil but prefers a water retentive and reasonably nutritious one, such as the rich borders of woodlands. I have however grown *A. vulparia* (and other species) in an extremely well-drained soil that was prone to drying out in summer and they suffered only from a slightly smaller stature and smaller flowers. *Aconitum vulparia* grows in both full sun and light shade which makes it suitable for a woodland garden where it can be allowed to ramble freely, supporting itself on lower growing plants nearby.

It germinates readily from seed, and the tuberous roots can also be divided when dormant.

A M S O N I A T A B E R N A E M O N T A N A

W a l t.
FAMILY
Apocynaceae
ORIGIN
North America
HEIGHT AND SPREAD
75cm (2ft 6in) × 1m (3ft)
FLOWERING TIME
Midsummer
SPECIAL FEATURES
Pale lilac flowers, glossy foliage
CLIMATIC ZONE
Zone 5

The *Apocynaceae* family is an interesting one whose members mostly grow in tropical regions. The name means 'against dogs' referring to the poisonous nature of a milky latex produced by certain species; in the tropics certain kinds of rubber are made from plants in this family. It also gives us some very useful medicinal plants, such as *Catharanthus roseus*, the Madagascar periwinkle whose latex yields anti-cancer alkaloids; and some beautiful hardy plants, such as the genus *Vinca*, whose blue starry periwinkle flowers are typical of the family.

The genus has twenty species of herbaceous perennials, but *A. tabernaemontana* is the species most often cultivated. It is a variable species whose leaves may be quite broad or narrow and willow-like, which gave the plant its former name of *A. salicifolia*, the specific name meaning leaves like willow. Some botanists call the narrow-leaved plant a natural variety of the species: *A. tabernaemontana* var. *salicifolia*.

Amsonia tabernaemontana has a rigid form of growth, spreading slowly from stolons below ground. The shoots are green and sappy but they are almost woody at the base which creates the appearance of a shrub. This is combined with narrow, willow-like glossy leaves which look as though they should be evergreen. A clump over 1m (3ft) in diameter of *A. tabernaemontana* in bloom is a lovely sight, the panicles of flowers in palest blue carried above the glossy shining foliage. The five flat, radiating petals of each

Amsonia tabernaemontana.

A NEMON E RUPICOLA

Camb.

FAMILY
Ranunculaceae

ORIGIN
West China

HEIGHT AND SPREAD
25cm (10in) × 10cm (4in)

FLOWERING TIME
Early summer

SPECIAL FEATURES
White flowers, then fluffy seed heads

CLIMATIC ZONE
Zone 4

flower are very narrow, only a few millimetres (fraction of an inch) wide and about 2cm ($\frac{3}{4}$in) long. In common with other species of *Amsonia* the plant exudes a milky latex when cut, and care should be taken when handling the plant; the latex is not dangerous but could cause skin irritation.

Amsonia tabernaemontana is effectively used in a Sussex garden where the beds are edged with local sandstone paving stones and 1m (3ft) wide clumps are surrounded and indeed invaded by the silvery carpet of *Acaena argentea*. The silvery creeping stems of the latter provided a marvellous contrast to the pale blue flowers and glossy green leaves of the *Amsonia*.

Amsonia tabernaemontana turns a lovely bright yellow in autumn before dying back. The clumps are easily grown in full sun or partial shade and like a light, well-drained soil. They do not need staking. Propagate by lifting and dividing dormant plants, from softwood cuttings taken in early summer and inserted in a closed frame in 50:50 peat and sand, or from seed sown in the spring.

The mythology connected to the genus is fascinating. In one Greek version, Adonis, the embodiment of male beauty, was killed by a boar and from his spilled

Anemone rupicola.

blood sprouted *Anemone*. It flowers in open places, its seed spread by the wind. 'Anemos' means wind in Greek, and the sea anemone certainly derives its name from the wind-like effect of its tendrils as the waves and currents wash over it.

Anemone rupicola is one of several very pretty species on the fringes of cultivation. Every old-fashioned cottage garden relied heavily in late summer on the beautiful Japanese anemone and this is an equally lovely species, just as easy to grow, requiring little or no attention from year to year except weeding and containing its growth. It makes a delightful deciduous woodland undercarpet.

In common with other plants of the buttercup family, *Ranunculaceae*, *Anemone rupicola* has deeply dissected palmate leaves, and petal-less flowers. The colour comes from the five petal-like sepals which form a white, cup-shaped flower, with a purple flush on the outer sepals, and a mass of rich golden yellow stamens. The flowers are borne singly on stems which rise above the verdant undercarpet of foliage.

Rupicola means of the rocks, and it is best grown in shallow soil and shade, though I have seen it flourish where it received the morning sun. It thrives in dry conditions where its dark green leaves can add a luxuriant note to otherwise barren ground. It grows from short, slowly creeping rhizomes, forming a thick carpet.

A whole mass of this plant in flower is a fine sight, the white flowers shining against the green foliage. The extraordinary fluffy seedheads persist for several months like upright drumsticks, making obvious the relationship between *Anemone* and *Clematis*, for both produce this 'old man's beard' effect. The fluffy seedheads carry a few nutlets to regions further afield, but seeds are rarely viable. Propagate by offsets dug up at any time.

ASPHODELINE LUTEA

Reicht.

FAMILY
Liliaceae

ORIGIN
Southern Europe

HEIGHT AND SPREAD
1m (3ft) × 45cm (18in)

FLOWERING TIME
Early to midsummer

SPECIAL FEATURES
Sword-like silver foliage and yellow flowers

CLIMATIC ZONE
Zone 5

The asphodel meadows of ancient Greece were supposed to have been the famed Elysian fields inhabited by the souls of warriors. The fields' name, asphodiles, referred to both the yellow and white asphodel and also *Narcissus*, which was called 'asphodilus' by the Romans and eventually became daffodil. Fuch's drawing of asphodel in *De Historia Stirpium*, 1542, resembles one of the martagon or Turk's cap lilies, to add to the confusion. Asphodeline is distinguished from its close allies in the lily family by its erect branching stems which produce foliage and then bear the inflorescences above this.

The genus has fifteen species, all of which are native to the Mediterranean. They are often found in extremely hot, sun-baked positions, in limestone rocky outcrops or sandy areas. Most of the species are yellow-flowered and have narrow greyish foliage which gives *A. lutea* its other common name, king's spear. It is a rhizomatous plant which spreads slowly outwards to make new rosettes of soft, grey grassy foliage. Each narrow leaf can be as long as 45cm (18in) with a prominent keel giving it a characteristic central dark line. The young rosettes of radiating foliage are a handsome sight in early spring, long before the inflorescences are made. These flower spikes are stiff and narrow and can reach 1m (3ft) in height.

Although there are many buds on each spike, seldom more than a few open at a time, which is a pity,

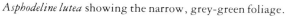

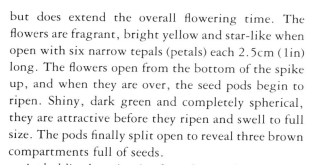

Asphodeline lutea showing the narrow, grey-green foliage.

Close-up of the inflorescence.

but does extend the overall flowering time. The flowers are fragrant, bright yellow and star-like when open with six narrow tepals (petals) each 2.5cm (1in) long. The flowers open from the bottom of the spike up, and when they are over, the seed pods begin to ripen. Shiny, dark green and completely spherical, they are attractive before they ripen and swell to full size. The pods finally split open to reveal three brown compartments full of seeds.

Asphodeline lutea is a hardy and easy plant to grow although it hates waterlogged soils in winter and requires maximum sun. Plenty of water at the rosette stage will encourage free flowering.

This species has an elegant later-flowering cousin, *A. liburnica*, from the Eastern Mediterranean. This has very fine, almost filigree-like, grey foliage and a similar growth habit. It produces short, 10cm (4in), spikes of yellow flowers branching from an inflorescence reaching 1m (3ft). This distinguished plant likes similar conditions to the more robust *A. lutea* but spreads more slowly. Both can be divided in early spring. Transplant quite a few rosettes during division, as this plant re-establishes itself more quickly from a clump than a single bud.

CALTHA POLYPETALA

Hochst.

FAMILY
Ranunculaceae

ORIGIN
Caucasus

HEIGHT AND SPREAD
60cm (2ft) × 45cm (18in)

FLOWERING TIME
Late spring

SPECIAL FEATURES
Vigorous, golden flowered, wet-loving plant

CLIMATIC ZONE
Zone 4

The marsh marigolds are splendid buttercups of which *Caltha polypetala* is the biggest and possibly the best. Curiously, the showiness of the large flowers of the twenty or so species of *Caltha* is due to petal-like sepals, as the true petals are absent. The vigour of the species lends itself to the colonization of stream sides and the boggy areas found around ponds and rivers. It is well planted in the water garden at Sezincote in Gloucestershire, and also around the ponds in Savill Garden at Windsor, but all too often it is vainly restricted to some paltry patch where its natural stature is unable to develop.

The giant marsh marigold, *C. polypetala*, has large rounded heart-shaped leaves over 30cm (12in) across, dark glossy green on both surfaces. They look like a larger version of the leaves of the related *Ranunculus ficaria* (lesser celandine). The clear golden-yellow flowers appear through and above the leaves, like a plane rising through clouds. Each flower may be more than 7.5cm (3in) across with five shining sepals and a mass of central stamens like an enormous buttercup — in fact, one of its common names is giant kingcup.

Unlike its close relation, the smaller *C. palustris*, which is clump forming and spreads largely from seed, *C. polypetala* is a vigorous creeping plant, with rooting stems, so must have plenty of room to spread. It grows well on moist stream banks, in boggy ground or on sodden clay. It even extends its succulent white rhizomes out over the surface of a pond or stream, and needs to be severely checked in small areas. It prefers sunny places, where its mass of flowers make a spectacular display against the dark green foliage in the last days of spring. *Caltha polypetala* can be easily lifted and divided or grown from seed sown as soon as it is ripe.

Giant kingcups bordering a pond.

CENTAUREA MACROCEPHALA

Puschk.

FAMILY
Compositae

ORIGIN
Caucasus

HEIGHT AND SPREAD
1m (3ft) × 1m (3ft)

FLOWERING TIME
Midsummer

SPECIAL FEATURE
Particularly large flowers

CLIMATIC ZONE
Zone 5

Close-up of the inflorescence.

I always associate knapweeds (or hard-heads as they are sometimes called), with cornflowers, found near unspoiled hedgerows in late summer. These hard-heads are usually maroon red with silvery foliage. However, the genus *Centaurea* contains some 600 or so species which are widely distributed. *Centaurea macrocephala* is a massive, clump-forming plant which originated in the meadows of the Caucasus region in the Soviet Union. Its size makes it a good candidate for large gardens. I first saw it in bud in John Piper's garden and realized the value of his artistic choice when I caught the sun shining on the plants' golden 'heads', some 5cm (2in) across. These golden buds are actually made up of papery scales and enclose a mass of tightly packed flowers which burst like sulphur from the bracts. It is certainly worthy of the name 'macrocephala' which means 'large head'. A decent-sized clump may be anything up to 1m (3ft) across, sometimes more, and carries fifteen or twenty of these masses of yellow flowers about 1m (3ft) above the ground. The pale green foliage is soft and downy right up to the stiff, flowering shoots.

Centaurea macrocephala prefers a fairly heavy moisture-retentive soil but will tolerate a lighter, sandy one, providing manure or compost is added every two or three years.

Although the actual flowering period in midsummer is over very quickly, the growth of the bright golden buds is slow and it is these which give the plant its common name of giant golden hard-head. After flowering, remove the spent heads to encourage the plant to concentrate its energies on growth. As well as a good plant for the herbaceous border, I have seen it growing with great success at the edge of a pond or stream where its vigour is increased by the readily available moisture, and it keeps competition from other plants at bay.

It is best divided in autumn or spring as it takes many years to flower from seed. However, once established, the plant will grow quite quickly and flower well the second year after transplanting.

A large clump of the giant knapweed.

CIMICIFUGA DAHURICA

(Turcz) Huth.

FAMILY
Ranunculaceae

ORIGIN
North-east Asia

HEIGHT AND SPREAD
1.8m (6ft) × 1.2m (4ft)

FLOWERING TIME
Early autumn

SPECIAL FEATURES
Attractive foliage, delicate flowers, doesn't need staking

CLIMATIC ZONE
Zone 4

Tight white flower spikes of the *Cimicifuga dahurica* rising above its palmate leaves.

It is unfortunate that the fifteen marvellous species of *Cimicifuga* are forever branded as the 'bugbanes'. 'Cimex' means a bug and 'fugo' to flee, referring to the use of the aromatic foliage of *Cimicifuga foetida* in Russia. The genus is distributed in the northern woodlands of Asia and North America with a few species in Japan.

Cimicifuga dahurica is a fine species, as yet less well known in gardens than its relations. Its bold, shining, dark-green leaves are made up of nine serrated leaflets on three lateral leaf stalks which arise from one central leaf stalk. The leaves can be as much as 60cm (2ft) long.

The branching flower spikes soar above the foliage on strong blackish flushed stems, which create a strong contrast with the dark-green foliage. The tiny flowers are creamy white with small, red-flushed petals and a mass of white stamens which produce a delicate feathery lightness. The seedpods continue the display after the flowers are over.

Cimicifuga dahurica will grow in any soil that is deep, with adequate moisture (especially in summer), and plenty of rotted leaf mould. It likes some sunlight but prefers filtered, dappled light for a good part of the day. *C. dahurica* is suitable for the back of a sheltered herbaceous border, where its tall flower spikes will arch gracefully over shorter perennials. At Hidcote Manor, Gloucestershire, it pushes up its long-stemmed drumsticks high above periwinkles and other smaller, shade-loving plants. Equally fascinating is the *Ranunculaceae* bed in the shade of a large tree at the Oxford Botanic Garden where three or four species of *Cimicifuga* offer their own differences to the discerning eye. *Cimicifuga dahurica* flowers before many of the other species.

Lift and divide when dormant. The ripe seed is usually viable for a short time and should be sown quickly before chemical dormancy renders it difficult to germinate.

CONVALLARIA MAJALIS

L. 'ROSEA'

FAMILY
Liliaceae

ORIGIN
Europe and Asia

HEIGHT AND SPREAD
22.5cm (9in) × 30cm (12in)

FLOWERING TIME
Early summer

SPECIAL FEATURE
Unusual, scented pink flowers

CLIMATIC ZONE
Zone 4

The pink flowered lily-of-the-valley.

Once encountered, the lily-of-the-valley is never forgotten. It certainly enraptured Colonel C. H. Grey in war-torn France, who wrote: 'I shall never forget it in May 1918 in the woods between Chemin des Dames and the Aisne, presenting a dense carpet of green and white, and so scenting the air as to dominate the smells of the shell-devastated area less than half a mile away. It was a most astonishing experience rendered the more astonishing by the fact that through the wire, which we had been at pains to put up, burst two wild boars, apparently as unconcerned by war and tumult as the lilies of the valley themselves.'

The plant he described was the species, found quite commonly there, but there are two rarer cultivars which I think are even more exquisite: the pink-flowered *C. m.* 'Rosea' and the variegated *C. m.* 'Variegata'. Both have flowers as highly scented as the white form. They take their name from 'convallis', Latin for valley, and 'majalis' or more accurately 'maialis', meaning May, which succinctly sums up their habitat and time of flowering.

The pink form *C. m.* 'Rosea' has identical foliage to the species: erect, pointed, glossy green leaves, which spread in ideal conditions to create an impenetrable carpet some several metres (yards) across. The flowers, opening from red-tinged buds, are an unusual dull reddish pink and look very attractive en masse. The flowers are slightly narrower and less urn-shaped than those of the species, but have similar bright orange fruits which are very poisonous.

The pink-flowered form of *C. majalis* is one of the best woodland carpeters I know, but it also grows extremely well and flowers prolifically in cooler parts of the rock garden, such as a north-facing site under the lee of a rock. (The pink flowers can look very effective against white stone.) It doesn't spread quite as readily as in the woodland and a sprinkling of leaf-mould encourages faster growth.

The beautiful, vertically streaked leaves of the variegated form, *C. m.* 'Variegata', are equally impressive especially when sited in full sun. (In shade the leaves tend to revert.) They are among the most attractive of all variegated foliage and last well, fading only slightly, until autumn starts to turn the leaves. They are handsomely striped in yellow and green with parallel creamy yellow lines and flourish in full sun on the more level ground at the foot of the rock garden or bordering a pond or stream. *Convallaria majalis* 'Variegata' has white flowers and also has

Convallaria majalis 'Variegata'.

a less spreading nature, as it has less green chlorophyll, which is necessary to the growth of all plants.

Convallaria may be propagated by division of the rhizomes at any time of the year. They normally adapt to their new surroundings very quickly.

DICTAMNUS ALBUS

L. 'PURPUREUS'

FAMILY
Rutaceae

ORIGIN
South Mediterranean

HEIGHT AND SPREAD
1.2m (4ft) × 1m (3ft)

FLOWERING TIME
Early summer

SPECIAL FEATURES
Unusual shaped flower and fragrant oils

CLIMATIC ZONE
Zone 5

Dittany is my favourite colloquial name for this plant, although it is better known as 'burning bush', 'candle plant' or 'fraxinella'. This latter name is a reference to an earlier synonym, *Dictamnus fraxinella*, 'fraxinella' meaning little ash and referring to the

ash-like pinnate leaves of the plant. Burning bush and candle plant are allusions to the immense quantity of volatile oils which are produced, particularly on the inflorescence just when the seed capsules are ripening. The great Reginald Farrer said (although I must admit I've never tried it myself) that on the hottest, stillest days in late summer, towards evening: 'it will blaze unconsumed in a supernatural glow, if a match be applied to kindle the volatile essences that hover in a halo round the petals that distil them'.

Dictamnus albus is one of half a dozen species of highly commendable herbaceous perennials, being tough, stately, interesting to look at and very long lived. Its ash-like foliage and stems are reddish tinged. The stems grow rapidly upwards, each culminating in a large inflorescence in early summer. This inflorescence is a spike sometimes 60cm (2ft) long, made up of orchid-like flowers. They are irregular in shape, with long narrow curving petals, and are loosely crowded. There is a pink form of the species and a white one. The purple form has dark red streaks

Dictamnus albus 'Purpureus'.

faintly noticeable on the petals.

The fruit capsules, or follicles, of *D. albus* and indeed of all *Dictamnus* species, are rather spectacular. The pods open only on one side to reveal jet black, shiny lozenge-shaped seeds. The seed pods are grouped in clusters up the inflorescence and when ready, explode and eject their seeds.

Dittany does have the most amazing scent. It smells faintly lemony if caught fleetingly, but is like a heavy dose of camphor if breathed in properly, leaving the unwary nose quite desensitized for several minutes. It is characteristic of the *Rutaceae* family, of which dittany is a member, that many of its relations have oil glands on the leaves and in other parts of the plant. This is obvious in dittany's cousins, the citrus tribe — oranges, lemons and limes — and in rue, *Choisya* and *Skimmia*.

Dittany loves the sun, does not mind a neutral or slightly acid soil but thrives in dry alkaline soils and needs a hot, well drained position. It does extremely well grown against a hot wall. Because it resents being moved, it is a bad subject for division but will grow slowly from seed, making a flowering sized clump in five or six years — well worth the wait in my opinion.

ERYNGIUM DECAISNEANA

Urban

FAMILY
Umbelliferae

ORIGIN
Central and South America

HEIGHT AND SPREAD
2.7m (9ft) × 1m (3ft)

FLOWERING TIME
Autumn

SPECIAL FEATURE
Statuesque evergreen perennial

CLIMATIC ZONE
Zone 6

South and Central American species of *Eryngium* are

all greatly appealing, as much for their fascinating size, variation and architectural qualities as for their lovely flowering habits and colour.

Much of the stunning effect of this species is due to its long, jagged-edged narrow leaves emerging from a very large centre. These leaves can be up to 1.5m (5ft) long and the plant may reach 1.2m (4ft) in height before the inflorescence starts. There can be more than two dozen leaves per plant and several plants in a mature clump: a mass several metres (yards) across. Each pointed green leaf has a series of serrations along the edge and in some forms there is a slight glaucous sheen. The former name for the plant is *E. pandanifolium* after the foliage of *Pandanus* — the tropical screw pines. The genera *Pandanus* and *Eryngium* are in fact completely unrelated, sharing only their sword-like leaves, together with such plants as *Yucca* and *Agave*. Until I saw this species in flower I found it hard to believe that it is related to cow parsley and hogweed.

The flowering spikes of *E. decaisneana* do not

Eryngium decaisneana.

emerge until late summer and if autumn is late in coming, they will flower at full height before the first frosts arrive, although their lofty height often protects them from ground frosts. The inflorescences have a majestic and rather strange appearance with many compound umbels. Each flower cluster at the end of its own stalk is globular and about 2.5cm (1in) across, a unique browny-red colour with greyish stamens. Quite a sight! The inflorescence makes a spectacular dried flower arrangement for a large hall and lasts for months, its stem up to 7.5cm (3in) thick.

Eryngium decaisneana grows well in mild and sheltered gardens without winter protection. Like so many similar plants, it will survive even the hardest winter once the clump is large enough. When this happens, the outer foliage is frosted and dies, protecting the living foliage beneath. Simply clear away the dead outer matter in spring to make way for new growth. Sun and well drained soil are necessary. It is a good centrepiece for a large border around which smaller plants can be grouped to excellent effect.

Propagate by division of the clump or by seed sown in spring.

ERYNGIUM VARIIFOLIUM

Coss.

FAMILY
Umbelliferae

ORIGIN
Morocco

HEIGHT AND SPREAD
60cm (2ft) × 15cm (6in)

FLOWERING TIME
Late summer

SPECIAL FEATURE
Evergreen, variegated foliage

CLIMATIC ZONE
Zone 4

The sea hollies all have a distinct attraction. I recall a whole ridge of them creating a blue, spiny desert on the shore line of Kent, and another species with short spiny rosettes high up in the Pyrenees, rendering the meadow grasses unsafe to sit upon. By far the majority of the beautiful and architectural sea hollies are handsome herbaceous perennials. *Eryngium variifolium* is a completely hardy evergreen perennial and, unusually, native to North Africa.

This tap-rooted plant forms a rosette of evergreen foliage of dark green heart-shaped leaves with toothed edges. Prominent white veins give the leaves their variegated appearance, most noticeable in winter when little else is visible. The dark green summer foliage which appears on the stiff flower stems is different in shape, 3.5cm (1½in) long, deeply dissected and spiny.

There are many flowering branches off a single central stem with the largest and often most conspicuous teasel at the top. Smaller teasels are carried on the surrounding branchlets. With its spiny stem leaves and a spiny bract under each teasel, *E. variifolium* looks very prickly indeed. The teasels are faintly flushed with blue and are only 1.5cm (½in) long, small for the genus. Yet the combined effect of many teasel-topped stems in a clump, and the spiny foliage, can make a very spectacular display.

All species of *Eryngium* prefer a well drained and

Eryngium variifolium, spiky blue and silver.

GENTIANA ASCLEPIADEA

L.

FAMILY
Gentianaceae

ORIGIN
Europe

HEIGHT AND SPREAD
1m (3ft) × 1.2m (4ft)

FLOWERING TIME
Late summer

SPECIAL FEATURES
Tall, long-lived ground cover with intensely blue flowers

CLIMATIC ZONE
Zone 4

open soil. They like full sun and *E. variifolium* is unaffected by frost. Lift and divide established clumps every five years or so for the easiest method of propagation. However, seed is not difficult to raise, although collecting the seed from the prickly flower heads may be painful. Seedlings grow fast and flower in less than two years.

Some of the species produce spectacularly coloured stems, invaluable for everlasting displays, and nearly all parts of these species are strongly coloured. Marvellous blue-stemmed species include *E. amethystinum* and *E. coeruleum*.

The name gentian probably conjures up alpine summits and great difficulty with cultivation, but the willow gentian, *Gentiana asclepiadea* is a woodland plant which has very few of the problems normally associated with many of its siblings. The genus is associated with intensely blue flowers, from which a dye is made, but is much more diverse than it first appears. There are some 400 species in all, ranging from 1.8m (6ft) high gentians with yellow flowers to dwarf species from the Andes with reddish blooms.

Gentiana asclepiadea is a herbaceous perennial emerging in spring from white tuberous, slowly spreading underground stems. 'Gentiana' comes from the name of a south-east European king, while 'asclepiadea' means like the genus *Asclepias*, the milkweeds, certain species of which have willow-like foliage. There is a beautiful symmetry about the foliage which is carried horizontally, dipping slightly from time to time. Each pair of tapered, willowy leaves is the same size, with a lovely dark green lustre on the upper surfaces, and prominent almost parallel veins on the paler undersurfaces. The enchanting flowers are usually borne in pairs in the upper leaf axils, bringing the already arching branches down to the ground with their weight. Until the flowers are produced, the species bears little resemblance to the alpine meadow gentians, but as soon as the buds are formed, the evidence is unmistakeable. The fabulous

Blue flowers of the willow gentian.

blue flowers are fully flared, deep trumpets, the outer surface streaked and indented. Inside are the characteristic white lines or white throat. There may be a dozen such flowers per stem.

Gentiana asclepiadea loves a cool, moist semi-shaded position. It has no preference as to acidity or alkalinity, but loves rich leaf-mould or peat-laden soils. The plant detests drought which can seriously set it back, sometimes at the expense of the flowers. There is a highly effective display of this plant in a narrow, semi-shaded border against the dark-red brick walls at Great Dixter, the home of the plant artist Christopher Lloyd. The gentian is surrounded by green grass in front and red walls behind; nearby is the golden-leaved autumn colour of *Schizophragma integrifolia*, a relation of the climbing *Hydrangea petiolaris*.

There are various different cultivars of this species, the best being the dark blue forms. There is also a light blue and a beautiful white form, *G. a. alba*, as well as shorter and taller forms.

Propagate by lifting and dividing the white fleshy roots in early spring. Seed is an alternative but seedlings vary in colour and quality.

GERANIUM PHAEUM

L.

FAMILY
Geraniaceae

ORIGIN
North Europe

HEIGHT AND SPREAD
60cm (2ft) × 30cm (12in)

FLOWERING TIME
Late spring

SPECIAL FEATURE
Nearly black flowers

CLIMATIC ZONE
Zone 4

The dark-red flowers of *Geranium phaeum*.

This plant is sometimes known as the mourning widow, presumably because the flowers are almost black and hang their heads down in assumed sorrow. To me, it seems far from lugubrious with its gently marbled, soft green leaves and great vitality of shape and habit.

To clear up the widespread confusion over the name geranium: it refers to the true perennial geraniums, not the florist's pelargoniums, which are tender evergreen sub-shrubs from South Africa. I prefer the common names, cranesbill for geranium and storksbill for pelargonium, both of which refer to the extraordinary rostrum, or beak-like, structure to which the seeds are attached.

Cranesbills are such a likeable group, being remarkably easy to cultivate and offering a wide range of flower colours. I can only assume that it is the slightly smaller flower size of the *G. phaeum*, compared to some others, which explains its comparative lack of appearance in many gardens. It has been available for many years and has even naturalized in certain woodlands quite successfully. The colour and shape of the flowers are stunning: the five petals are such a dark red that they look almost black, and they spring back from the central rostrum to present a bloom resembling a cyclamen.

Geranium phaeum prefers shade and will survive under relatively dark, sunless conditions, colonizing readily to form convenient ground cover throughout spring and well into summer. Its lush green foliage is about 30cm (12in) high and will cover a large area most effectively if allowed to grow unchecked. There is a wood near Boar's Hill just outside Oxford, the floor of which is a carpet of dusky mourning widow further than the eye can see. It follows on from the earlier bluebells, which are better known as England's woodland carpet.

There is also a white form, var. *album*, and a much paler subspecies of *G. phaeum, G. p. lividum*, which has cloudy mauve flowers, and less reflexed petals. Closely related is *G. reflexum* which has pinkish, very reflexed flowers. It hybridizes very easily with *G. phaeum* to produce *G. × monocense*, a promising plant very useful for the garden with large, dark mauve, unreflexed flowers and a vigorous growth habit.

All the plants mentioned above will tolerate most soils, provided there is adequate moisture during the growing season. In full sunlight, the blackish marks between each lobe of the leaves will become much more prominent. They can be raised from seed except *G. p. album* which is best divided to ensure true colour of the flowers.

GERANIUM PSILOSTEMON

Ledeb.

FAMILY
Geraniaceae

ORIGIN
Turkey, Armenia

HEIGHT AND SPREAD
To 1.5m (5ft) × 1.5m (5ft)

FLOWERING TIME
Midsummer

SPECIAL FEATURES
Tall-growing geranium, with attractive foliage and flowers

CLIMATIC ZONE
Zone 5

'Geranos' is Greek for the crane bird from which we get the vernacular name for the genus: crane's bill, referring to the beak-like seed structure.

Geranium psilostemon.

Geranium psilostemon is one of the largest plants in the genus, growing to a height and spread of 1.5m (5ft). As students at Kew we visited the now famous nursery run by Alan Bloom at Bressingham in Norfolk. There, among the many island beds of herbaceous perennials, was this giant species. The sheer volume of flowers on such a large plant was a memorable sight and one which stood out for me amongst so many new plants seen for the first time that day.

Apart from its striking magenta flowers, the foliage is equally handsome. Each large, five-lobed palmate leaf is carried on a tall stalk, and is serrated, with deeply cut margins. Its beautiful autumn leaf colour is rare among herbaceous perennials, let alone the geraniums. The colour is predominantly dark claret red, which picks out the areas between the veins and eventually covers most of the leaf.

The flowers of *G. psilostemon* are like a flattened cup, bright magenta with a dark violet black centre and a blackish basal zone.

Geranium psilostemon is vigorous and can become rather untidy, swamping smaller plants if unsupported. Stake the plants before the leaves reach 50cm (20in); either hazel branches or split bamboo canes will provide sufficient support without the necessity for a full branch and/or strings support. The hazel branches pushed into the ground all the way around the clump will provide support for the plant to grow up and through, leaving few signs of the branches.

Geranium psilostemon grows in any soil but loves a hot sunny spot enriched with plenty of manure early in the year. I have seen it look stunning slightly trailing over the edge of a wall. It grows easily from seed and, like all *Geranium* species, can be lifted and divided once dormant. There is an attractive hybrid between *G. psilostemon* and *G. procurens, G.* 'Ann Folkard', which is shorter, scrambling and with a darker, almost purple flower, still showing the distinctive violet blotch.

HAKONECHLOA MACRA

(Munro) Makino
'AUREOLA'

FAMILY
Gramineae

ORIGIN
Japan

HEIGHT AND SPREAD
30cm (12in) × 45cm (18in)

FLOWERING TIME
Autumn

SPECIAL FEATURE
Golden-striped ornamental grass

CLIMATIC ZONE
Zone 4

I have always held this grass in high esteem, for its compactness and softness. Hakon is a region of Japan and 'cloa' is the Greek for grass which aptly describes the genus of just one species: *macra*. Often confused with 'mega', meaning big, 'macra' means long, as well as large, and this is a grass long in stem, in relation to its rather diminutive overall size. Its nearest relation is the common reed, *Phragmitis*, altogether a much more massive plant with a certain attraction of its own but nothing like as charming or useful as its smaller cousin.

Hakonechloa macra 'Aureola' is a yellow-variegated form of the shiny green-leaved species similar to some dry shade-loving 'brome' grasses, with flexible arching foliage. (The brome grasses are oat like – 'bromus' is Latin for oats – and are commonly found all over Europe.) The yellow stripes appear on all parts of *H. macra* 'Aureola': leaves, nodes and even the inflorescences. The contrast between the green and yellow is stunning seen en masse, and is at its best in late summer and early autumn, when the stems are longest and the plant flowers. Wispy panicles of maroon-red flowers are carried about 20cm (8in) above the ground on the ends of arching stalks, and make a splendid colour contrast to the mass of foliage.

Hakonechloa macra 'Aureola' likes a rich well-

Compact growth of *Hakonechloa macra* 'Aureola'.

manured or composted soil with adequate moisture throughout the growing season. The plant dies down to a clump of hard rhizomes during winter with almost nothing visible above ground level. The ideal site is one which receives full sunlight yet never completely dries out, such as the bottom of a south- or west-facing slope. However, the grass survives very cold weather and short periods of drought with little detriment. It survives in shade, though its colouring is less vivid.

H. macra 'Aureola' must be divided because seed does not necessarily produce the same variegated leaves.

HELICTOTRICHON
SEMPERVIRENS

(Vill.) Pilger
FAMILY
Gramineae
ORIGIN
South-west Europe
HEIGHT AND SPREAD
60cm (2ft) × 1m (3ft)
FLOWERING TIME
Midsummer
SPECIAL FEATURES
Blue-grey foliage, attractive shape
CLIMATIC ZONE
Zone 5

Helictotrichon sempervirens is a superb ornamental perennial grass which was known for a long time as *Avena candida* and may still be found under this name in one or two nurseries. It now belongs to the genus *Helictotrichon*, a diverse group of grasses, most of which are European weeds. *Candida* means white, and *sempervirens* means always alive, and *H. sempervirens* is one of the bluest of the grasses. It is a similar blue to sheep's fescue (*Festuca glauca*) but the plant is far more robust. Its graceful habit of growing upwards and outwards, without being the least invasive, makes it a useful specimen plant. The narrow, erect leaves are over 40cm (16in) long.

Blue-grey leaves of *Helictotrichon sempervirens*.

The panicles of flowers, like stiff glaucous oat ears, are equally eye-catching, and hang from thin grey stems. The flowers have no petals but visibly emit pollen when ripe and it is the cumulative effect of the pollen from such grasses in summer which makes pollen count so high. The flower spikes remain until the stems fall over in autumn and they should then be cleared away.

The plant is hardy and easy to grow but needs dividing and replanting every other year, otherwise it becomes rather tatty and shapeless, full of dead thatch smothering the healthy new growth. It is also worth pulling out any thatch produced in the first year to encourage new growth. In my family home in Yorkshire, a circle of it is planted around an urn and it looks most effective rising above the surrounding sandstone paving.

Propagate by division in early spring. It can also be grown from seed but takes much longer to produce an effective display.

HELLEBORUS PURPURASCENS

Waldst. & Kit.

FAMILY
Ranunculaceae

ORIGIN
Russia, Eastern Europe

HEIGHT AND SPREAD
20cm (8in) × 15cm (6in)

FLOWERING TIME
Late winter to early spring

SPECIAL FEATURE
Very early, unusually coloured flowers

CLIMATIC ZONE
Zone 4

No winter would be complete without the intrepid flowers of the hellebores. They are so neat and useful, last so long and offer such a good contrast to other winter-flowering plants. All the hellebores are poisonous, as their name tells us: the Greek word 'helein' means to kill, and 'bora' means food. *Helleborus purpurascens* is a flowering gem worthy of better recognition, especially as it has given us many excellent hybrids, such as *H. × torquatus*.

This genus has twenty species of which the *H.p. orientalis* hybrids and *H. niger*, the Christmas rose, are the best known. I have always been intrigued by the

way the sepals and bracket (petals) of *H. niger* go green after the flower has been fertilized and also how long they remain on the plant while the seeds ripen. The five-petalled flowers of *H. purpurascens* are rich purple on the backs only and duck-egg green on the inner surface. (The only other purplish species, *H. atrorubens*, has the same colour on both sides.) The purplish back may also have a greyish bloom although this is not always very pronounced. The flowers, 2.5cm (1in) across, are smaller than those of *H. niger*, but larger than those of *H. foetidus*, the English wild hellebore.

H. purpurascens has a habit of producing flowers with only a single bract-like leaf on the flowering stem, well before the emergence of the true, deeply cut leaves. Many of the *Helleborus* species produce their foliage at the same time as the flowers and at least one species – *H. lividus* – spends two years just producing its flowering shoots independent of its foliage.

Helleborus purpurascens is a useful plant to grow in partial shade in a woodland, at the front of a border, or in a wild garden in association with other early plants, such as snowdrops and scillas. It dislikes very dry, shady positions but will thrive unprotected almost anywhere else. It increases slowly but large clumps can be divided immediately after flowering. Ripe seed germinates readily, but is a less reliable means of propagation, as the seed may hybridize with nearby *Helleborus* species.

Curious flowers of *Helleborus purpurascens* at Kew Gardens.

Highly-scented white flowers of *Hosta plantaginea*.

HOSTA PLANTAGINEA

(Lam.) Asch.

FAMILY
Liliaceae

ORIGIN
China

HEIGHT AND SPREAD
60cm (2ft) × 60cm (2ft)

FLOWERING TIME
Late summer

SPECIAL FEATURE
Highly scented flowers

CLIMATIC ZONE
Zone 5

Hostas are generally well known for their attractive lilac flowers carried high above large, often grey-green, leaves. Hostas all, with the exception of *H. plantaginea*, lack scent.

Hosta plantaginea was introduced from China in about 1780 and, inexplicably, has remained in obscurity ever since. It is certainly unique among its race. Its lovely heart-shaped leaves are a very bright green and positively shine in the sunlight that tends to scorch the foliage of its woodland cousins. Once established, each plant produces half a dozen flowering shoots, all bearing seven or eight flowers opening from the bottom upwards. The flowers are like an elongated Madonna lily (to which the plant is distantly related); its flowers have the same pure whiteness and a similar fragrance which can be heady and intoxicating on a still evening. For such flowers to bloom in that awkward period between the end of summer and beginning of autumn is a real bonus.

It grows well in any soil but needs a fairly high level of moisture. Even so, I have seen this plant survive extremely dry spells on a light, sandy soil, showing only faint signs of damage. There is a large-flowered form, *H.p.* 'Grandiflora' which I believe is sterile. 'Honeybells' is an excellent hybrid between this species and *H. fortunei* raised recently. Its pale lilac flowers have the lovely fragrance of *H. plantaginea*.

It is not often that one comes across a really stunning plant association at the time of year when this plant flowers, but I shall never forget my first sighting of *H. plantaginea* in the Chelsea Physic Garden where it was set amid the maroon red foliage of *Cotinus coggygria* 'Foliis purpureis' – a large clump of some dozen plants with over thirty flowering shoots.

Lift and divide established clumps when dormant, or alternatively sow seed in spring to flower in three or four years' time.

IRIS UNGUICULARIS

Poir. 'ALBA'

FAMILY
Iridaceae

ORIGIN
Algeria, Greece and Asia Minor

HEIGHT AND SPREAD
60cm (2ft) × 60cm (2ft)

FLOWERING TIME
Autumn and winter

SPECIAL FEATURES
Long flowering period, good for cutting

CLIMATIC ZONE
Zone 5

The genus *Iris* has been known and used since ancient times. *Iris florentina*, for instance, goes back at least as far as the Romans and is familiar today as orris root, whose rhizomes with their strong smell of violets are an important ingredient in perfumery. *Iris unguicularis* (syn. *Iris stylosa* Desfont) is a much more recent, but valuable, introduction. It used to be known as *Iris stylosa* because of the prominent claw-like endings to the style, part of the female organs of the flower; in fact, its current nomenclature, *I. unguicularis*, means 'containing little claws'. It is these and its unusually wide open petals which instantly distinguish it from other iris. Its special feature is the delicate, fragrant flowers it produces once established, from October or November through until March when the weather begins to get milder.

The great plantsman and gardener E. A. Bowles certainly held this plant in high esteem. He used all the coloured variants of this species as cut flowers for their delicious fragrance and their ability to last for over a fortnight without withering in a vase. Although sometimes listed as 'Bowles' White', the larger-flowered and splendid form which he described is probably no longer grown, and *I. unguicularis* 'Alba' is equally desirable.

Iris unguicularis 'Alba' makes a handsome display if planted thickly so that the shiny grassy foliage forms a dense clump. The white flowers appear barely peeping over the foliage and as such are scantily protected from decimating winter winds.

Iris unguicularis is best grown in a large clump at the foot of a wall, in front of a protected herbaceous border, or between two large boulders in the rock garden. It likes shelter, poor, well drained soil and plenty of sunshine in summer. It withstands a considerable degree of frost and retains its evergreen grassy foliage even if the delicate flowers are killed. The species is variable in flower shape, size and colour and several distinct forms exist. The most usual has lilac flowers with a slightly darker colouring to the outer petal surfaces, and an almost soft, grey tinge. There is a paler form, 'Walter Butt', but I find the white cultivar 'Alba' the loveliest of all, its white petals set off by rich golden yellow lines converging on the flower's centre.

Iris unguicularis 'Alba', which flowers in winter.

Once included in *I. unguicularis*, but now considered a separate species, is the enchanting *I. cretensis*. It has smaller, narrower, dark blue flowers and glaucous, almost grass-like foliage. It grows to a height of about 15cm (6in) and, like *I. unguicularis*, is slow to flower.

Propagate by division of the rhizomes at any time and replant in clumps to encourage flowering. Seed-grown plants may take many years to flower and old, undisturbed clumps flower best.

KIRENGESHOMA PALMATA

Yatabe

FAMILY
Saxifragaceae (or *Hydrangeaceae*)

ORIGIN
Japan

HEIGHT AND SPREAD
1m (3ft) × 1m (3ft)

FLOWERING TIME
Early autumn

SPECIAL FEATURES
Stiff handsome leaves, yellow flowers

CLIMATIC ZONE
Zone 5

This plant is a one-off, an outsider, and yet blends readily with almost anything in the woodland or shady garden. It is in a genus consisting only of itself, but is distantly related to others in the large and diverse *Saxifragaceae* family. It was once classed in a moment of botanical invention as *Kirengeshomiaceae*, but related also to *Hydrangea*, it could equally well pass in *Hydrangeaceae*.

There are minor variations in the species and *K. koreana*, once recognized as a second species, has since been reduced by most people to a variety of *K. palmata*, distinguished only by its smaller flowers and more upward-facing buds.

The Japanese genus *Anemonopsis* is known by them as 'rengeshoma' and our plant is referred to as the yellow (ki) version of it, although totally unrelated

Kirengeshoma palmata.

botanically. The similarity lies in their mutual need of a deep, moist woodland soil. The Latin 'palmata' refers to the palmate or hand-like leaves. There are as many as eleven shallow lobes on the dark green, prominently veined leaves which can measure 20cm (8in) across. The leaf and flower stalks are often tinged with black and lightly covered in short hairs. The inflorescence is often 30cm (12in) long, composed of fifteen or twenty big yellow drooping flowers in a wide much-branched panicle. The petals are thick and softly leathery, each overlapping the next and curling back at the tips once the flowers open. This happens only in warm weather and I find that much of the flower's life is spent unopened. Nevertheless, the flowers are still alluring and when open are startlingly beautiful.

Kirengeshoma palmata must never be allowed to fully dry out while it is growing. It will not tolerate lime and prefers acid soils; sunlight encourages flowering, provided the soil remains moist.

Lift and divide when dormant, or grow from seed sown as soon as ripe in the autumn.

KNIPHOFIA TRIANGULARIS

Kunth.

FAMILY
Liliaceae

ORIGIN
South Africa

HEIGHT AND SPREAD
45cm (18in) × 60cm (2ft)

FLOWERING TIME
Late summer, autumn

SPECIAL FEATURES
Hardy, dwarf red hot poker with subtle colouring

CLIMATIC ZONE
Zone 5

The genus *Kniphofia* (pronounced nye fo feea) is much better known as red hot pokers and these usually conjure up images of giant grape hyacinth-like spikes of fire, yellow, orange and red on the hottest summer days, held above sword-like foliage. I first encoun-

Kniphofia triangularis, a small red hot poker.

tered *Kniphofia triangularis*, a subtle dwarf version of its gaudy cousin, growing sedately in the front of an autumn flowering herbaceous border in Berkshire. In the last twenty years a whole range of cultivated dwarf pokers, as they are called, have been bred. Most have got some *K. triangularis* blood in them, all are pretty, unassuming and very desirable. They tend to prefer well drained, hot situations like their larger relation, only asking for the soil around them to be forked once a year to keep it loose.

Kniphofia as a genus is almost exclusively South African, apart from one or two species from tropical East Africa. There are seventy five species in total, all of which, including *K. triangularis*, have the characteristic tufted narrow foliage and central spike of almost stemless flowers. These have a long narrow tube ending in a narrow opening through which certain insects, notably bees, sometimes force themselves and are then unable to withdraw. *K. triangularis* has flowers which vary from yellow through orange to reddish and the inner mouth of the

Kniphofia galpinii at the University of London Botanic Garden, Egham, Surrey.

tube is always paler in colour than the outer part.

K. triangularis gets its name from its distinctly three angled leaves. Dark green on all three surfaces, the leaves have a central ridge or keel with two flanges on either side whose edges are coarsely toothed. They are usually 1m (3ft) long by 1cm ($\frac{1}{3}$in) wide and a certain flaccidity makes them drop at the ends.

K. triangularis is a fine, small clump-forming plant which may reach 60cm (2ft) across and can make six or more spikes of flowers, either together or sequentially. It is a hardy species surviving the very worst frosts, as long as its dead foliage is left to provide protection for the squat stems and roots below. It comes from well over 1000m (3000ft) high on South African mountains so prefers an open position in well drained soil, though in dry positions some watering may be necessary in summer. The most common flower colour of this species is orange with reddish buds.

K. galpinii is another charming small, red hot poker which is closely related and also reliably hardy, so worthy of inclusion. It too comes from high on the South African mountains and will thrive under similar conditions. The foliage of this plant is narrower than that of *K. triangularis* and lacks the coarse-toothed edge to the leaf. Its flower spikes are the same height, but the flowers themselves are much more condensed on the spike and the length of the flowering portion of the spike often no more than 10cm (4in). The buds, which are rarely as long as 3cm

($1\frac{1}{4}$in), are much darker in colour than the flowers.

All species of Kniphofia hybridize readily so unless a single species only is grown, the seed which is copiously produced in spherical capsules would be of hybrid value only. Propagate by lifting and dividing large clumps with a spade in the spring.

LAMIUM ORVALA

L.

FAMILY
Labiatae

ORIGIN
Southern Europe

HEIGHT AND SPREAD
30cm (12in) × 45cm (18in)

FLOWERING TIME
Late spring and early summer

SPECIAL FEATURE
Non-invasive ground cover plant

CLIMATIC ZONE
Zone 4

I always thought of *Lamium* as a vigorous roadside weed of creeping habit or an insignificant weedy annual on waste ground. The roadside weed is *Lamium album*, the white dead-nettle, and it is very like a stinging nettle but with white tubular flowers and no sting. *Lamium orvala*, with its handsome flowers and foliage, couldn't look less like a weed. As a first-rate herbaceous border and woodland plant, it never fails to attract interest, on account of its splendid thickly rounded clump and impressively large flowers for its size. It is also one of the hardiest and easiest plants to grow.

Lamium is Latin for throat, a reference to the throat-shaped corolla; the specific name comes from the Old French 'orvale', a sage plant (*Salvia*) in early French mythology. *Salvia* is distantly related to *Lamium* and their flowers have a superficial resemblance to each other.

Lamium orvala makes large, slow-spreading clumps; several clumps undulating over the ground

Lamium orvala and *L. orvala* 'Alba' growing together.

look particularly impressive. The tubular flowers are flushed maroon red and the tube expands to form the characteristic upper and lower jaws (the lips) of the *Labiatae* family. The lower jaw is beautifully streaked with dark maroon lines running from the curled lobe down to the throat of the tube. The flowers are borne in whorls around the opposite leaves on the stem.

There is a lovely symmetry about nearly all the parts of *Labiatae* plants: the square four-angled stem, the opposite leaves which emerge spiral fashion up it, and the circular whorls of flowers called verticillasters. The leaves of the species are rounder than those of white dead nettle, and have a hint of stinging nettle with their serrated edges and hairy upper surfaces.

They are dark green, shiny on the upper side and with a characteristic musty odour redolent of their white-flowered cousin.

Lamium orvala 'Alba' does not, as you might expect, have white flowers, but palest pink-flushed ones. These are the same size as those of the species, and have no hint of streaking along the throat.

L. orvala is a useful plant as it does not mind dry shade, although it is happier in the open on heavier, water-retentive soils, and is also happy in woodland. It is indifferent to acidity or alkalinity. It may droop (as other plants will do) on light soils in particularly dry spells. It is easily increased by division or from seed.

LINUM NARBONENSE

L.

FAMILY
Linaceae

ORIGIN
Central Mediterranean

HEIGHT AND SPREAD
50cm (20in) × 30cm (12in)

FLOWERING TIME
Summer

SPECIAL FEATURE
Stunning blue flowers

CLIMATIC ZONE
Zone 5

I have included several species of flax in this book and for good reason; it is one of the few genera which produce superb examples of blue, red and yellow flowers. They are not the easiest plants to grow, but worth the extra effort.

Linum narbonense represents the best of the true flaxes. It is not cultivated for flax fibres – that is an annual, *L. usitatissimum* – but it does have some of the richest sky blue flowers of any plant I know, enhanced by their large size – 2.5cm (1in) across – in relation to the short narrow leaves. The plant sends up many stiff, leaf-covered stems from a basal rosette of leaves. The grey, pointed leaves are smooth and not more than 1.5cm ($\frac{1}{2}$in) long. On the ends of these wiry stems the flowers are produced in cymes, and each opening flower follows the next.

The stiff branches can go on producing flowers in succession for several weeks, but *L. narbonense* tends to reach a sensational flowering peak when many buds open at once. Each saucer-shaped five-petalled flower unrolls from the bud, the pale blue undersides of the flower in contrast to the rich dark blue open flowers.

Linum narbonense is a sun lover; in fact its flowers will only open when the sun is out. It is one of the easier species to grow and thrives in a hot sunny

Linum narbonense, one of the bluest flaxes.

situation. It is a superb candidate for that 15cm (6in) strip of soil beside the house wall, at the foot of a light and airy rock garden or in between stones of a path. *Linum narbonense* takes up little space for the area of top growth it makes each year, bushing out to nearly 60cm (2ft) from the 15cm (6in) strip of soil. Its worst enemy is cold temperatures following wet weather which, if severe, may cut it back hard and in very severe conditions may even kill it.

Propagate *Linum narbonense* from cuttings in early summer, especially if you have a particularly good form. Mind you, I have never come across a bad form of this plant.

LIRIOPE MUSCARI

(Deane) L. H. Bailey 'MAJESTIC'

FAMILY
Liliaceae

ORIGIN
China, Japan

HEIGHT AND SPREAD
35cm (14in) × 60cm (2ft)

FLOWERING TIME
Autumn

SPECIAL FEATURE
Excellent ground cover in sun or shade

CLIMATIC ZONE
Zone 5

Liriope in Greek mythology was a water nymph and the mother of Narcissus, who eventually drowned as a result of falling in love with his own reflection. This genus, ironically, is one of the few I know which actually likes very dry shady areas, though it is generally very versatile. There are arguably five or six species, all East Asian. They have evergreen grassy foliage, a densely bushy habit and flowers borne in tight clusters carried on spikes just above the foliage, followed by bluish, whitish or black shining berries. This species is named after *Muscari*, the grape hyacinth genus, which is also in the *Liliaceae* family, very appropriately, as the flowers do resemble grape

Flower spikes of *Liriope muscari* 'Majestic'.

hyacinths. In America this plant is charmingly called lily turf.

The shining dark green leaves are narrow, tough and leathery, 30cm (12in) long, and each clump makes a thick mat like a soft hedgehog, bristling with many such leaves. There is a peak period of new growth in midwinter, provided the weather is not *too* cold. In autumn, the clustered spikes of stemless flowers are unmistakable. Several dozen tiny violet purple flowers appear on each spike which is carried on a violet-coloured stem. Each flower is typical of *Liliaceae*, with six petal-like tepals and six yellow stamens. This species is reluctant to fully open its flowers, probably due to the low temperatures when it begins to flower. This does not detract from its beauty, but only emphasizes its 'grape hyacinth' like appearance. Eventually the buds behave rather like the autumn leaves of so many plants, dropping off as soon as the slightest breath of wind rocks the stems.

Liriope muscari 'Majestic' is a large-spiked, purple form. The species is variable, with several flower colours, and there is also an excellent variegated form the foliage of which is streaked whitish or creamish with very little green. There is a pale-pink cultivar and also a white-flowered cultivar, 'Munro White'.

Liriope muscari 'Majestic' grows on any soil, wet or dry, in full sun or dense shade. It flowers best in full sun where a clump 45cm (18in) across can easily produce a dozen flower spikes.

Lift and divide established clumps then keep the new clump well watered until established. The plant may also be propagated from seed, when it will set, although the variegated form may not breed true.

LUNARIA REDIVIVA

L.

FAMILY
Cruciferae

ORIGIN
Europe

HEIGHT AND SPREAD
1m (3ft) × 1m (3ft)

FLOWERING TIME
Early summer

SPECIAL FEATURES
Fragrant flowers and everlasting seed pods

CLIMATIC ZONE
Zone 4

There are only three species of *Lunaria*, of which two are in general cultivation: the first is honesty, *Lunaria annua*, the familiar biennial (once called *L. biennis*) which tends to spread round the garden. *Lunaria rediviva* is perennial but resembles its biennial cousin in several ways; the flowers are produced in a similar manner and both are followed by silicula seed pods useful for flower arranging.

Lunaria comes from the Latin word 'luna' which means the moon and refers to the shape of the seed pods; the orbs are like little moons. *Rediviva* means coming back to life, as opposed to dying back like the biennial species. *Lunaria rediviva* grows rapidly to nearly 1m (3ft) and produces plenty of stems. The leaves are softly hairy on both surfaces and look like elongated hearts with a dentate margin. The flowers

are a pale lilac, verging almost on white. The inflorescence sits at the end of the shoots and has branches of flowers spirally arranged round the stem in twos and threes. The flowers are 2cm ($\frac{3}{4}$in) across and are typical of the *Cruciferae* family, with four petals and four stamens between, enhancing the cross-like shape of the flowers that gives the family its name: *Crucifera*, meaning cross bearing. The flowers are deliciously fragrant.

Shortly after the flowers die, the seed pods begin to develop. These are slightly elongated versions of those of biennial honesty and can measure up to 5cm (2in) long by 2.5cm (1in) wide. They sit on the branches like stiff sentinels until they become softened by rain or battered by the wind and drop off.

Perennial honesty is one of the easiest of herbaceous perennials to grow, happy on any soil, completely hardy and tolerant of drought, cold and almost anything people and nature can hurl at it.

Lunaria rediviva is easily propagated by division when dormant. It also seeds itself but not quite as vigorously as its biennial cousin, which makes it more controllable. It is a sun lover, completely indifferent to soil but growing better with manure and plenty of moisture early in the season.

The pale flowers of perennial honesty.

MISCANTHUS SACCHARIFLORUS

(Maxim) Hack.

FAMILY
Gramineae

ORIGIN
East Asia

HEIGHT AND SPREAD
To 2.5m (9ft) × 1.8m (6ft)

FLOWERING TIME
Autumn

SPECIAL FEATURE
Huge ornamental grass with attractive flowers

CLIMATIC ZONE
Zone 5

The Greek 'mischos' means a stalk or stem and 'anthos' a flower: a perfect description of the flower panicles of this remarkable grass. The flower stems tower above the rich green foliage, so unexpected in autumn when everything else is turning shades of red and brown. *Miscanthus* lies halfway between the woody bamboos and the herbaceous grasses and is a fairly small genus consisting of about twenty species, of which three are in general cultivation: *M. sinensis* (and its cultivars); *M. nepalensis*; and *M. sacchariflorus*.

Miscanthus sacchariflorus grows by means of thick, woody, slowly spreading rhizomes into an impenetrable clump over 1m (3ft) thick and reaching 1.8–3m (6–10ft) in height. It has partially woody stout stems sheathed by finely indented leaves, covered in a white bloom. The leaves are dark, glossy green, 1m (3ft) long with the characteristic white mid-vein which gives the plant a resemblance to another very widely grown grass, *Saccharum officinarum*, more commonly called sugar cane. This has led to confusion over the name of *M. sacchariflorus*, whose flower panicles are allegedly also similar to *Saccharum*; *sacchariflorus* means flowers like *Saccharum*. I have seen the plants wrongly labelled *saccharifolium* more than once.

Miscanthus sacchariflorus flowering in summer.

Miscanthus sacchariflorus in winter.

The flowers are freely produced after hot, dry summers. They are complicated, small and insignificant, but are surrounded by a mass of soft silvery hairs. The flowers are borne in chains or spikelets which emanate from a central spike and the whole inflorescence can be more than 30cm (12in) long with an attractive wispish purple-silver appearance.

Miscanthus sacchariflorus is excellent for cutting, the inflorescence lasting for months, long after the flowers have fallen, while in the garden the woody, brown, dead leafy stems stand firm in winter even during snow. It is, in this respect, not unlike a diminutive pampas grass, but is much tougher.

Miscanthus sacchariflorus should be cut back before new growth begins. It also has a remarkable speed of growth, not emerging as it does sometimes until early summer. *Miscanthus sacchariflorus* can be grown as a specimen in any open, exposed position, creating a focal point. It can fill a corner of the herbaceous border or several clumps can be grown along a path to form a sort of oriental corridor. The plant can even make an evanescent hedge lasting only six months of the year, and is useful for associating with early spring-flowering plants.

An experiment of mine at Chelsea was to plant a 1m (3ft) square dormant clump of this plant in a very exposed, well drained corner of the garden, in the right angle where a path and lawn meet. Every year since planting, the grass has flowered, and remained a splendid winter presence, still standing months after all the top growth had died.

Divide when dormant into large clumps rather than small pieces, which would take several years to make a sizeable clump and would be far more prone to damage from frost or summer drought.

PACHYPHRAGMA MACROPHYLLUM

(Hoffm.) Busch.

FAMILY
Cruciferae

ORIGIN
Northern Turkey, Caucasus

HEIGHT AND SPREAD
35cm (14in) × 30cm (12in)

FLOWERING TIME
Late spring

SPECIAL FEATURE
Excellent ground cover for shade

CLIMATIC ZONE
Zone 4

Pachyphragma macrophyllum growing in a woodland at the RHS Garden at Wisley, Surrey.

For a long time, this plant was in the cress-like genus *Thlaspi*, but it is now designated the only species in the genus *Pachyphragma*, 'pachys' meaning fat and 'phragma' a partition or division. This refers to the seed capsule which is unusually thickly divided.

The *Cruciferae* family is mainly known for its edible plants: cabbage, radish, mustard, cress, kale, watercress and so on. All these are linked by their cross-shaped, or cruciform, four-petalled flowers with four stamens. Another feature of many of the *Cruciferae* is their sulphur-laden mustard oils which give us that 'hot' flavour in radishes and cress, and the onion or garlic smell and flavour particularly associated with *P. macrophyllum*, the young leaves of which would no doubt make a tasty addition to a spring salad. (This group of oils with its characteristic aroma is also found in totally unrelated genera, such as *Tropaeolum* and of course *Allium*.)

Pachyphragma macrophyllum is a handsome and hardy herbaceous perennial with creeping rhizomatous roots, which form large clumps. The dark-green heart-shaped leaves are carried facing upwards on petioles 20cm (8in) or more long. The leaf surface is regularly veined and the margins are wavy. The white, sweetly scented flowers are carried on long racemes which are almost pyramidal in shape. The flowers make a spectacular show against the leaves in dappled shade. There is a woodland, many metres (yards) across, in the garden of the Northern Hor-

ticultural Society, Harlow Car, at Harrogate, which is carpeted with *Pachyphragma macrophyllum*. In late spring its delicious, honey-like scent is enticing.

Pachyphragma macrophyllum thrives on leafmould in partial shade, with a superficial root system that feeds on the surface debris, seemingly impartial to the soil type or rock beneath. Propagate by lifting and dividing the dormant rhizomes, as it does not set seed readily.

PAEONIA MLOKOSEWITSCHI

Lomakin

FAMILY
Paeoniaceae

ORIGIN
East and Central Caucasus

HEIGHT AND SPREAD
1m (3ft) × 1m (3ft)

FLOWERING TIME
Early spring

SPECIAL FEATURE
Lemon-yellow flowers

CLIMATIC ZONE
Zone 4

Surprisingly only two of the thirty species of *Paeonia* have become well known and from *P. lactiflora* and *P. officinalis* many garden hybrids and cultivars have been developed. *Paeonia officinalis* has long been used medicinally as a tonic. Paion was a physician to the gods of ancient Greece and the plant to which he gave his name provides many rare beauties for the garden. *Paeonia mlokosewitschi* is a tongue twister of a name — sometimes known as 'Molly the witch' — for a tremendous plant. It is one of the earliest paeonies to flower, producing clear, pale lemon blooms and rounded lobed leaves. The large, single flowers are typical of the wild paeony species. In this species they are spectacularly large, between 7.5–10cm (3–4in) in diameter with a conspicuous mass of golden yellow stamens. A good sized clump of *P. mlokosewitschi* may have over a dozen of these lemon cups facing upwards.

The foliage is attractive in its own right, green on top and slightly downy grey beneath. The leaves are large and made of several leaflets.

Paeonies resent being moved, but a large plant can be transplanted successfully provided it is dormant. Large clumps of *P. mlokosewitschi* may be lifted and divided in early spring. Sever the tuberous roots, using a knife, into two or three smaller clumps, each with growth buds. Do not cut off small individual tubers as it will be some years before they flower. *Paeonia mlokosewitschi* is hardy and tolerant of all soils, and responds well to a winter mulch of manure placed around the clump. The manure can be dug in during mild winter weather, allowing plenty of space around the clump, to avoid damaging the tubers. It is a plant worthy of special care, and though it flowers only for a short time early in the season, its foliage is attractive for many months. The species can be grown from seed. In late summer or early autumn, the plant produces bright red seed capsules which split to reveal jet black seeds, glistening attractively in the sunlight.

(An interesting footnote is that many species are pollinated by beetles.)

Paeonia mlokosewitschi.

PENNISETUM ALOPECUROIDES

(L.) S p r e n g .

FAMILY
Gramineae

ORIGIN
Eastern Asia

HEIGHT AND SPREAD
1m (3ft) × 45cm (18in)

FLOWERING TIME
Summer or early autumn

SPECIAL FEATURE
Ornamental grass with blue-black flower spikes

CLIMATIC ZONE
Zone 5

Pennisetums are sometimes known as feather grasses, their name coming from 'penna' which means feather in Latin. Of all the grasses in cultivation they are amongst the most spectacular, with their unique display of graceful flowers, but unfortunately not all are reliably hardy. However, they are quite easy to grow and, if positioned carefully, survive for many years unharmed, although they do need a little extra care during the coldest weather.

Pennisetum alopecuroides is the toughest of the bunch (sharing this distinction with the closely related *P. orientale*) and produces large inflorescences. These resemble those of meadow foxtail grass (*Alopecurus pratensis*), to which it allegedly owes its name. But growth of *P. alopecuroides* is in complete contrast to its namesake. Where the meadow foxtail produces comparatively small inflorescences at the top of a tall stem above a small plant, *Pennisetum alopecuroides* makes striking large spikes of unique blue-black flowers on a short stem. The flower spikes are soft and feathery to the touch, 7.5cm (3in) long and 2.5cm (1in) wide. A healthy plant may produce over a dozen of these in an area less than 45cm (18in) across.

The clumps of this grass are a splendid feature at Hidcote Manor garden in Gloucestershire. There, they break up the comparative similarity of many herbaceous plants. *Pennisetum alopecuroides* is effective

Pennisetum alopecuroides with its soft feathery flowers just emerging.

grown in the front of a herbaceous border where the beauty of its flowers carried above neat, more compact plants may be appreciated. It grows easily on most soils but performs best on clay loams or soils containing plenty of organic matter, which helps retain moisture during the driest summer months. The moisture tends to encourage the production of more flowers later in the summer. Like those of several grasses, the flowers will remain on the plant well after the first frosts scorch the foliage to the ground. They are useful for adding a little interest to a winter garden. The flower spikes last for a month or two if picked but eventually disintegrate.

This species prefers full sunshine and benefits from the protection of a thick layer of straw, compost or leafmould in cold weather. The clumps can be divided easily in early spring before too much growth has been made, but after the worst of the winter weather is past. (A larger clump will protect itself much better than several smaller groups.) *Pennisetum alopecuroides* can also be raised from seed; they germinate readily but take several years to develop into sizeable plants.

PHLOMIS RUSSELIANA

Benth.

FAMILY
Labiatae

ORIGIN
Syria

HEIGHT AND SPREAD
1.2m (4ft) × 60cm (2ft)

FLOWERING TIME
Midsummer

SPECIAL FEATURE
Excellent ground cover for exposed and shaded areas

CLIMATIC ZONE
Zone 4

Confusingly, *Phlomis russeliana* has been known by two other names in the past, one of which is totally erroneous and refers to a completely separate species. This is *P. samia* the foliage of which is very like that of

P. russeliana but is greyer in colour and much hairier. Their flowers are totally dissimilar however, *P. samia* having creamy blooms with pink centres and *P. russeliana*, clear butter yellow flowers. The latter are eye catching when fully out, shining even in dull weather above the green carpet of their foliage. I first saw them in the family beds at Kew, and immediately thought that they deserved a more aesthetic site than amongst their many *Labiatae* cousins.

Phlomis russeliana was also called *Phlomis viscosa* for many years, and still occasionally is, although this name is now invalid. The genus encompasses over a hundred species, the majority originating from countries round the Mediterranean and well into Eastern areas. Many of these species are quite large shrubs but one or two make growth which dies back to the ground during winter. *Phlomis russeliana* is one, but is quite hardy, its basal foliage remaining consistently evergreen after the flowering stems have been cut back for winter.

Phlomis russeliana shows all the true characteristics

Phlomis russeliana with its yellow whorls of flowers.

of the genus. It produces the hairy leaves and distinctive hooded flowers which seem to give the bees a frustrating time as they try to enter. The flowers are arranged in beautiful circular clusters, intermittently spaced up the central stem; these circular whorls are particular to the *Labiatae* family. In a healthy plant, the flowering stems may reach over 1.2m (4ft) and are four angled, again a feature of many plants in the *Labiatae* family. The clear butter yellow, two-lipped flowers contrast well with the large green heart-shaped leaves bristling with stiff hairs beneath and a lighter coating above. The leaves grown en masse have a bold, almost sculptural appearance.

Phlomis russeliana is quick growing but not particularly invasive, making it a useful ground cover plant in less shady parts of a woodland garden, for example. There, the leaves will grow larger but it will not flower quite as profusely as when grown in full sun. The plant is also well suited to the herbaceous border. Because it spreads by means of rhizome-like stems above and slightly below the ground, it is extremely useful for thin, patchy soils and will grow over almost rocky ground, finding its way along crevices and

using its large leaves to preserve moisture and shade the creeping stems from the sun. It prefers alkalinity and a dry soil to a damp one. Propagate from division of the clump or from seed, which is freely set.

POLEMONIUM CARNEUM

Gray

FAMILY
Polemoniaceae

ORIGIN
North America

HEIGHT AND SPREAD
60cm (2ft) × 45cm (18in)

FLOWERING TIME
Midsummer

SPECIAL FEATURE
Flowers changing colour as they age

CLIMATIC ZONE
Zone 5

Polemonium carneum whose flesh-pink flowers change colour with age.

Polemonium 'Lambrook Mauve'.

Pliny recorded that two kings fought over the discovery of a European species of *Polemonium*, each claiming that he had found the plant first. It was accordingly named *Polemonium* after the Greek 'polemus' meaning war. There are some fifty or so species of *Polemonium*. Some of the loveliest come from North America and one of these, *P. carneum*, is a fine herbaceous perennial and a must for this book. I have also included elsewhere the alpine species *P. reptans* to show the garden worthiness of this genus.

The marvellous blue Jacob's ladder, *Polemonium caeruleum*, has a major drawback which *P. carneum* fortunately lacks: that of seeding itself into every possible nook and cranny to the extent of being a menace. *Polemonium carneum* is less fecund, producing fewer seeds, which tend to germinate near existing clumps. Its flower colour is so unique that it does not mix well with other plants. I find it most effective against foliage such as that of *Yucca, Phormium* or certain irises.

Carneum means flesh coloured, but in fact the flowers of *P. carneum* have many hues, each flower changing colour as it ages. The bud is clear creamy-white; it opens slowly into a five-petalled cup 2.5cm (1in) across which begins as cream and very slowly fades through flesh pink to lilac. The very old flowers are pinkish mauve. Each flower has five bright orange anthers. The flowers are borne in loose cymes in a range of shades. Each pinnate leaf of *P. carneum* is composed of between five and ten pairs of leaflets. These, and indeed most parts of the plant, often have a sort of rosy hue which adds to the *carneum* effect.

Polemonium carneum is a true herbaceous perennial, withstanding several degrees of frost unscathed and remaining dormant during the winter. Unfortunately, it has a habit of flopping over when in flower so needs staking or the support of nearby plants. Common to all species of *Polemonium*, it needs the sun and prefers a full open situation. It is easy to grow on any soil that does not completely dry out; a mulching with compost or manure helps retain soil moisture. It is happiest in alkaline soils.

Propagate from seed sown in spring or divide large clumps when dormant.

P. carneum has been crossed with *P. caeruleum* to produce the rich, clear mauve-flowered *P.* 'Lambrook Mauve'. (*Polemonium* 'Dawn Flight' is possibly a paler coloured variant of this.)

PULMONARIA RUBRA

Schott.

FAMILY
Boraginaceae

ORIGIN
East Europe

HEIGHT AND SPREAD
30cm (12in) × 15cm (6in)

FLOWERING TIME
Spring

SPECIAL FEATURES
Early flowering, excellent ground cover

CLIMATIC ZONE
Zone 4

The genus *Pulmonaria* is named from the Latin 'pulmonis', meaning for the lungs, and includes ten species of lungwort. One, *P. officinalis*, was grown as an officinal plant – sold as a dried herb in the 'officina' or office – on the basis that its spotted leaves suggested lungs, and therefore were useful in curing afflictions of that organ. Several species have spotted leaves and although the true *P. rubra* does not, the form 'Bowles variety' has faintly spotted markings.

The majority of species have blue or pink flowers, the pink turning to a sort of muddy blue. This is quite common in the *Boraginaceae* family, particularly with some *Symphytum* species and also with borage. *Pulmonaria rubra* is aptly named: its flowers are a rich light red, somewhere between brick red and a very dark salmon colour. The bell-shaped flowers consist of five petals, and two or three flower clusters are carried on each branch. The flowers open in sequence, and the flowering period is long; *P. rubra* may start to flower before the end of winter, and continue to flower consistently into early summer.

The whole plant is coarsely hairy and the large leaves are an attractive light green. The plant remains evergreen in shaded woodland, growing slowly during mild spells in winter. It is deciduous in more

Pulmonaria rubra, the red-flowered lungwort.

exposed situations, where it comes into growth later and consequently flowers later, too. *Pulmonaria rubra* spreads in moist, shaded woodland, covering several metres (yards) in a few years, and usually produces a great abundance of fertile seed. It tolerates quite dry conditions but spreads less rapidly from its short fat stolons. It is very attractive grown near the equally vigorous *Anemone ranunculoides*, the yellow flowers of which contrast with the lungwort's red.

Propagate by lifting and dividing established clumps or from seed sown as soon as ripe.

ROSCOEA CAUTLEOIDES

Gagnepain

FAMILY
Zingiberaceae

ORIGIN
China

HEIGHT AND SPREAD
30–40cm (12–16in) × 15cm (6in)

FLOWERING TIME
Mid to late summer

SPECIAL FEATURE
Orchid-like flowers

CLIMATIC ZONE
Zone 5

William Roscoe, a founder of the Liverpool Botanic Garden, is commemorated by these glorious (and curious) plants. Although related to ginger they appear very orchid-like. The first time I saw a clump of them at Chelsea Physic Garden I was bowled over by their floral display and have since learnt how easy they are to grow. There are nineteen species as yet classified but much uncertainty as to how many there really are, particularly from China. *Roscoea* is one of the most northerly genera in the *Zingiberaceae* family, occurring at high altitudes in the Himalayas and Chinese mountains. The scent of their crushed leaves is a reminder that they are cousins, not only of ginger but also of cardamum, turmeric and East Indian arrowroot.

Roscoea cautleoides is a pale yellow-flowered plant, but there are also purple, white and, less frequently, pink forms in the wild. It is the yellow form which is most commonly referred to under this name.

The plant has a tuberous rootstock which, in summer, sends up a flowering stem comprised of three or four sword-like, folded leaves, each one 20–30cm (8–12in) long. The orchid-like flowers are borne at the top and two or three may open at any one time.

Roscoea cautleoides will grow in dry, exposed situations and is indifferent to acidity or alkalinity, but prefers a light, sandy or gritty soil. Normally a woodland plant, I have known it to grow in full sun on dry sandy soil as well as on the fringe of a woodland in well mulched soil and partial shade. I should also imagine it would do well in a rock garden, as it has been collected from open meadows and rocky slopes as well as limestone cliffs and shady glades. It seems a very tolerant plant and certainly has not succumbed, in my knowledge, to the coldest temperatures in the south of England over the last few years.

The yellow orchid-like flowers of *Roscoea cautleoides*.

Roscoea cautleoides has an interesting cultivated variant, possibly a hybrid with *R. auriculata*, sold under the name of 'Beesiana'. The flower is yellow but the two lower petals are streaked and flushed with purple. *Roscoeas* may be raised from seed which is produced copiously. Sow the seed outdoors as soon as it is ripe; wintering breaks any dormancy and the seed should germinate in the following spring. Large clumps of *R. cautleoides* can also be lifted and divided.

SALVIA HAEMATODES

L.

FAMILY
Labiatae

ORIGIN
Greece

HEIGHT AND SPREAD
1.2m (4ft) × 1m (3ft)

FLOWERING TIME
Early summer

SPECIAL FEATURE
Sprays of clear blue flowers

CLIMATIC ZONE
Zone 4

Salvia haematodes is a herbaceous perennial related to the shrubby culinary sage (*S. officinalis*). They bear little resemblance to one another, though both are fine, worthy species for the garden.

Salvia haematodes produces slightly wrinkled leaves, 15cm (6in) or more long, from a large, squat rosette which hugs the ground during winter. In late spring the plant begins to send up half a dozen or more square stems which in turn produce a mass of pale blue flowers in early and midsummer. The colour of these flowers is quite remarkable: a soft, clear blue made all the more stunning by the sheer number produced on each spray. Individual flowers are only 1.5cm ($\frac{1}{2}$in) long and have the distinctive two-lipped structure characteristic of salvias.

Salvia haematodes is an easy plant to grow, preferring full sun and thriving on alkaline soils. It will

tolerate most soils but does not like to be waterlogged in winter. I have seen it in good form on the edge of woodland, where it does not flower quite so prolifically but looks delightful against a background of dark greenery. To my surprise it did not seem to mind its partially shady situation and I was informed that it had been flourishing there for many years. At Pusey House in Oxfordshire one of the glories of its long herbaceous border is this plant. It grows in large clumps on a chalky clay soil, its tall pale blue sprays contrasting well with the dark green foliage.

One of the drawbacks of many herbaceous salvias is that they are short lived. Some can be lifted and divided after two or three years, but they seed prolifically and are healthier plants grown from seed, providing the parent plant is not allowed to hybridize with another nearby *Salvia* species. In this case, the results may well be very interesting, but *S. haematodes* will not be the outcome.

Salvia haematodes.

SAXIFRAGA ROTUNDIFOLIA

L.

FAMILY
Saxifragaceae

ORIGIN
Europe, Asia

HEIGHT AND SPREAD
60cm (2ft) × 60cm (2ft)

FLOWERING TIME
Midsummer

SPECIAL FEATURE
Easy-going plant for damp shade

CLIMATIC ZONE
Zone 4

Saxifraga rotundifolia, a delicate cloud of starry flowers.

The cosmopolitan genus *Saxifraga* includes some 370 species of almost exclusively alpine or mountain plants. The origin of the name is confused, but I prefer the theory that it comes from the Doctrine of Signatures belief that, as the plants grew in rocky crevices, they can somehow cure kidney or gall stones: 'saxa' means stone, and 'fraga' comes from 'frango', to break. Other unrelated plants, such as *Pimpinella saxifraga*, the burnet saxifrage, were often used in a similar context and sold in apothecaries' stores.

Saxifraga rotundifolia, the round-leaved saxifrage (*rotundifolia* meaning round leaf) is one of the larger species. It grows abundantly in cool, moist alpine woods in many countries and varies in size, growth, foliage and flower. It has a stubby, swollen stem which sits above ground level. The scallop-edged, kidney-shaped leaves form a rosette and are slightly fleshy, revealing their alpine origins.

The much-branched panicle of single flowers, white speckled with pink or red, is very large in relation to the rosette below, reaching 60cm (2ft) and sometimes as much as 1m (3ft) tall by 30cm (12in) across. The whole inflorescence is a marvel of symmetry, each five-petalled flower in its cup-shaped, green five pointed calyx.

The seed capsules release many small, highly fertile seeds, equipped to survive wherever they land, be it bog, rock or fertile rock crevice, and the ensuing plants develop in size according to where they fall.

Saxifraga rotundifolia is easy to grow in cool moist conditions and thrives in partial shade, although the latter is not essential. Its fluffy white flowers would lighten up any damp, cool corner of a garden. It needs very little attention or depth of soil, as it grows along the surface. It is indifferent to soil pH but, unlike its species siblings, does not have the capacity of exuding excess lime through chalk glands on its leaves. Propagate from seed.

SCHIZOSTYLIS COCCINEA

Backh. and Harv.

FAMILY
Iridaceae

ORIGIN
South Africa

HEIGHT AND SPREAD
1m (3ft) × 7.5cm (3in)

FLOWERING TIME
Autumn

SPECIAL FEATURE
Free flowering late in the season

CLIMATIC ZONE
Zone 4

The Kaffir lily or crimson flag is better known than it used to be, but still needs publicity as one of the loveliest autumn-flowering plants. It is the only species of *Schizostylis*, a near relation to the enormous genus *Gladiolus*. *Schizostylis* means split-style and refers to this plant's split female style, normally a single protrusion in the *Iridaceae* family. Also uncommon are this plant's white fleshy rhizomes, instead of the distinct corms or rhizomes of its cousins *Gladiolus, Crocus* and *Iris*.

Schizostylis coccinea is a clear bright scarlet, *coccinea* meaning scarlet. In the wild it grows just short of 1m (3ft), producing stem-sheathing, sword-shaped, grassy leaves 30cm (12in) long. The flowering shoot dominates the plant, rising out of the foliage with two ranks of flower buds, each held in a prominent pair of green bracts. The red, cup-shaped, starry flowers open from the base of the inflorescence upwards. There may be as many as ten or twelve such flowers on a spike, and flowering lasts a month or more; they are excellent cut flowers.

Schizostylis coccinea is easily grown in a moisture-retentive, acid soil. It thrives in areas of high rainfall, although full sun, with adequate moisture, encourages the production of flowers. I have known the plant

Schizostylis coccinea, the pink form, called 'Viscountess Byng'.

grow very well near an old vinery house where mulch for the grape vines (planted outside the glasshouse) undoubtedly gave vigour to the neighbouring *S. coccinea*. The heat reflected from the glass must also have contributed and this patch produced several dozen spikes each year. I have also seen it quite happy in the barer patches of a herbaceous border, protected during winter with a layer of peat (a simple precaution like this so often saves the life of a tender plant) and it thrives unprotected at Newby Hall, North Yorkshire.

Schizostylis coccinea has several cultivars, including the late-flowering 'Viscountess Byng' and pale-pink 'Mrs Hegarty'. The species can be propagated from seed provided the long thin seed capsules are produced, or by lifting and dividing established clumps when dormant.

SMILACINA RACEMOSA

Desf.

FAMILY
Liliaceae

ORIGIN
North America

HEIGHT AND SPREAD
1m (3ft) × 60cm (2ft)

FLOWERING TIME
Early summer

SPECIAL FEATURE
Fragrance

CLIMATIC ZONE
Zone 4

I was well and truly caught out by the indomitable gardener Major Hardy, when visiting his woodland garden at Sandling Park in Kent in my earliest gardening days. He referred me to a plant which to all intents and purposes looked exactly like a Solomon's seal (*Polygonatum multiflorum*) but with completely the wrong flowers. These were so strongly scented like lily-of-the-valley and so resembled old cottage cobweb brushes that they made a lasting impression. In North America *Smilacina racemosa* is known as false spikenard, spikenard being a plant from India with

highly aromatic foliage from which incense has been made for over a thousand years.

Smilacina racemosa is a majestic woodland plant, growing rapidly when the conditions are right, to 1m (3ft) high and making large clumps several metres (yards) across. The stems emerge from Solomon's seal-like rhizomes to make a dense thicket of bright green foliage, the leaves alternating along the stems and featuring many prominent parallel veins. Each leaf is some 15cm (6in) long by 10cm (4in) wide, similar in size and shape to the lily-of-the-valley, and with a dozen or more to a stem. *Smilacina racemosa* is a bit of a misnomer as the flowers grow in panicles, not racemes. I presume it took its name because the Central American species, *S. paniculata*, was already in existence. Strictly speaking, a raceme is only a single stem of flowers on stalks rather than several branched clusters of flowers along the main stalk.

The inflorescence is usually 10cm (4in) long by 7.5cm (3in) wide and consists of up to thirty panicles each 5cm (2in) long and carrying several six petalled,

Sweetly scented *Smilacina racemosa*.

star-shaped flowers of creamy white. The individual flower is tiny and its starry shape is emphasized by six ray-like stamens with globular cream anthers at the ends. The fragrance from a single inflorescence made up of hundreds of these tiny starry flowers is quite delectable and floats through the woodland on a still summer evening. Occasionally, in drier summers, bright red globular fruits are produced after the flowers die.

Smilacina racemosa is an easy plant to grow, but does not tolerate lime. It likes a well-drained, acid soil and given ideal conditions, will spread slowly each year. It thrives in damp, shady spots and loves a damp start to the year, encouraging it to produce larger panicles and vigorous growth. It is very hardy and is easily divided when dormant.

Smilacina racemosa has an invasive cousin, *S. stellata*, which produces rapidly spreading rhizomes. This grows only to a height of 30cm (12in) and produces a few white, star-shaped flowers in early summer, a raceme at the end of each stem. Its petals are slightly longer than those of *S. racemosa* and are not as fragrant. It needs plenty of space in a wild area of the garden where its spreading habit will not be a menace.

STIPA GIGANTEA

Link.

FAMILY
Gramineae

ORIGIN
Spain, North Africa

HEIGHT AND SPREAD
1.8m (6ft) × 1m (3ft)

FLOWERING TIME
Mid to late summer

SPECIAL FEATURE
Huge ornamental grass

CLIMATIC ZONE
Zone 5

Stipa comes from the Greek word 'tuppe' meaning tow, a kind of rope made predominantly from the fibres of one of the *Stipa* grasses. It was probably originally *S. tenacissima* – Esparto grass – used for making rope, mats and paper, but there are many other European species which could have been used.

The genus is affectionately called feather grass or sometimes needle grass, a more sinister name given to those species which have needle-like fruits with backward-pointing hairs on their tips. Many species have long feathery awns or bristles which curl up when dry and uncurl when wet, the object being to drive the needle-like seeds forward into the ground, corkscrew fashion. Sadly, this process can go awry and the wet needles are sometimes driven through the skin of sheep and cattle and into their vital organs, causing death or severe discomfort.

Stipa gigantea is a gentle giant in comparison to its aggressive siblings; the awns are shorter and innocuous, the seeds rarely set. It looks like a cross between pampas grass (*Cortaderia*) and oat (*Avena*), and grows in a large, weed-proof clump of leafy stalks. The semi-evergreen leaves are rough, thin and greyish-green, arching up and over towards the ground; they can be over 1m (3ft) long but rise only about 60cm (2ft) from the ground.

There is a bed of *Stipa gigantea* at Logan Botanic Garden in south-west Scotland which is as decorative as any bed of pampas grass, lacking only the enormity

Stipa gigantea.

of the latter. The bed fronts a forest of the giant leaves of *Gunnera manicata*, making a very memorable combination.

The erect flower spikes, over 1.8m (6ft) high, appear in succession with sometimes as many as a dozen spikes from a single clump 30cm (12in) across. Each spike carries a panicle over 30cm (12in) long, with the branches radiating around the spike from top to bottom like a pyramid. The flowers are reddish brown when they first open, giving the inflorescence its distinctive colouring. The empty flowers and the stems end up a true corn-yellow colour, remaining so well into autumn.

Stipa gigantea is a hardy, easy to grow grass which prefers a light soil with a good drainage and full sun. It should not be allowed to get too wet in winter or too dry in summer, but tolerates almost anything else which nature can muster, and does not need staking.

Lift and divide once the clump is large enough, and stems which have rooted can also be removed and planted elsewhere. Plants raised from seed will flower in two years, but seed is scant.

STYLOPHORUM DIPHYLLUM

(M i c h x .) N u t t .

FAMILY
Papaveraceae

ORIGIN
North America

HEIGHT AND SPREAD
60cm (2ft) × 60cm (2ft)

FLOWERING TIME
Summer

SPECIAL FEATURE
Long-flowering woodland plant

CLIMATIC ZONE
Zone 4

The celandine poppy is one of three species of *Stylophorum*, the other two coming from China and

Yellow poppy-like flowers of *Stylophorum diphyllum*.

Japan, and is ideal for the woodland or shady garden. It is extremely adaptable and like certain other woodland herbaceous perennials, benefits more from the damp cooler climate than from the shade. Provided *Stylophorum diphyllum* doesn't dry out or bake in hot sunshine it will be quite happy in the open. It is a great seeder and produces many small seedlings which are protected when young by the mother plant's leafy mantle. It has shy but beautiful flowers and a long flowering season as if to make sure they are not overlooked. Like many members of the poppy family, *S. diphyllum* exudes a curious yellowish orange liquid when broken which was once used as a dye.

Every winter *Stylophorum diphyllum* dies back to a thick fleshy mass of enlarged buds which are hardy and often rest on the surface of rock or soil. In early spring the foliage appears. Each large leaf is usually deeply dissected into five lobes and is bright green on top and glaucous beneath, rather like those of the sessile oak, *Quercus petraea*.

The cup-shaped flowers are rich dark yellow and closely resemble those of the greater celandine from which the plant takes its common name, but they are more spectacular and at least three times the size. These lovely flowers are borne intermittently on stems which emerge through the large foliage and are sometimes partially hidden by the leaves. There are often buds, flowers, unripe and ripe hairy capsules on the same plant.

Stylophorum diphyllum prefers cool moist woodland conditions but tolerates less sheltered positions, suffering only slightly from periods of drought. It thrives best on acid soil but tolerates neutral soils. Lift and divide established clumps when dormant. It sets seed but not in large amounts, which should be sown in a peat-based compost as soon as ripe.

UNIOLA LATIFOLIA

Michx.
FAMILY
Gramineae
ORIGIN
North America
HEIGHT AND SPREAD
1m (3ft) × 60cm (2ft)
FLOWERING TIME
Late summer
SPECIAL FEATURE
Everlasting
CLIMATIC ZONE
Zone 4

The flattened flowers of *Uniola latifolia*.

Most people are aware of the great food value of members of the *Gramineae* family — corn, maize, rice, sugar cane and bamboo are grasses — but there are also one or two which make excellent herbaceous perennials. The ubiquitous South American pampas grass is one, and *Uniola latifolia* is another. The latter is small and unobtrusive when growing actively and has excellent autumn colour after flowering, to provide a good display for many months. It takes very harsh weather or a human hand to topple these sturdy stems. I first saw this plant in the Botanic Garden of London University at Egham. Initially I thought it was a flattened type of quaking grass (*Briza media*) then noticed it was stiffer and more colourful.

The plant's shape and foliage are typical of most clump-forming grasses and can be unobtrusively hidden at the base of a larger, more spectacular plant or wall during early summer. The grass starts to come into its own later in the season, when the broad, glossy green leaves offset the strange flattened flower panicles. Each tall stalk carries a large, loose panicle of twenty to thirty flowers.

In autumn, the whole plant turns a wonderful dull coppery colour and it is at this time that the plant is at its elegant best. It is also an excellent plant for flower arrangers, the flowers remaining fixed long after picking and drying. I have some flower spikes which I picked over two years ago displayed in a vase and not a single flower has dropped off.

The plant spreads by its creeping root system which, although not invasive, makes a sizeable clump in a few years. During winter, it dies back completely to ground level and can be safely lifted and divided. It is fully hardy and long lived.

UVULARIA GRANDIFLORA

Smith

FAMILY
Liliaceae

ORIGIN
North America

HEIGHT AND SPREAD
75cm (2ft 6in) × 30cm (12in)

FLOWERING TIME
Late spring

SPECIAL FEATURES
Ground cover with hanging yellow lily flowers

CLIMATIC ZONE
Zone 4

Uvularia consists of four North American species which are fairly similar and are affectionately known as bellwort or merrybells. Merrybells is an apt name as these nodding yellow lilies brighten the edge of any woodland. There are various theories of the origins of the generic name and I suspect that the plant was once used to cure ailments of the throat which is where you will find the uvula. The genus is closely related to *Disporum*, *Tricyrtus* and *Polygonatum*, or Solomon's seal, all graceful woodland plants. *Uvularia grandiflora* has a shyness and gentleness which belies the inherent tenacity and vigour of its creeping root system. It reminds me of the potential power of seemingly vulnerable femininity to which many a male is unavoidably drawn, similarly the beauty which is there to be appreciated. A whole bank side of *Uvularia grandiflora*, such as in the woodland garden at Kew, is a breathtaking sight in late spring.

Uvularia grandiflora shares with the rest of the genus the knack of the stem twisting as both the foliage and the lemon-yellow flower tepals uncurl. The lance-shaped leaves clasp the stem, have several prominent parallel veins and are a smooth dark green on top and faintly glaucous below. The flowers are borne at the end of the arching stems, forcing them slightly downwards with their weight. The bell-shaped flowers are relatively large, often 5cm (2in) long, and the six tepals flare outwards, like a narrow miniature lily.

Uvularia grandiflora can make quite large clumps many metres (yards) across with dozens of flowers opening as the leaves unfurl. It prefers a sandy acid soil, but also tolerates lighter, more alkaline soils. In both cases, provide a generous mulch of organic matter. Sun or light shade is equally suitable. To propagate, lift and divide the rhizomes when dormant.

Uvularia grandiflora.

VERATRUM VIRIDE

Ait.

FAMILY
Liliaceae

ORIGIN
North America

HEIGHT AND SPREAD
1.8m (6ft) × 1.2m (4ft)

FLOWERING TIME
Midsummer

SPECIAL FEATURES
Immense stature and strikingly pleated leaves

CLIMATIC ZONE
Zone 4

The stately green flower spikes of *Veratrum viride*.

Of the twenty-five species of *Veratrum*, a handful are among the most stately of all herbaceous plants. 'Vere' means true in Latin and 'ater' means black, a meaning that has two connotations: the roots of all species are truly black, and the powerful drug 'Veratrium' obtained from the plant is (or was) a black or unknown quantity. There has always been something both beautiful and vaguely sinister about this plant when in flower. The foliage of all species is highly attractive regardless of the strange appearance of the unusual green flower, which I for one find curiously irresistible.

Veratrum viride, or Indian poke, is a rigid, erect clump-forming plant. Its stems emerge from ground level early in winter, protected by a mass of golden fibres which permanently clothe the thick vertical rhizomes beneath. These rhizomes and those of the very closely related European *V. album*, yield the drug Veratrium, which has a powerful purgative effect, causing vomiting and diarrhoea when taken internally; it is also a mild skin irritant. The drug is sometimes called white hellebore powder as opposed to black hellebore, which is extracted from the genus *Helleborus*. *Helleborus* simply means fatal (killing) food: a straightforward statement on their shared lethal properties. (Although the plants are totally unrelated, *Veratrum* species are sometimes called false hellebores, or helleborines, for this reason.)

Veratrum viride grows rapidly, uncurling its pleated hosta-like leaves which clasp the emerging stem. A basal leaf can be 30cm (12in) long and 10cm (4in) wide. The oval leaves decrease in size up the stem and are wonderfully structured, with conspicuous parallel veins running from base to tip. The flower stem can reach 1.8m (6ft) or more, and carries a 30cm (12in) long panicle with a prominent central spike and smaller side branches. Each star-shaped flower is bright greenish white, hence the name *viride*, which means green. This strange colouring, coupled with the size of the inflorescence, is most impressive.

Veratrum viride prefers heavy damp soils in full sun, where the leaves can soak up the moisture available during spring and early summer. It is remarkably tolerant of dryness however, merely showing its discomfort by not growing as tall or by producing less flowers. It is ideal for the water garden, wild garden or herbaceous border. *Veratrum nigrum* is also very spectacular, with maroon red to black flowers.

Veratrum viride is slow to grow from seed, which can take six or seven years to produce a flowering-

Close-up of flower spike of *Veratrum viride*.

VERONICASTRUM VIRGINICUM

(L.) Farw.

FAMILY
Scrophulariaceae

ORIGIN
North America

HEIGHT AND SPREAD
1.8m (6ft) × 1m (3ft)

FLOWERING TIME
Mid to late summer

SPECIAL FEATURE
Architectural form

CLIMATIC ZONE
Zone 4

The Culver's physic or Culver's root has long been cultivated in North America for its emetic and cathartic properties and it was once used extensively as a body purgative or internal cleanser. Quite apart from this, it is a highly ornamental hardy perennial better known in its native North America than in Europe. This species looks like a bumper-sized *Veronica spicata* but its rings of leaves and taller spikes of flowers have much more style and architectural form. *Veronicastrum* is sometimes included in *Veronica*, a huge genus of 250 species, but I prefer to keep it separate because of its distinctive whorled leaves and more tubular-like flowers. There are only two species in the genus: *V. virginicum* from North America and *V. sibiricum* from North Asia.

Veronicastrum virginicum has circular whorls of large leaves set at regular intervals up its tall rounded stems. There may be as many as fifteen whorls on a stem and each whorl usually has five, six or seven lance-shaped leaves.

The attractive flowers are borne on a long narrow terminal spike. Each flower is composed of a small mauve blue tube, out of which similar coloured stamens emerge. The inflorescence, 15cm (6in) or more long, has a fine feathery effect with the stamens appearing all around the spike. On large stems, a whorl of smaller flower spikelets forms around the central spike. There is also a lovely white form, *V. v.* 'Album', with a narrower spike up to 30cm (1ft)

sized plant. The plant is best lifted and divided as soon as it dies back in autumn, when next year's buds will have already been produced and lie just below soil level.

Close-up of flower spike of *Veronicastrum virginicum*.

VIOLA
GLABELLA

Nutt.
FAMILY
Violaceae
ORIGIN
North America
HEIGHT AND SPREAD
15cm (6in) × 10cm (4in)
FLOWERING TIME
Early to mid-spring
SPECIAL FEATURE
Yellow violets
CLIMATIC ZONE
Zone 4

long, and the slightest hint of pink in the petals. It has darker, smaller leaves and a shorter stature than the species. *Veronicastrum sibiricum*, from Asia, has pale blue flowers on smaller spikes; this plant is sometimes regarded merely as a variant of *V. virginicum*.

V. virginicum likes rich soil in full sun and plenty of moisture to grow to its full, impressive size. It spreads slowly from a creeping stoloniferous root system and doesn't need staking. Propagate from seed sown in spring or autumn, or by division of the mature clumps.

Violets, pansies and heartsease are well known and well loved, but they are only a few of more than 500 species of *Viola*, most of which grow on alpine scree and meadow or in rich, deep woodland. Of this enormous number, there are some real beauties, as well as uninteresting weeds. Many are herbaceous perennials while some are annuals. A large number come from North America and quite a few of those are yellow flowered, including *Viola glabella*. This easy-to-grow but little known woodland plant is also known affectionately as the stream violet. This name no doubt applies in North America to its natural habitat but in the Chelsea Physic Garden its home is quite a dry shady one, under the evergreen canopy of three middle-aged holm oaks (*Quercus ilex*). There is a small gap of light between each tree but the area is otherwise shaded all year round. The yellow violets give a light and airy feel to the shady ground and are encouraged by a mulch every two years of well rotted leafmould. Surprisingly some seedlings appeared nearby in between some limestone rocks where they receive full sun for most of the day. These plants are proving much happier than I expected and indicate the versatility which this charming violet possesses.

Viola glabella has thick creeping rhizomatous roots which rest on or just below the surface of the ground. Its top growth consists of many loose stems carrying smooth dark-green, deciduous leaves, *glabella* meaning smooth. The stems usually end in a cluster of kidney-shaped leaves in the axils of which the flowers

The yellow flowering *Viola glabella*.

are produced. The fully grown stems are relatively leafless in the middle, although this isn't obvious when seen from above as there is so much foliage growing on the tips.

The flowers resemble those of the dog violet or fragrant violet, except that they are bright yellow with the bottom petal streaked with dark brown veins. The flowers, which appear in great numbers, make a fine contrast against the rich dark green foliage. The plant flowers before the branches are fully extended, which means that the flowers sometimes bloom at ground level.

Viola glabella spreads very rapidly by both runners and from seed when given no ground-cover competition and plenty of leafmould. The plant is also quite content in a shady area of the rock garden, where it remains more compact. I have known it survive dry spells with little more than a slight wilting, and it soon picked up once watered. The plant tolerates alkaline soils but prefers a more acid woodland soil. Lift and divide the rhizomes or raise from seed sown in the autumn.

SHRUBS AND SMALL TREES

A concise definition of a shrub might be a woody perennial that does not attain the same size and stature as a tree and which often produces several stems from the ground. However, as with all aspects of natural history, there are notable exceptions, such as large single-stemmed shrubs or Bonsai trees. Shrubs do tend to have low-growing branches which reach the ground.

Many more shrubs than trees are included simply because many more shrubs are grown in today's smaller gardens, where there may be room for only one tree. I have, however, selected a handful of smaller trees which are certainly worth growing but are seldom seen in cultivation.

GROWTH
Like some herbaceous plants, most shrubs can spread great distances by means of their creeping root systems. *Ceratostigma* and *Clerodendrum bungei* are two examples. Shrubs can spread by layering, the process by which a branch touches the ground and forms roots there, eventually making a new plant; *Fuchsia magellanica* var. *molinae* and *Illicium floridanum* layer themselves naturally. Many shrubs also increase and spread themselves far from the parent plant by seed.

SHAPE AND HABIT
Shrubs vary in overall shape and outline, according to the type of stem and general branch network. Horizontally-growing branches have an entirely different visual effect from a mass of vertically growing stems, and shrubs can look as different as the bushy, many-stemmed, dome-shaped *Ribes speciosum* and the single, gnarled and twisted-stemmed *Poncirus trifoliata*.

FOLIAGE
The foliage also adds to the diversity of shrubs. It can be thick, glossy green and evergreen or woolly, grey and evergreen. There are deciduous leaves, which annually reveal the skeletal superstructure of the branches, and there is variegated and coloured foliage. Foliage is essential to a plant's character, and

lasts, in most cases, much longer than any flowers. Leaf shapes range from the tight, rounded leaves of box (*Buxus sempervirens*) which lends itself to topiary and hedging, to the beautiful, multi-divided palmate leaves of *Paeonia lutea*, the tree paeony. Foliage scent may be pleasant or over-powerful, but is an important feature and one which is often the key to a plant's identification.

CLIMBING AND TRAILING SHRUBS
All the shrubs in this section are self-supporting and free-standing, either as a solitary specimen or collectively as part of a shrub border. Climbing and trailing plants are dealt with in a separate chapter although technically many of them are classified as shrubs. There is a group of ground-hugging or sprawling shrubs which could be classed as trailers; the only plant in this chapter which falls into that category is *Ceratostigma plumbaginoides*.

PRUNING
Even within the confines of an inspirational book such as this, a general knowledge of pruning is essential. It is a subject much open to dispute but I would recommend adopting two courses of action: an annual clean-up and individual pruning according to the needs of the plant. Again, climbing plants are a separate case.

The annual clean-up involves tidying up the plant by removing any dead wood, untidy growth or weak and undesirable growth, in spring or autumn. Most shrubs need no other treatment than this, and additional pruning should be restricted to the removal of any branches that might block the path. Branches heavily laden with seed can be removed unless the seeds are a desirable feature. The production of seed takes an enormous amount of energy out of the plant which is better directed into growth for flower production later on; and some plants, such as *Buddleia* and *Lavatera olbia* seed themselves prolifically all over the garden, making extra work for the gardener.

Individual pruning may be necessary to keep certain plants, such as *Stachyurus chinensis*, in good shape, although *Cistus* and shrubs with most of their growth at the ends of the branches suffer if pruned too hard. Generally, pruning keeps a shrub strong and young; *Buddleia*, for example, flowers on growth made the same year and is vigorous enough to take a hard annual pruning in spring. *Fuchsia magellanica* var. *molinae* can also be pruned annually to encourage plenty of flowering growth although the weather may prune this plant and *Indigofera heterantha* naturally. Most shrubs do not need pruning every year.

Pruning can be used to maintain a good balance between the amount of growth made and the number of flowers produced. Proceed with care, so you do not prune off all the next season's flowers: individual species flower at different times of the year, and on wood of different ages.

PLANTING

Careful planting of any plant is absolutely crucial to its survival, and timing is vital. Evergreen shrubs can be planted at any time of year providing the weather is not too severe: deciduous are best planted when dormant. Container-grown plants can be planted any time of the year, as long as the soil is not frozen or waterlogged, but they tend to need very careful watering if moved when in active growth.

The ideal conditions for planting are soft, persistent rain which helps the plant stay moist and prevents the roots drying out. Rain also helps firm the transplanted root system into position. The worst weather for planting is blazing hot and sunny, with the ground baked hard, or freezing conditions in winter. Drying winds are equally unhelpful.

Always dig a hole deeper and wider than the rootball of the shrub. Make sure the soil in the bottom of the hole is not compacted and mix with leafmould or well rotted compost if available; it is important that this is well mixed and not too concentrated. Insert the shrub with the stem upright and the top of the root system below the level of the surrounding soil. Handle the root system gently and make sure it is spread out. With container-grown shrubs, prise out any long roots that encircle the container. Return the soil to the hole making sure there are no gaps, and firm with your foot. This soil may also be mixed with compost if available.

Make sure the top of the soil is level with the surrounding ground, and water well. In heavy soils, it helps to mound the soil round the stem of the shrub to ensure water does not collect round the root system; in dry soils, a shallow crater helps collect water.

PROPAGATION

Most shrubs can be propagated by division of creeping rootstock, layering or from seed; full details on these techniques are in the chapter on propagation.

AESCULUS PARVIFLORA

A . W a l t .

FAMILY
Hippocastanaceae

ORIGIN
South-east USA

HEIGHT AND SPREAD
3.5m (12ft) × 4.5m (15ft)

FLOWERING TIME
Late summer

SPECIAL FEATURES
Attractive stems, flowers and foliage

CLIMATIC ZONE
Zone 4

Most of us know and love the horse chestnut tree, *Aesculus hippocastanum*, one of the glories of early summer with its hand-like foliage and flower clusters like red and yellow torches waving all the way to the top of even the largest trees. *Aesculus parviflora* is a very different species but one which deserves better recognition and equal praise in its own way.

Aesculus parviflora is a shrub, never reaching tree proportions and, as its name *parviflora* — small flowered — suggests, has much smaller flowers than many other species. The flowers are, however, very attractive, and produce an effective display. Each flowering spike, or panicle, is about 15cm (6in) long and half as much across, comprised of many white flowers with prominent red stamens.

Aesculus parviflora in flower.

This plant is often grown as a single clump in a lawn where, given the space, it will produce a beautiful dome-shaped bush of many stems, taller in the centre and shorter round the edge. I have never seen it grown as a single stemmed plant, but would imagine it gives the effect of a miniature horse chestnut tree. I have seen a marvellous stand of *A. parviflora* fringing the edge of an evergreen woodland, where it simply shone out in flower.

The species is remarkably hardy and will tolerate most soils; the only drawback is that, being deciduous, it loses its leaves in winter. It needs a little imaginative under-planting, such as *Arum italicum* for its marbled foliage or *Anemone apennina* which has lovely blue or white flowers in early spring. Both of these will have died back by the time the attractive palmate foliage of the *Aesculus* unfolds in late spring. A clump will grow to about 3.5m (12ft) in height and can exceed that in breadth – there is a clump at the Royal Botanic Gardens in Kew which has a diameter of some 4.5m (15ft).

Aesculus parviflora is propagated by the removal of rooted suckers any time during the dormant season.

Young foliage of *Aesculus parviflora*.

AZARA DENTATA

Ruiz & Pavon

FAMILY
Flacourtiaceae

ORIGIN
Chile

HEIGHT AND SPREAD
3m (10ft) × 2.1m (7ft)

FLOWERING TIME
Mid to late summer

SPECIAL FEATURE
Unusual orange flowers

CLIMATIC ZONE
Zone 5

Fragrant golden balls of *Azara dentata*.

There are a dozen or so species of *Azara* and they come from the cooler regions of South America. They are not particularly hardy but will survive all but the harshest winters if carefully sited and given adequate protection. For this reason, they are not recommended for very cold districts, but *Azara dentata* offers such attractive and unique features that it deserves inclusion in the book. This shrub is well suited for sunny, sheltered corners in city gardens, where wind cannot ravage and frost does minimum damage.

Azara dentata is one of the larger-leaved and larger-flowered species. It is not quite as hardy as the more widely known *Azara microphylla*, which can be grown as a free-standing shrub, so *A. dentata* requires wall protection, particularly from easterly winds. It has shiny oval evergreen leaves which give the shrub a kind of lustre on hot sunny days. The bitter-tasting leaves are downy on the undersides and toothed, giving the plant its name – *dentata* means toothed or indented. The shrub may reach 3m (10ft) or more in height if allowed to grow unchecked, and forms a reasonable shape after only a few years.

The real glory of this plant is its flowers; they have no petals and are in fact a globular mass of both sterile and fertile male stamens enclosing the female parts. These globular flowers resemble superficially the flowers of mimosa (*Acacia* species) but are much larger, nearly 2.5cm (1in) across. They are a rich orange and have a strong scent very like that of the lime tree (*Tilia*). This scent is wonderful for filling the air on a hot summer's day, attracting many bees. Luckily, *Azara dentata* is without the black sticky drips exuded from lime trees which reduce anything beneath them to a cloying mess in midsummer.

Frost damage is easily recognized by the leaves turning black almost instantly, with no trace of brown. This is a peculiar attribute of several species of *Azara*, particularly in frost driven hard by wind. Given adequate protection though, these shrubs grow steadily and quite rapidly in all types of soil. Propagate from cuttings of new growth taken in early summer and inserted in the usual 50/50 peat and sand mixture in a closed frame. Cuttings of semi-ripened wood also root if placed in a cold frame. Apparently seed will set although I have never seen it.

BUPLEURUM
FRUTICOSUM

L .

FAMILY
Umbelliferae

ORIGIN
Mediterranean

HEIGHT AND SPREAD
1.8m (6ft) × 1.2m (4ft)

FLOWERING TIME
Mid to late summer

SPECIAL FEATURE
Blue-green evergreen foliage

CLIMATIC ZONE
Zone 5

Members of the *Umbelliferae* family are instantly recognizable by their characteristic umbels of white or yellow flowers, such as those of cow parsley, angelica, hogweed, hemlock, carrot, fennel, dill, coriander and a host of other related plants. *Bupleurum fruticosum* is the only shrubby member of the family which can be grown easily outdoors in cool temperate climates.

Bupleurum fruticosum has leathery evergreen foliage with a bluish-green tinge if the plant is grown in full sun; this sheen tends to be reduced where the plant is grown in the shade. It spreads prolifically by means of layering where its branches touch the ground, and forms attractive domed mounds which by midsummer are smothered in buds. The individual flowers themselves are dull yellow and rather small although the overall effect of the mass of flowers on the inflorescence is quite pleasing. These inflorescences are 7.5cm (3in) in diameter and are typically *Umbelliferae*, each one slightly convex.

Bupleurum fruticosum has a rather tenuous and interesting allegiance with ivy. *Hedera helix* produces two different types of growth, one which is climbing and sterile and which is the only kind seen in shade. The other, in exposed areas, makes shrubby branches of flowering shoots. These are a haven for wasps which

Bupleurum fruticosum in flower.

Close-up of *Bupleurum fruticosum* flowerhead.

CERATOSTIGMA WILLMOTTIANUM

Stapf.

FAMILY
Plumbaginaceae

ORIGIN
China

HEIGHT AND SPREAD
1m (3ft) × 1m (3ft)

FLOWERING TIME
Late summer through autumn

SPECIAL FEATURES
Compact shrub, intensely blue flowers

CLIMATIC ZONE
Zone 4

seem attracted to the flowers. Similarly, the growth of *Bupleurum fruticosum* will produce far more inflorescences in exposed conditions and the flowers are again very attractive to wasps. There is believed to be a relationship between the *Araliaceae* family, to which the ivy belongs, and the *Umbelliferae* family. The wasps are too busy with the flowers to be any kind of nuisance to the observer and the blooms of *B. fruticosum* are quite pleasantly scented.

Bupleurum fruticosum grows well on any soil but it particularly likes an alkaline one; I have seen it thrive in a very chalky garden in the Chiltern Hills. In exposed places it may be scorched by severe frosts and is best protected by neighbouring shrubs. It flowers best in full sun but will grow in quite shady areas under large trees or near tall buildings, although it may not flower. It is not easy to grow from cuttings although new growth in spring will root slowly if put in a peat and sand mix in a closed frame. It is easily raised from seed, however, and a plant will seed freely, given a hot summer. I am told that this plant is one of the few that is salt tolerant and like *Griselinia littoralis*, will thrive near the sea.

It is grown as a wall shrub to 1.8m (6ft) at Pylewell Park in south Hampshire where its glaucous foliage and lush growth look fine against the red brick orchard walls.

Two or three hardy species of *Ceratostigma* are grown in cool temperate climates, and are sometimes known as hardy plumbagos because of their relationship with that tender plant. However, of these, *C. willmottianum* is the hardiest and I think the most spectacular. When I worked for C. R. Rassell Ltd, nurserymen in the west end of London, this plant was highly sought after, together with *Caryopteris × clandonensis*. Both have remained old favourites of mine because of their long Latin names with no English counterparts and also their rich blue flowers.

Ceratostigma willmottianum made its entry into England via Ernest Wilson who sent his enthusiastic gardening friend Miss Ellen Willmott some seeds from China in 1908. Miss Willmott succeeded in raising two plants at Warley Place in Sussex, from which the majority of plants in cultivation are derived. They turned out to be spectacular and took their name from her in recognition of her success.

Ceratostigma willmottianum produces many branches radiating out from a central mass of wiry stems to make a fine rounded dome. In severe winters, its branches may be killed back to ground level, but new growth develops as soon as spring arrives. These grow rapidly and by midsummer should be 60cm (2ft) tall and clothed in slightly hairy pale green oval leaves. Even before flowering, this plant is to be admired for its neat, compact habit.

The flowers of *C. willmottianum* are as blue as a clear

Ceratostigma willmottianum.

summer sky and are a similar shape to those of its close relation, *Plumbago auriculata*, from the Cape of South Africa. The flowers are borne in corymbs, or clusters, at the end of each branch. The length of the flowering period is remarkable, due to the continual opening of new flowers; flowering can continue for several months until frosts destroy new growth. This and the outstanding blue of the flowers is memorable enough, but *C. willmottianum* will often add the bonus of reddening foliage as the weather begins to cool towards the end of the season.

This plant thrives on a chalky soil, so much so that it has the facility to liberate excess chalk from the so-called 'chalk glands' on its leaves, particularly in dry weather. It likes sun and prefers a well drained soil, living happily on a steep bank or in crevices in a wall or rock garden. Propagate from cuttings of semi-ripe wood taken in late summer or by division of the clump. Prune hard to near ground level in late winter or early spring, if the woody growth survives the winter, or once it has become old and sprawling.

Other species worth growing include the shrubby grey-leaved *C. griffithii*, which is tender and requires wall protection; and the reliably lovely but rampant creeping *C. plumbaginoides*, which is really a rhizomatous herbaceous plant.

Ceratostigma plumbaginoides – close-up of the flowers.

CHIMONANTHUS PRAECOX

(L.) Link.

FAMILY
Calycanthaceae

ORIGIN
China

HEIGHT AND SPREAD
3m (10ft) × 3m (10ft)

FLOWERING TIME
Midwinter

SPECIAL FEATURE
Fragrant flowers in winter

CLIMATIC ZONE
Zone 4

Chimonanthus praecox, the scented wintersweet.

My inquisitive nose first led me to this plant so aptly known as wintersweet. I came upon it clipped to within 15cm (6in) of a wall on a Dorset farmhouse, under a kitchen window. It was planted in almost solid chalky clay and its spurs of yellow wax-like flowers with their curious opaqueness were instantly attractive. I have since found it in its free-sprawling form in many gardens. The name tells us all but its fragrance: 'Chima' is Greek for winter, 'anthos' is a flower, and *praecox* means early.

The wintersweet has featured in our gardens for a long time, but is still not very widely known. It is related to Carolina allspice, *Calycanthus floridus*, a plant from North America with aromatic leaves and wood, and not surprisingly, *Chimonanthus* also has fragrant foliage. However, its leaves are nothing like as aromatic as its American cousin's, and it is the flowers of *Chimonanthus* which have delicious fragrance in winter.

The scent is not pungent but soft and seductive, and unlike some fragrances, can never be too strong. It is a pleasure to encounter when the garden is at its lowest. The slightly opaque, urn-shaped flowers appear to have two layers of petals. These are actually petal-like sepals called tepals and the inner tepals of the true species are a reddish colour while those of the cultivar 'Luteus', a bright sulphur yellow. Seeing these flowers on a bright sunny day in the middle of winter is positively alluring. Only the cultivar 'Grandiflorus' has particularly large flowers, 5cm (2in) across. As is so often the case when the size of flower increases, the fragrance is diminished.

Chimonanthus praecox and its forms perform well on all types of soil and grow adequately in either partial shade or sun. They can also be grown to good effect against a wall, in which case thin the growth immediately after flowering. This helps encourage new growth on which flowers will be produced the following winter. The lanceolate, dark green leaves look particularly handsome during the summer months, with the attractive large, brown, papery seed capsules up to 7.5cm (3in) long.

Propagate *C. praecox* either by seed, which is readily set and germinates to produce flowering-sized plants in three years; or by division of the main clump once it is well established. Earthing up soil over the mass of central stem growth encourages rooting along the branches which can then be removed for transplanting.

CISTUS INCANUS

L.

FAMILY
Cistaceae

ORIGIN
Southern Europe

HEIGHT AND SPREAD
1.2m (4ft) × 1m (3ft)

FLOWERING TIME
Midsummer

SPECIAL FEATURES
Aromatic leaves and showy flowers

CLIMATIC ZONE
Zone 5

The common name sun rose refers to the genera *Halimium* with yellow or white flowers in midsummer; *Helianthemum*, with yellow, orange, pink, white or red flowers; and *Cistus*, whose large rose-like flowers epitomize the heat of the Mediterranean summer and whose aroma is a heady reminder of sunburnt days and the whirr of cicadas. The twenty or so species of *Cistus* are all attractive shrubs, with individual flowers evanescent, falling usually after only a day. There is, however, a succession of flowers in midsummer.

Cistus incanus creticus was once the main source of a resinous substance called gum labdanum or gum ladanum which was used medicinally. It is still used today in perfumery, collected as it always was by the Cretans who comb it from the fleece of sheep, which browse among the plants. The Spanish *C. ladanifer* is another source. The oils which many species produce probably act as a deterrent to grazing animals as well as protecting the plants from moisture loss in the intense Mediterranean sun.

The pink flowers of *C. incanus* are five-petalled; each petal overlaps the next and is crinkled as it unfolds (a characteristic of the genus). Each petal has a

Cistus incanus.

Close-up of flower of *Cistus* × *purpureus*.

butter-yellow area at its base surrounding the dark yellow cluster of filaments. The 2.5cm (1in) leaves are greyish green with prominent netted veining.

Cistus love a limey soil and in the wild often smother a rocky limestone hillside. *Cistus incanus* is not as hardy as *C. laurifolius*, the toughest, white-flowered species, but given a sunny position sheltered from bitter easterly winds, the former should survive most winters with only superficial damage. Make sure it is not planted in a frost pocket.

Cistus incanus is one parent of the beautiful hybrid *C.* × *purpureus* which has green leaves and rich dark pink flowers over 7.5cm (3in) across, with maroon blotches on each petal. The centre of the flower is yellow blotched, with yellow filaments. There is a particularly fine form raised by Messrs Taudevin of Cheshire called 'Betty Taudevin', which has larger petals and is relatively hardy.

Propagate from semi-ripe cuttings inserted in a frame in late summer or from soft cuttings in early summer. Cistuses are notorious interbreeders so seed is never reliable, although results may be interesting.

CLERODENDRUM BUNGEI

Steud.

FAMILY
Verbenaceae

ORIGIN
North China

HEIGHT AND SPREAD
1.5m (5ft) × 2.1m (7ft)

FLOWERING TIME
Late summer

SPECIAL FEATURE
Fragrant, richly coloured flowers

CLIMATIC ZONE
Zone 5

This showy species is related to a group of plants which live mainly in the tropics, yet it is hardy even in the colder regions. Like several other shrubs, *Clerondendrum bungei* behaves more like a herbaceous perennial in hard winters: the woody top growth simply dies off, to sprout anew in spring from the persistent and often far-reaching root system. This prolificity and hardiness makes it a difficult plant to kill, even if you want to. Given room to spread, the plant produces a thicket of stems and a mass of blooms. A 1m (3ft) thick border planted solidly with *Clerodendrum bungei* outside a health clinic in Chelsea is particularly awesome when in flower. Though pruned back to the ground one year for no apparent reason, this proved merely to encourage vigour the following year and since then it has continued to flourish.

The spectacular flower heads of *Clerodendrum bungei* are 10cm (4in) or more across, and made up of densely packed, dark-pink buds which open to smaller, pale pink trumpet-shaped flowers with a strong, sweet fragrance. The flower heads are carried facing upwards at the ends of the main branches. A large clump of *Clerodendrum bungei* will produce many flowers; I have never seen the plant set seed.

The large, heart-shaped foliage has purple-reddish midribs. Its only drawback is that the leaves have a strong, fetid smell, rather like boiled milk, if touched. As a result, I would recommend that it is

The bright pink flowers of *Clerodendrum bungei*.

planted away from a terrace or path, and that you avoid touching the plant when smelling the flowers.

Clerodendrum bungei quickly spreads by means of its suckering root system; I have seen a young sucker emerge some 3m (10ft) away from its parent. Such shoots can be severed and transplanted. It tolerates a wide range of soils, surviving even in poor, dry conditions, but prefers some sun and an unrestricted space. In a very exposed site, the plant tends to be smaller and more prone to dying back to the ground each year; I have seen it surviving well in a woodland and light shade.

COLQUHOUNIA
COCCINEA

Wall.
FAMILY
Labiatae
ORIGIN
Himalayas, W. China
HEIGHT AND SPREAD
2.4m (8ft) × 1.8m (6ft)
FLOWERING TIME
Late summer, early autumn
SPECIAL FEATURES
Fragrant silver foliage and rich red flowers
CLIMATIC ZONE
Zone 5

The six species of *Colquhounia* (pronounced Cahoonia) are natives of the eastern Himalayas and West China. These aromatic shrubs of varying degrees of hardiness are named after Sir Robert Colquhoun of Luss (on the shores of Loch Lomond), a patron of the Calcutta Botanic Garden and a keen naturalist. *Colquhounia coccinea* is a fairly hardy shrub, although in the harshest weather it remains squat and flowers shyly. (Severe frost will cut it back to ground level, but it usually recovers the following spring.) When grown well it excels many plants in beauty particularly for a shrub flowering so late in the season.

The pointed leaves are typical of the *Labiatae* family, carried opposite each other alternately at 90° up the stem. The stem is also typical of the *Labiatae* in that it is four angled although rather more rounded and often further obscured by a coating of dense short hairs which cover the entire plant. The upper surface of the leaf is finely covered with hairs so that it appears rich dark green, but it is grey, almost white, with hairs on the undersurface. Before the flowers open and, to some extent, after they are open, the shrub has a distinct superficial resemblance to the totally unrelated genus *Buddleia*. The funnel-shaped flowers are tubular and bright orange red, with flame-like markings from the red lips to the bright orange throat. The flowers are borne in the circular whorls, typical of the *Labiatae* family, and the branches can be crowded with up to six layers of these flowering whorls, all in flower at once.

Flame-red flowers of *Colquhounia coccinea*.

One of the most delightful attributes of *C. coccinea* is the delicious fresh smell of eating apples that the foliage emits when pressed: it always reminds me of baskets full of freshly picked apples.

Colquhounia coccinea grows on acid or alkaline soils, preferring lighter soils. It grows quite large if protected from easterly winds and its lax stems can be effectively trained against a wall. Protect with straw or bracken in harsh weather. It will strike very easily from softwood cuttings taken at any time in the growing season. *Colquhounia* produces viable seed if the autumn frosts are not too early and a flowering shrub can be easily grown from seed in two years.

C Y D O N I A
O B L O N G A

Mill.

FAMILY
Rosaceae

ORIGIN
West and Central Asia

HEIGHT AND SPREAD
6m (20ft) × 3m (10ft)

FLOWERING TIME
Early summer

SPECIAL FEATURES
Silvery foliage, apple-blossom flowers and edible fruit

CLIMATIC ZONE
Zone 4

The so-called common quince makes an extremely attractive garden plant yet doesn't seem as well known as it should be. Its curious name has evolved from Cydonia, an area of Crete where the plant was grown in ancient times. The Romans later changed the Greek word Cydonia into Cotonium and this was further modified by the early French to *cooin* and thence probably in the 14th century to *cuince* (plural for a *quin*). The quin was the fruit of the plant, then as now, valued for its flavour and setting qualities in making jams and jellies.

Cydonia oblonga, the only species in the genus, is often confused with the Japanese quince (*Chaenomeles japonica*). The latter is widely grown and produces quince-like fruits of a very inferior flavour but it has equally attractive flowers. *Cydonia* is better known commercially than ornamentally, and is widely grown as the rootstock on which pears are grafted. It is a shame that quince is not equally popular for the splendid ornamental plant it is.

Quince is attractive from the beginning of the year when it starts putting out new leaves of a delicate silver, tinged with green. (The silvery felted effect is due to many tiny hairs on the undersides of the new leaves.) By early summer, large, pale-pink flowers start to emerge, each one 5cm (2in) across and a fine contrast to the still young foliage. The flowers look a little like apple blossom superficially, but are larger and a more delicate shade of pink. The ovate leaves,

SHRUBS AND SMALL TREES

Close-up of the pale pink flowers of the true quince, *Cydonia oblonga*.

dark green on their upper surface, can reach 10cm (4in) in length.

The autumn fruits of this purposeful plant are 10cm (4in) or more long and are shaped like a rather woolly fattened pear. They turn a rich golden yellow when ripe, as do the leaves before they fall. In the cultivar 'Maliformis' the fruits are more apple shaped but both it and the species are highly fragrant and make delicious quince jelly or sauce.

Cydonia oblonga is hardy but needs warm summers to ripen its fruit and wood, and does not set fruit in cold areas unless it is given the protection of a south or west-facing wall. (It can be trained against a wall as a single stem with horizontal lateral branches, espalier style.) In the open, it makes a large shrub or even a small picturesque tree and can be grown as a fine specimen plant. It prefers full sun and a moist but well drained soil, and is alkaline tolerant.

Propagate from seed which germinates after the cold of winter, or from hardwood cuttings taken in autumn and plunged to half their depth in sand for the winter. Rooting takes several months.

DAPHNE
MEZEREUM

L. forma ALBA

FAMILY
Thymeleaceae

ORIGIN
Europe and Central Asia

HEIGHT AND SPREAD
1.2m (4ft) × 1m (3ft)

FLOWERING TIME
Winter and early spring

SPECIAL FEATURE
Fragrant, long-lasting flowers

CLIMATIC ZONE
Zone 5

Mezereum is an ancient medicinal plant whose fruits and bark have been used as a stimulant and diuretic

Daphne mezereum.

Daphne mezereum alba comes true from seed and produces flowering-sized plants in three to four years. It prefers sun but plenty of moisture at the roots, not easy conditions to provide in the garden. The best compromise is to plant the shrub in light shade at the edge of a woodland or lea of a building. It resents root disturbance and once planted should not be moved. The plant is remarkably hardy and tolerates a wide range of well drained soils although it prefers chalky ones. I have seen mature specimens withstand very dry conditions which finished off nearby shrubs, although flowering was diminished the next year.

Sow seed as soon as ripe in summer preferably in situ in a shady part of the garden.

for hundreds of years. As is usually the case with many medicinal plants, parts of this plant are in fact poisonous and have been at times mis-used. The genus has nearly seventy-five species distributed throughout Europe and Asia, and provides our gardens with many marvellous flowering plants. This particular plant is one of the best, the white form being still little known.

Daphne mezereum and its forms have beautiful, unforgettable scent. It is at its best on a mild day in winter when the fragrance seems to cling to the air, sweet but never sickly. The species has flowers which range from dark magenta to maroon and many shades of pink, and produce bright red berries lasting throughout autumn and into winter. The white form, however, has translucent yellow fruits which age to a rich brown. As is so often the case with white forms, the stems and foliage are a brighter, paler green than the type, with no sign of reddening or browning of the wood and young growth. The leaves are narrow and smooth, often more than 2.5cm (1in) long. They are rather willow-like in appearance and, although deciduous, persist well into winter, masking the beginnings of the floral display. These flower buds are often so modest that when the first flowers open the uninitiated may spend time trying to locate the source of the fragrance. Once discovered, however, never forgotten.

The tubular flowers of *D. m. alba* are milky white, and are carried in clusters at the ends of the erect, leafless stems, densely packed to lengths of up to 15cm (6in).

The white variety, *Daphne mezereum alba*.

ELAEAGNUS ANGUSTIFOLIA

L.

FAMILY
Eleaganaceae

ORIGIN
West Asia

HEIGHT AND SPREAD
12m (40ft) × 6m (20ft)

FLOWERING TIME
Early summer

SPECIAL FEATURES
Silver leaves, fragrant flowers and fruits

CLIMATIC ZONE
Zone 5

This is the true oleaster, although all forty-five species of the genus *Elaeagnus* are known collectively under that name. It has an interesting origin, from the word 'elaia' which is Greek for olive, and 'agnos', meaning pure. The origin of purity dates back to when Greek women used to strew the leaves of the unrelated plant, *Vitex agnus castus*, on their beds to induce fertility without the need for sex first. 'Oleaster' is derived from its superficial resemblance to the olive's foliage and scented flowers; the generic name *Elaeagnus* means olive of purity.

Elaeagnus angustifolia is a large, silver-leaved deciduous shrub or small tree, up to a height of 12m (40ft). However, it usually forms a spreading shrub over 6m (20ft) or more wide when fully grown. Its branches are silvery (in other *Elaeagnus* species they can be golden) due to hundreds of overlapping scales.

The leaves of *E. angustifolia* are long and narrow, dark green on top and silvery, almost white and shining with scales underneath. The specific name *angustifolia* means narrow-leaved and is aptly descriptive. The flowers are also scaly and rather inconspicuous, as the scales tend to make them appear dull and

A mass of flowers on *Elaeagnus angustifolia*.

Close-up of the *Elaeagnus angustifolia*'s fruit.

the same colour as the silvery foliage and branches. The flower clusters are, however, produced in such enormous quantity that their fragrance soon leads the eye to search for the source of the scent. The small lozenge-shaped fruits which follow can also cover the plant. They are a dull orange brown and fleshy, again lightly covered in scales and rather tasteless but quite sweet; they are often sold in Turkey as snacks.

Eleagnus angustifolia prefers a dry sandy soil in which the roots can penetrate deep to reach water reserves. It is completely hardy, flowering best in full sun.

Raise from seed sown in autumn and over-wintered to break dormancy. The plant may also be layered if branches grow long enough to reach the ground.

FUCHSIA MAGELLANICA

Lam. var. MOLINAE

FAMILY
Onagraceae

ORIGIN
Chile

HEIGHT AND SPREAD
1.8m (6ft) × 2.1m (7ft)

FLOWERING TIME
Midsummer to autumn

SPECIAL FEATURE
Hardy, pale-flowered fuchsia

CLIMATIC ZONE
Zone 5

Close-up of the flowers of *Fuchsia magellanica molinae*.

The great sixteenth-century German botanist Fuchs is commemorated in the hundred species of mainly South American shrubs, with one or two originating in New Zealand. Most have large ornamental pendant flowers, often with a coloured tubular calyx. *Fuchsia magellanica* is the only species generally grown in cultivation. Virtually hardy, it is seen in one or more of its crimson red forms as a hedging plant in Cornwall, Ireland and Western Scotland, but the pale pink form, *F.m. molinae* is rarely seen. This has been erroneously called *F.m. alba* for many years and is not

white, as its varietal name suggests, but a very pale pink. It has been in cultivation since 1926 but is as yet relatively unknown. The occasional pale-flowered *Fuchsia magellanica molinae* always catches the eye of the traveller along the south-west Irish roads, largely hedged with the red *Fuchsia magellanica*.

F. magellanica molinae exhibits many of the characteristics which white forms of otherwise coloured plants show: pale-green leaves, green-tinged stems and pale-green unripe fruits, with no hint of red or brown. The oval leaves are 1.5–2.5cm ($\frac{1}{2}$–1in) long. The flowers, although produced in fair quantity, do not stand out as vividly as the dark red flowers of the species, which are produced in such profusion. Flowers are carried in the leaf axils, a green ovary sitting firmly behind each one, waiting for fertilization to fatten it up. The flowers, which are borne in continu-

remarkably wind tolerant but will succumb to the ravages of a hard frost. A large plant is seldom killed, however, as it revives each spring, and is capable of making a trunk several centimetres (inches) thick. Propagate from softwood cuttings taken in late summer and inserted in a warm or cool frame. The species in all its forms naturally layers itself and these layers may simply be removed with adequate roots.

HALESIA TETRAPTERA

L.

FAMILY
Styracaceae

ORIGIN
North America

HEIGHT AND SPREAD
6m (20ft) × 4.5m (15ft)

FLOWERING TIME
Early summer

SPECIAL FEATURE
Graceful pendulous flowers

CLIMATIC ZONE
Zone 4

ous succession, consist of a tubular pale-pink calyx which ends in four points and a pale lilac pink corolla of four petals which make a circular tube-like centre, one petal overlapping the next. The eight stamens and single style project from the centre, and are so pale a pink as to be nearly white; it is easy to see why the plant was once known as var. *alba*. The green, four-angled fruits which follow have little chance of ripening and I have never seen fertile fruit set, although I have seen and indeed eaten the delicious fruits of the species. The seeds can be gritty but otherwise the fruits are tasty and sweet. By far the best fruits are produced by the New Zealand tree fuchsia, *F. excorticata*, which are as good as blueberries or gooseberries.

Fuchsia magellanica molinae prefers acid, sandy soils and thrives on plenty of moisture. The plant is

The snowdrop tree, *Halesia tetraptera* (syn. *Halesia carolina*), does not normally grow a straight trunk, but produces erratic growth to make it a most distinctive and graceful character in the garden. Before the pale green, ornate leaves appear each year, the spreading branches produce marvellous pendulous, nodding blooms, up to 1.5cm (½in) across, which resemble snowdrops and justify its common name.

More often than not, the flowers smother the bare branches in white blooms with a hint of yellow in the petals, producing a faint creamy appearance. In autumn the plant makes an equally spectacular display: the leaves fall to reveal hard, nut-like fruits, sometimes 5cm (2in) long with four longitudinal wing-like flanges, hanging along the branches. These may remain on the plant well into winter.

This is one of three or four species of *Halesia* which are easy to grow in cool temperate climates providing

Halesia tetraptera, the snowdrop tree.

HALIMIUM LASIANTHUM

Spach. 'CONCOLOR'

FAMILY
Cistaceae

ORIGIN
Southern Portugal

HEIGHT AND SPREAD
1m (3ft) × 1m (3ft)

FLOWERING TIME
Summer

SPECIAL FEATURES
Hardy sun rose with long flowering period

CLIMATIC ZONE
Zone 4

Of the dozen or so species of *Halimium, H. lasianthum* and its cultivar 'Concolor' described here, are by far the hardiest of the sun roses. *Halimium* is closely related to both *Cistus* and *Helianthemum* and bridges the gap between the two. The genus is named after the sea orach plant, *Atriplex halimus*, whose silvery-grey foliage is very similar to at least one species of *Halimium*. A great grower of sun roses and specialist nurseryman, John Coke, has a twin border of *Cistus* species and cultivars, and *H. lasianthum* 'Concolor' in his garden in Hampshire. There, the value of *Halimium* is particularly striking; its flowering season is far longer than that of the *Cistus*, and it seems always to be in flower, as it sprawls over the paved path.

Halimium lasianthum has rich butter-yellow flowers 3.5cm (1½in) across and each petal has a dark brown blotch at the base giving the flower a characteristic brown centre. In the form 'Concolor', there is no brown blotch, the flowers irradiating their pure yellow among the greyish foliage. Its growth habit resembles some of the *Cistus* species rather than that of *Helianthemum*: it makes a sprawling, dense shrub up to 1m (3ft) or more high and 1.2m (4ft) across. It needs full sun to flower over a long period during the summer months. The flowers, like flat, doll-sized plates of yellow, are made of five petals, each one overlapping the edge of the next. They are produced on the ends of the twigs and open in succession

the soil is not too dry or alkaline. There is another less well-known but larger growing species worth mentioning, *H. monticola*, the mountain snowdrop tree; its flowers are even bigger. *Halesia* flowers best in full sun and enjoys a situation against a wall. There is a beautiful specimen of the snowdrop tree near one of the ponds in the Isabella Plantation in Richmond Park near London. Its show of flowers immediately caught my attention and to my mind resembled a fictitious white flowering weeping willow.

Halesia tetraptera can be grown from seed but like its relative, *Styrax*, the hard seed should be cracked or split open to encourage germination. The plant can also be grown from branches pegged and layered onto the soil or from hardwood cuttings taken after the leaves have fallen in the autumn. These may be left to root slowly over the winter months in a cold frame or sheltered corner of the garden.

Pure yellow flowers of *Halimium lasianthum* 'Concolor'.

throughout the summer. The oval leaves are rarely over 2.5cm (1in) long, and are covered with hairs, which give them a greyish appearance. The twigs are also covered with hairs, which gives the whole plant a downy look. As is often the case with Mediterranean sun-loving plants, hairs on the foliage prevent excess evaporation from the leaf surfaces and thus keep the leaves cooler. (The leaves are actually green underneath their hairy surfaces.)

The plant came originally from southern Portugal and it is surprising how hardy it can be. I dare suggest it is hardier than nearly all the *Cistus*, and have never seen it severely damaged by the coldest frost-laden winds, even when growing in an exposed open site. It is perhaps more susceptible to damage from very wet weather followed by an extremely cold spell. The cold

penetrates far more when there is water surrounding the root system of the plant.

Halimium lasianthum 'Concolor' is happiest in a dry well drained position and is equally content on a light or heavy soil. I have noticed a slight yellowing (chlorosis) of the leaves if there is a high level of lime in the soil which can result in some lack of vigour, but the plant will be content to bask in the sun.

Halimium lasianthum 'Concolor' can be propagated from softwood cuttings in spring or from semi-ripe cuttings of the current season's growth taken in late summer. The plant can be raised from seed, but the genus *Halimium* and its ally *Cistus* have a natural propensity for hybridization. If there are other closely related plants nearby, you cannot expect *H.l.* 'Concolor' to come true from seed.

ILEX CORNUTA

L i n d l.

FAMILY
Aquifoliaceae

ORIGIN
China, Korea

HEIGHT AND SPREAD
3m (10ft) × 4m (13ft)

FLOWERING TIME
Insignificant flowers; fruiting in autumn

SPECIAL FEATURES
Graceful shape and unusual foliage

CLIMATIC ZONE
Zone 4

Ilex cornuta, showing its horned leaves.

The horned holly, *Ilex cornuta*, is a slow-growing shrub, only reaching large proportions when very ancient, and even then its small size and dome-shaped habit look nothing like its stronger-growing cousin, the common holly, *Ilex aquifolium.* There are some 400 species of holly, most of which are evergreen shrubs and trees; one or two are deciduous and one, *I. paraguiaensis*, provides the dried leaves for making yerba maté, a type of green tea from South America. I once had a Brazilian friend who used to offer a popote of maté from which one drank the tea using a metal tube-like structure called a bombilla; the tea was delicious.

Ilex cornuta is slow growing by holly standards, but throughout its long life always remains an attractive plant, its dome shape and tightly packed branches giving it what architects call 'form'. I have never tried to clip it but imagine it would respond well. It is very hardy in both full sun and shade. There is a splendid specimen in the Duke's garden at Royal Botanic Gardens, Kew.

Ilex cornuta gets its common name from the Latin *cornuta* which means horned. This is a reference to the prominent horns or points which make the corners of the lobes on the leaves. These leaves are attractive, both individually and seen en masse: they cover the shrub so densely that it looks like an impenetrable thicket, reaching more than 3m (10ft) and usually spreading to about 4m (13ft). The individual leaves

are more or less rectangular in shape with four or five spines, shiny dark green and rather stiff. The flowers are insignificant and do not contribute much to the merits of the plant; they are small and greenish-white, appearing in late spring. The berries are rich scarlet red and although sparsely produced contrast beautifully with the leaves.

Ilex cornuta fruits best in a sheltered sunny corner, but, in common with most hollies, it tolerates very dry soils and quite shady situations. It is happiest in sandy soils, and can be found flourishing in both alkaline and acidic conditions. It is this reliable toughness and its comparatively compact habit that make this plant so potentially useful in the garden.

Ilex cornuta can be grown from seed but this takes a long time and it is best propagated from semi-ripe cuttings. However, it is not the easiest plant to propagate oneself and it is worth buying instead.

ILLICIUM ANISATUM

L.

FAMILY
Illiciaceae

ORIGIN
China and Japan

HEIGHT AND SPREAD
3m (10ft) × 1.5m (5ft)

FLOWERING TIME
Late winter, spring

SPECIAL FEATURES
Attractive flowers, evergreen aromatic foliage

CLIMATIC ZONE
Zone 5

The white starry flowers of *Illicium anisatum* in early spring.

The forty-two species of *Illicium* are the sum total of the *Illiciaceae* family and are somewhat out on a limb, being only distantly related to *Drimys winteri* and *Schizandra* and, more distantly, *Magnolia*. Only two or three species are hardy enough to be grown outside in cool temperate climates, as most come from warmer regions of North America and East Asia.

Illicium is a good name for the genus, 'illicius' meaning to allure, but *I. anisatum* is misleadingly named. *Illicium verum* is the species which yields the star anise popular in Eastern cooking, although *I. anisatum* does have a marvellous aroma to its bruised foliage, redolent of a kind of sweet aniseed. Its strange fruits are burnt as incense in Chinese temples, which gave the plant its earlier name, *I. religiosum*.

Illicium anisatum is a handsome evergreen shrub, with fleshy but shiny lance-shaped evergreen leaves. The branches bend gracefully down to the ground and quite often extend out from the plant like a wave, layering themselves as they go. The flowers and later the fruits are equally remarkable. The flowers vary from a clear white through yellowy green and are 3.5cm (1½in) across. Many strap-shaped, narrow petals form a fringe around the centre, which is composed of a strange fringe-like structure of its own. The fruits which develop after flowering look very like the so-called star anise. They are star-shaped in a three dimensional way, radiating in a dozen different directions, each ray holding a single, large brown seed.

Illicium anisatum is one of the toughest species, vying with *I. henryi* for hardiness. I have known it survive hard frosts, protected against cold winds only by surrounding shrubs. Its aromatic oils must prevent the penetrating cold from damaging the evergreen foliage. It is a very fine sight covered in white blossom in early spring.

Illicium anisatum is acid loving, preferring a soil with plenty of peat and leaf mould, and likes a sunny, sheltered position. It flowers on five-year-old plants and requires little attention except the removal of dead or unsightly wood. Propagate from the layered branches.

INDIGOFERA HETERANTHA

Wall. ex Brandis.

FAMILY
Leguminosae

ORIGIN
Himalayas

HEIGHT AND SPREAD
3m (10ft) × 1.8m (6ft)

FLOWERING TIME
Midsummer to autumn

SPECIAL FEATURE
Hanging flowers late in the season

CLIMATIC ZONE
Zone 4

Indigofera means literally making indigo and alludes to the blue dye expressed from the flower buds and young shoots of the true indigo plant, *Indigofera tinctoria*. (The substance extracted is a dark blackish blue and is washed several times and then dried into cakes.) There are more than 700 species of *Indigofera*, most of which are typical herbaceous plants or shrubs; there are a handful which are completely hardy, and these give us some of the showiest shrubs in the pea family. The hardy species behave as shrubs in a sheltered position against a wall, or as herbaceous perennials, because of their sappy branches, if grown in exposed positions. There are a number of shrubs in the *Leguminosae* family which can behave in this way: *Lespedeza* and *Desmodium* are both genera with species which will die back each year.

Indigofera heterantha has been known for a long time as *I. gerardiana*, although the former is the earlier and more valid name. If the plant is cut to the ground by frost, up to 1m (3ft) of annual growth is made before the racemes of flowers are produced. Each beautiful leaf has fifteen to twenty-one oval, bright green leaflets. The racemes of small, rosy pink pea-shaped flowers are spiky and reach a length of 7.5—10cm

The pink pea-flower of *Indigofera heterantha*.

(3–4in). Seed is often set and is usually viable. The seedlings put on a good 45cm (18in) of growth, often more, in the first year.

Grown out in the open as a herbaceous perennial, this species can be cut back to the stool in late autumn once the flowers have fallen off, or it can be left until early spring. It is particularly effective grown with winter and early spring-flowering plants such as *Anemone ranunculoides* or spring bulbs, whose leaves have faded by the time *Indigofera* puts on growth in early summer.

Indigofera heterantha likes a well-drained soil but will tolerate lime soils. Given the shelter of a wall and sun, it can reach 3m (10ft) high by 1.8m (6ft) wide. A hard prune every spring, cutting back by half all last year's main branches, will encourage the growth of lateral branches and thereby increase the amount of flowers.

ITEA
ILICIFOLIA

Oliver.

FAMILY
Iteaceae (or *Saxifragaceae*)

ORIGIN
China

HEIGHT AND SPREAD
3.5m (12ft) × 3m (10ft)

FLOWERING TIME
Mid to late summer

SPECIAL FEATURE
Long, drooping flowers

CLIMATIC ZONE
Zone 5

It is the strong scent exuded by *Itea ilicifolia* which catches the attention of passers-by and draws them to trace its origin. The tassels may at first glance appear to be seed vessels as their greenish colour belies their catkin nature. *Itea ilicifolia* produces a spectacular display and is reasonably hardy once it has reached sufficient size, although it may be cut hard to the ground in exposed gardens during hard winter conditions. Its name comes from *itea*, meaning willow, and

ilicifolia, meaning holly-leaved, so it comes as no surprise that the spiny, evergreen leaves are very like holly.

The drooping flowers, giving the shrub a weeping appearance, provide the willow connection. These pendulous blooms, up to 30cm (12in) long, are truly remarkable. Each flowering shoot, comprised of many bright, green-yellow flowers with reduced petals and a sweet scent, hangs gracefully down from the vigorously growing branches. Standing near the plant I am always reminded of the fresh honeycomb smell of some buddleias. A mature specimen in full flower looks like something from an old Chinese flower painting and the strange greenish colour of the flowers looks beautiful against the dark, holly-like foliage. The bright green shoots grow as much as 1.8m (6ft) long in one season, in preparation for the waterfall of flowers that follows.

The plant can be grown in partial shade, but looks spectacular grown against a wall, even in full sun. It is certainly the pride and glory of the genus, exceeding

The green honey-scented tassles of *Itea ilicifolia*.

the other species in showiness and is far more tolerant of cool climatic conditions. *Itea ilicifolia* does not like too alkaline a soil, although it will tolerate a small degree of chalk or limestone. It is easily propagated from new growth in the spring by inserting 15cm (6in) long cuttings in a cold frame. Cuttings may also be taken in autumn and treated in the same way, left to root more slowly during the winter under the protection of the frame.

It flowers quickly after propagation – sometimes in the same season – and may be used as a pot plant in a cool greenhouse or conservatory for the first year before planting more safely in its permanent position the following year.

Lavatera olbia, a tree mallow.

LAVATERA OLBIA

L.

FAMILY
Malvaceae

ORIGIN
South-west Mediterranean coasts

HEIGHT AND SPREAD
3m (10ft) × 1.8m (6ft)

FLOWERING TIME
Midsummer to autumn

SPECIAL FEATURES
Vigorous shrub with long flowering season

CLIMATIC ZONE
Zone 5

Lavatera is a genus of twenty-five species which are collectively referred to as the 'tree mallows'. Strictly speaking, this title only belongs to the tallest of the species, *L. arborea*, but has often been used for the others, particularly *L. olbia*. The genus was named after a pair of Swiss naturalists, the Lavater brothers, while *olbia* originates from the Roman name for the Iles d'Hyères off the south-west coast of France, where the plant grows wild.

This is a plant whose virtues are not totally reliant upon its flowers, though they are exquisite and long lasting. *Lavatera olbia* also has an attractive shape, form and foliage and a terrific growth rate; I don't know another shrub to match it. Defining any of this genus as a shrub may be a misnomer, for the woody content within the stems is not as high as in most other shrubs. The plant is really a large, extra-tough herbaceous perennial with a rather woody base. In a particularly severe winter, I have known all the top growth, 1.8–3m (6–10ft) high, cut back to this woody base, but the plant invariably recovers.

The young branches, the foliage and the flower buds are all softly felted with downy hair and this gives the new growth a very fine appearance. The leaves can be quite large when mature, up to 15cm (6in) long and distinctly three lobed, with a central lobe about twice as long as the two on either side. The flowers are borne singly and alternately up the branches, just above a leaf, in the leaf axil. (A curious feature of the genus is the presence of a kind of double calyx: the outer one is correctly termed an involucre of bracts or epicalyx.) There are five rich pink petals, streaked with a darker pink, each separate from the next. They are narrow at the base and widen out considerably to form a cap-like flower over 3.5cm (1½in) across. A mature shrub in flower can have many dozen flowers out at the same time from early or midsummer through to autumn.

Lavatera olbia can be grown quickly and easily from seed, producing a stronger plant than one struck from a cutting. It will almost certainly flower the year after germination, if not within the first year, and may easily grow to a metre (yard) or more in height within a few months. For this reason, siting of the plant is important and 1.8m (6ft) should be allowed for spread.

Lavatera olbia prefers an alkaline soil but will grow on almost any type except wet, clay soils. It may be slightly stunted on poor stony ground but this could be considered an advantage if you wanted to limit its growth. Allowed to grow to its full size, it makes a stately feature in the centre of an herbaceous border.

LONICERA FRAGRANTISSIMA

Lindl. & Paxt.

FAMILY
Caprifoliaceae

ORIGIN
China

HEIGHT AND SPREAD
2.4m (8ft) × 2.1m (7ft)

FLOWERING TIME
Winter and early spring

SPECIAL FEATURE
Winter fragrance

CLIMATIC ZONE
Zone 4

The highly-scented flowers of *Lonicera fragrantissima*.

Many of the plants which flower during winter have a particularly strong fragrance and often small flowers. The size of flowers can be attributed to harsh weather which would damage large blooms, but the exaggerated fragrance is presumably intended to attract those few insects which can be coaxed out on fine days.

Lonicera fragrantissima, a shrubby honeysuckle, has small scented blooms, produced in the cold winter months and resembling those of *Daphne mezereum*. The blooms, habit of growth and winter flowering belie the relationship of *L. fragrantissima* to those more familiar climbing honeysuckles seen in the bee-filled summer. On a warm, still day the scent can be almost intoxicating. *Lonicera fragrantissima* is a semi-evergreen or deciduous shrub, depending on the weather. It is free standing with a spreading, not climbing, habit of growth. (The only other winter-flowering species is the less showy *L. standishii*.)

The flowers of *L. fragrantissima* are creamy white and, although smaller than the more familiar flowers of many climbing honeysuckles, are attractive in their way. They are carried in the leaf axils, often several pairs to an axil, and a good branch may be covered along its length in flowers. Such a branch cut and stood in water in a cool room lasts for weeks, releasing a delectable fragrance.

The plant needs full sun to flower well. However, it tolerates light shade on the edge of woodland. When the foliage drops off in cold weather, the flowers become more visible. *Lonicera fragrantissima* can also be trained against a wall where it can reach quite a height and spread. In this position, the shrub should be pruned in spring after flowering, thinning out the old wood.

Lonicera fragrantissima tolerates any type of soil but responds best to damp ground. Layering is the best means of propagation, but cuttings of ripened wood may also be taken in late summer. *L. × purpusii* is an attractive hybrid between *L. standishii* and *L. fragrantissima* and has pink-flushed, larger flowers.

MALUS TRILOBATA

(L a b i l l.)   S c h n e i d.

FAMILY
Rosaceae

ORIGIN
Greece, Spain, Lebanon and Israel

HEIGHT AND SPREAD
_10m (30ft) × 3m (10ft)_

FLOWERING TIME
Early summer

SPECIAL FEATURES
Upright shape, attractive flowers and autumn colour

CLIMATIC ZONE
Zone 4

There can be few plants with such universal appeal as this large shrub or small tree. _Malus_ is the old Latin word for the apple as distinct from the genus _Pyrus_, meaning pear. Linnaeus, when classifying plants in the middle of the eighteenth century, lumped all the _Malus_ species under the umbrella of _Pyrus_. Philip Miller, one-time curator of the Chelsea Physic Garden, consequently wrote, 'I shall therefore beg leave to continue the separation of the apple from the pear, as both hath been always practiced by the botanists before'. His ruling still stands for the thirty-five species of _Malus_ today. The distinction between the two genera is easily recognized by the shape of the fruits and by the female styles which are joined at the base in _Malus_ but not in _Pyrus_.

Malus trilobata has a central stem with short lateral branches arising from it, giving the tree an erect, almost fastigiate outline. It has very downy new growth which in spring bursts like silvery green velvet from the ends of the branches where most of the leaves are carried. The youngest branches are also downy, ageing to a more typical smooth apple wool texture. In late spring or early summer, small clusters of the palest pink flowers appear. (The plant is sometimes described as having white flowers, but though white is the net result, there is a definite hint of pink.) The flowers are large for the genus, 3.5cm ($1\frac{1}{2}$in) across. The small, oblong fruit seldom ripens but those that develop are an attractive red or yellow.

Close-up of flower of _Malus trilobata_.

PAEONIA LUTEA

French. var. LUDLOWII

FAMILY
Paeoniaceae

ORIGIN
Tibet

HEIGHT AND SPREAD
1.8m (6ft) × 1.8m (6ft)

FLOWERING TIME
Early summer

SPECIAL FEATURES
Large yellow flowers, attractive foliage

CLIMATIC ZONE
Zone 4

The distinctive autumn foliage of *Malus trilobata*.

The leaves are equally unique, *trilobata* meaning three lobed. In fact, the plant was at one time thought to be a species of hawthorn, as many *Crataegus* species have three-lobed leaves. The fine woolliness on the leaf underside and its general constitution, however, are more apple-like. There are three main lobes: a long central one and two lateral lobes, each of which is further indented with two or three shallower lobes. To me, the total effect is more reminiscent of the *Acer* genus, to which maples belong, than *Malus*. The first time I saw the plant at Kew in full autumn colour, a brilliant flash of crimson, scarlet and maroon with only the barest hint of green, I did not recognize it as a *Malus*.

Malus trilobata grows on any soil but prefers a deep, rich one and thrives in full sun. It needs no pruning except to shape any misplaced branches and it makes a wonderful specimen in a lawn or shrubbery. It is difficult to propagate but can be grown from 25cm (10in) long hardwood cuttings inserted in sand or loam in a cold frame or sheltered bed.

Paeonia suffruticosa has given flower lovers some of the most enormous and beautiful blooms of all time. *Paeonia lutea* var. *ludlowii* is a yellow-flowered closely related plant, which has dipped mildly in and out of popularity, though it has never been a best seller. Apart from frost nipping the odd precocious leaf early in spring, neither the plant nor its cultivational requirements can be faulted. We once had a cottage 200m (650ft) up in the ironstone hills of South Warwickshire. Surprisingly the only plant which was content after ten years of neglect before we came there was a fine specimen of *Paeonia lutea* var. *ludlowii* which stood proudly through the rest of the melee.

Paeonia lutea var. *ludlowii* is the largest of the so-called 'tree' paeonies. These paeonies are not, strictly speaking, trees, but deserve their name because of the immensity of woody growth produced in contrast to their herbaceous cousins.

Paeonia lutea var. *ludlowii* is impressive all year round, even during winter, when the thick erect branches stand strong against the bitterest weather. The winter outline is very much reminiscent of the coral-like branches made by the heavenly frangipani plants. Like all *Paeonia* species, *P. lutea* var. *ludlowii* has beautiful foliage. The *Paeonia* genus is closely related to the buttercup family (*Ranunculaceae*); in fact, they are listed as members of *Ranunculaceae* in old books, though they have since been given a family, *Paeoniaceae*, of their own. Many species in both

The large single yellow flowers of *Paeonia lutea* var. *ludlowii*.

families have splendid compound divided leaves; one only has to glance at some *Actaea* or *Cimicifuga* species to make this comparison. *Paeonia lutea* var. *ludlowii* has leaves which are less dissected as in the other tree paeonies, and measure some 22.5 cm (9in) long by nearly the same wide. The smooth leaflets are bright pale green, making an attractive setting for the yellow flowers.

The flowers are large, often up to 12.5cm (5in) in diameter. They are a clear lemon yellow and have a column of green carpels as their centre. *Paeonia lutea* var. *ludlowii* originated in Tibet and is far more widely cultivated than the original species.

Paeonia lutea var. *ludlowii* tolerates a wide range of soils and grows rapidly and easily from seed to make flowering-sized plants in three years. Light shade, shelter and plenty of moisture are preferable. The only drawback, other than early frost damage, is that the flowers are sometimes obscured by the luxuriant foliage. It is completely hardy and so vigorous that a large site should be chosen for it.

Raise from seed or divide very large plants by removing rooted outer branches from below ground level.

PENSTEMON CORDIFOLIUS

Benth.

FAMILY
Scrophulariaceae

ORIGIN
California

HEIGHT AND SPREAD
2.1m (7ft) × 1.8m (6ft)

FLOWERING TIME
Late summer

SPECIAL FEATURE
Scarlet flowers

CLIMATIC ZONE
Zone 5

Penstemon cordifolius.

The penstemons have graced our gardens for many years and their reputation is for beauty and unreliable hardiness; by far the majority grown in cool temperate climates are slightly woody herbaceous perennials. *Penstemon cordifolius*, however, is a shrub and I have seen it reach over 2.1m (7ft) in height against a wall, where its identity baffled me completely. I hardly expected to find a large shrub in this genus, let alone one fan trained against the wall of a Warwickshire cottage. There, facing west, it was as surprising as the marvellous related *Phygelius capensis*, 6m (20ft) high on the wall of Hidcote Manor in Gloucestershire. Free-standing, the arching branches of *P. cordifolius* may spread more than 1.8m (6ft).

'Pente' is Greek for five and 'stemon' means stamen, and indeed the flowers possess five stamens. *Cordifolius* refers to the leaves which are heart shaped with serrated edges and about 2.5cm (1in) long. The plant has spectacularly long tubular flowers produced in very large panicles, appearing at the end of the present year's growth, which can be more than 1m (3ft) long. Each of the lateral branches also produces a small panicle so that the whole branch is smothered in scarlet, lipped flowers. The shrub in full flower is truly spectacular, and the scarlet flowers look particularly effective against a stone wall.

Penstemon cordifolius grows well on any light, well drained soil and tends to suffer more from cold, persistent dampness around the roots in winter than the cold itself. If the weather doesn't prune it, hard prune in mid spring. The resulting growth is rapid and copious and produces the next crop of flowers.

Penstemon cordifolius sets masses of small, grain-like seed in conical capsules which can be easily germinated in spring. Alternatively, propagate from soft tip cuttings taken in late spring. The tip cuttings strike well within a fortnight if kept in an enclosed humid environment, inserted in the usual 50:50 mixture of peat and sand.

PHLOMIS ITALICA

L.

FAMILY
Labiatae

ORIGIN
Balearic Islands

HEIGHT AND SPREAD
1.5m (5ft) × 1m (3ft)

FLOWERING TIME
Midsummer

SPECIAL FEATURES
Pink flowers above grey foliage

CLIMATIC ZONE
Zone 5

Pink whorls of *Phlomis italica*.

Phlomis is one of my favourite genera, and is largely made up of hardy and half-hardy grey-leaved shrubs with some green-leaved hardy herbaceous perennials. Its species are almost all ornamental, and most of them are good garden plants. 'Phlogmos' is Greek, meaning a wick, and the plants probably got their name from the use of the calyces, which are like small felted cones, as candles; the calyces were soaked in dishes of olive oil, and then lit at the tip. This genus is not the only one to be used for this purpose: *Ballota pseudodictamnus*, which means false burning bush, has also been grown and used likewise.

Phlomis italica is an interesting name for a plant wholly native to the Balearic Islands between Spain and North Africa. Linneaus believed the species to have come from Italy. Philip Miller of the Chelsea Physic Garden was evidently confused as well because in 1750 he called the species *rotundifolia* which means round-leaved, although the leaves are long and narrow. *Phlomis italica* is a hardy, grey-leaved shrub, the greyness having both a light silvery quality and a patina of gold. The whole plant − stem, leaf, calyx and even the flower − is densely covered with star-shaped hairs. *Phlomis italica* is a typical *Labiatae*, with four-angled, square stems (although the hairs round off the edges), opposite foliage and hooded flowers in whorls at the leaf nodes around the stem, sometimes more than a dozen pale lilac or pink flowers in each whorl. Often there is a small tuft of foliage terminat-ing each flowering branch above the topmost whorl of flowers. (The genus is usually represented by yellow-flowered Jerusalem sages and this pink species opened my eyes to the colour range of flowers available in other familiar plants.)

Phlomis italica flowers best in a very sunny position and does not mind a fairly poor soil; prune back after flowering. It is useful for spreading itself among rocks or between the gaps of paving stones on a terrace, its herbaceous creeping root system finding its own way among the cracks.

Phlomis italica is hardy but lies somewhere between shrub and herbaceous perennial. It spreads under-ground by means of white succulent herbaceous stems which become woody on contact with the surface air. In very severe weather, the above-ground growth may be killed, but I have never known a healthy mature plant die completely. Very young plants, however, can die as a result of winter weather.

Phlomis italica can easily be propagated from cut-tings of softish growth taken in spring. I always rub off any stellate hairs or bristles from the base of the cuttings. Place the cuttings in an airy frame and water from below, as water on silver foliage tends to encourage rotting. Alternatively, raise from seed or divide large clumps.

PITTOSPORUM TOBIRA

Ait.
FAMILY
Pittosporaceae
ORIGIN
China, Japan, Korea
HEIGHT AND SPREAD
3m (10ft) × 2.1m (7ft)
FLOWERING TIME
Early summer
SPECIAL FEATURES
Glossy evergreen shrub, fragrant flowers
CLIMATIC ZONE
Zone 5

The genus *Pittosporum* has 150 species, mostly found in New Zealand and Australia, although there are a few species, including the delightful *P. tobira*, which come from other parts of the world. 'Pittos' is Greek for pitch and 'sporum' means a seed, a reference to the green seed capsules which are often marked with black sticky pitch-like resin, particularly noticeable in this species. It is not reliably hardy as a free-standing shrub in an exposed site, but is hardier in a shrubbery or against a wall or hedge. It enriches the garden in winter with its lustrous, leathery evergreen foliage and in summer with intoxicating fragrance.

In southern Europe, *P. tobira* reaches tree-like proportions and is also commonly found as a hedge. It is smaller in cold temperate climates, but can be sizeable in very sheltered gardens. The stiff evergreen foliage is borne in tight terminal bunches from many radiating branches and it forms an impenetrable dome-shaped shrub, which lends itself to shaping. The glossy, dark-green leaves are 5cm (2in) long, and have a characteristic blunt tip. Underneath they are pale green. The flower clusters, 7.5cm (3in) or more

across, are produced at the ends of the branchlets from top to bottom of the shrub. The flowers open a pure creamy white, then slowly fade to a sort of yellowy ice-cream colour. Each tubular flower is about 2.5cm (1in) long and nearly as much across. The fragrance is unlike that of any other plant: thick and sweet, arresting without being cloying, like a cross between that of *Daphne mezereum* and *Citrus limon*. It is an almost edible fragrance like a banana-flavoured chewy sweet; I once tried tasting the flowers only to blanch at their surprising astringency. The green, egg-shaped fruits, with their black patches, follow the flowers. I have never come across seedlings growing naturally around the shrub, but presume that under favoured conditions, the seed would be viable.

Pittosporum tobira likes a sandy, well-drained soil but thrives quite happily on alkaline soils in fairly sheltered positions. It flowers best given full sun and wall protection, but is equally at home in a dryish part of the woodland or next to large shrubs in a shrubbery. A small, silver-variegated specimen was

Creamy scented flowers of *Pittosporum tobira*.

proudly shown to me by Lady Wimborne on a recent visit to Guernsey. Probably *P. tobira* 'Variegatum', it was a very handsome plant. *Pittosporum tobira* and its forms will strike easily in late summer from cuttings of slightly woody growth made that year.

PONCIRUS TRIFOLIATA

(L.)   R a f.
FAMILY
Rutaceae
ORIGIN
China
HEIGHT AND SPREAD
4m (13ft) × *3m (10ft)*
FLOWERING TIME
Early summer, often again in autumn
SPECIAL FEATURES
Unusual growth habit, fragrant flowers and fruit
CLIMATIC ZONE
Zone 4

The hardy orange is a very close relation to the well known genus *Citrus*. The plant is truly hardy in the coldest places and very nearly an orange in both flower and fruit. Apart from its extremely hazardous spines, it is one of the most desirable, easy-to-grow shrubs. The sharp spines do give the shrub added character, a kind of coral-like frenzy of branches, and also indicate the kindred genes which it has to the spiny lemon tree. *Poncirus* originates from the old French 'ponsire', which was a form of orange or tangerine.

Poncirus trifoliata when mature is unique in outline, as its branches grow straight for a very short distance before changing their direction. The plant often grows from a single trunk and produces a large dome-shaped canopy, as wide as it is tall and thinly clad with leaves. As the shrub comes into leaf late, this highlights the dark-green, shining branchlets and sharp, extremely rigid spines which may be 5cm (2in) long. The leaves are trifoliate, hence *trifoliata*, and comprise one large central leaflet with two much smaller leaflets on either side. These leaves are dark glossy green on both surfaces and, in common with nearly all *Rutaceae* plants, contain essential oils and so are aromatic when crushed.

Poncirus trifoliata may provide a sensational display of pure white flowers in early summer on leafless branches, then flower again more discreetly among the foliage before the autumn frosts turn it yellow. Each flower is 3.5cm (1½in) across and composed of usually five but sometimes four white petals, surrounding the golden yellow anthers.

The fruit takes a long time to develop and spends most of the summer in obscurity among the dark-green leaves. It is more like a tangerine than an orange in shape, flattened at one end and about 5cm (2in) across. It remains green until long after the foliage has fallen and then turns a striking lemon yellow and darkens to almost orange: a fine sight in winter on the bare branches. This very wrinkled, hard fruit is extremely bitter and unsuitable for eating raw, but quite interesting made into jam or pickle.

Poncirus trifoliata is easy to grow on any light soil in

Poncirus trifoliata, the hardy orange.

full sun, and makes an impenetrable hedge. The green young branches grow quickly but the older ones can be very slow to increase in size, resulting in top-heavy branches which may need careful pruning. Raise from seed sown in spring, or from cuttings of half-ripe wood taken in early or mid-summer.

RIBES SPECIOSUM

Pursh.

FAMILY
Grossulariaceae (Saxifragaceae)

ORIGIN
California

HEIGHT AND SPREAD
2.4m (8ft) × 1.8m (6ft)

FLOWERING TIME
Late spring

SPECIAL FEATURES
Early into leaf, fuchsia-like flowers

CLIMATIC ZONE
Zone 5

Ribes speciosum with its hanging fuchsia-like flowers.

The genus *Ribes* is immortalized in the commercial blackcurrant cordial Ribena. Its name comes from the Arabic 'ribas', meaning acid or astringent in flavour, which many of the currants are. The black, white or red fruits of *Ribes* should not be confused with the dried culinary currant, the fruit of *Vitis vinifera* var. *corinthiaca*, or the Corinthian grape.

Ribes speciosum has flowers carried in clusters of four from the leaf axils (the currant family normally produce racemes of flowers). *Ribes speciosum* was at one time known as *R. fuchsioides*, an appropriate name as the flowers are indeed fuchsia-like, but one that sadly has been superceded by *R. speciosum.* The red pendulous flowers have immensely long stamens which sometimes hang down more than 2.5cm (1in) from the flower.

The leaves are shiny bright green on top and a paler green below, very much the same size and shape as those of the gooseberry, to which it is closely related. The gooseberry-like spines on the younger growth are

bright red, frequently in sets of three with the central spine longer than the outer two.

Ribes speciosum is undoubtedly one of the glories of the genus. It comes into flower early in spring and can sometimes continue producing red fuchsia-like flowers for two or three months. The plant makes a 2.4m (8ft) high rounded shrub in three to four years and once established, can make annual new growth of almost 1.8m (6ft). Layering, which the plant often does naturally, is the easiest and most reliable means of propagation, as cuttings are slow and unreliable and seed rarely sets.

R. speciosum likes an open site with a rich soil and, although it comes from California, is a semi-evergreen shrub, becoming deciduous only in hard winters. In this case, it comes back into leaf very early. I have seen a beautiful specimen growing against a 3m (10ft) high flint wall, the brilliant red flowers offset by the greyish stone.

SALVIA MICROPHYLLA

H. B. K. var. NEUREPIA

FAMILY
Labiatae

ORIGIN
Mexico

HEIGHT AND SPREAD
1m (3ft) × 1.2m (4ft)

FLOWERING TIME
Midsummer to autumn

SPECIAL FEATURES
Aromatic foliage and long flowering season

CLIMATIC ZONE
Zone 5

The bright red flowers of *Salvia microphylla*.

The sages are special favourites of mine for the scope they offer, with potential introductions from Mexico and South America and also hybrids raised from cultivated plants. *Salvia microphylla* var. *neurepia* is included here because it is more widely cultivated than the original species. This variety is grown under several different names and to add to the confusion, there are various different forms in cultivation which have not been given cultivar names.

All forms of *S. microphylla* have semi-evergreen foliage which is strongly scented, rather like blackcurrant leaves on a hot day. The flowers of *S. microphylla* var. *neurepia* are bright scarlet, appearing first in midsummer and continuing until the first autumn frosts, sometimes more than four months later.

The flowers are carried on terminal racemes 15cm (6in) long, and open usually in pairs from the bottom of the raceme up. The flowers, nearly 2.5cm (1in) long, are typical for *Salvia*, with a narrow tube opening out into the two-lipped flowers of the *Labiatae* family. The species has similar flowers but dark carmine red, and there is a pale pinkish-carmine plant which I believe is of hybrid origin and will be called *S. microphylla* 'Oxford'.

Salvia microphylla var. *neurepia* has attractive pale green foliage borne in alternately opposite pairs giving the typical square-angled stems the marvellous symmetry of the *Labiatae* family: paired leaves, paired branches and paired flowers, perfectly distanced between each one.

All the forms of *S. microphylla* are easy to grow, develop fast and flower from seed in two years. The species represents some of the toughest Mexican sages but, even so, is too tender for the coldest positions. Frosts often cut it back hard but it is quick to recover.

Cuttings of soft tip growth root easily, in less than a week in summer, put into 50/50 peat and sand mixture in a heated frame. The plants grow best in a sunny but protected position, and love lime soils.

At Wootton Manor on the warm limestone of Oxfordshire there is a large shrub 1.8m (6ft) tall by as much across. The hot red flowers and pale green foliage go so well against the pale limestone walls and bright blue flowers of the nearby *Commelina caerulea*.

SARCOCOCCA HOOKERIANA

Baill. var. DIGYNA

FAMILY
Buxaceae

ORIGIN
West China

HEIGHT AND SPREAD
1.2m (4ft) × 1m (3ft)

FLOWERING TIME
Mid to late winter

SPECIAL FEATURES
Longevity and fragrance of flowers

CLIMATIC ZONE
Zone 5

Sarcococca hookeriana var. *digyna*, the sweet box, at Kew Gardens.

Evergreen low-growing shrubs are the sweet boxes, sweet because of their powerful fragrance which lingers thickly like honey in pockets of the winter air. *Sarcococca* refers to the fleshy berries which most of the species bear, often at the same time as they flower. Some species are more prolific than others. *Sarcococca hookeriana* var. *digyna* is shy to berry but flowers freely. The sweet boxes have marvellous tight shining evergreen foliage and are useful for very shady areas although they also grow in full sun.

Sarcococca hookeriana var. *digyna* is readily recognizable by the reddish purple tinge to its shoots and leaf midribs. The leaves are lanceolate and 7.5cm (3in) long, the flowers white with faintly pink-tinged stamens. These flowers have a very strong honey-like fragrance which, if picked on a warm winter's day, can emit a scent strong enough to permeate the whole house. The species *S. hookeriana* produces green-stemmed branches and glossy green leaves with flowers which are white with either cream coloured or dusty brown stamens. The species is generally taller than the variety *digyna*, varying from 60cm–1.2m (2–4ft), and not as hardy.

Sarcococca hookeriana var. *digyna* is a particularly useful plant. It produces scented flowers during mid- and late winter when there is little else of interest on display. It makes an attractive shapely evergreen shrub and produces large purplish, almost black fruits, 1cm ($\frac{1}{2}$in) across, which can remain on the plant for many months, even after the flowers.

Like the other species, *S. hookeriana* var. *digyna* thrives on chalky or alkaline soils but they are remarkably resistant and survive a wide range of soil and weather conditions. They prefer half-shade or sun with some shelter from cold winds and are least tolerant of highly acidic soils.

Sarcococca hookeriana var. *digyna* is closely related to *Sarcococca hookeriana* var. *humilis* which only grows to 60cm (2ft) and has very characteristic reddish stems when they first appear. The foliage is smaller than but similar in shape to that of *S. hookeriana*. These three plants have a creeping root system which annually increases the clump by a few centimetres (inches) and which provides an easy means of propagation by division. Alternatively, dry the fruits and sow the seeds in spring. A good flowering plant should result after two years.

SASA VEITCHII

Carr. Rehd.
FAMILY
Gramineae
ORIGIN
Japan
HEIGHT AND SPREAD
1m (3ft) × 60cm (2ft)
FLOWERING TIME
Insignificant flowers
SPECIAL FEATURE
Immensely useful ground cover in dry shade
CLIMATIC ZONE
Zone 4

Sasa veitchii with its scorched leaf edges.

I feel as though I am really sticking my neck out by recommending this plant as being of great garden value. Generally the most favourable literature you can find on it at the moment calls it 'a nuisance' or 'of little garden value'. Yet it is one of the very few plants I know which will steadily colonize an extremely dry shaded part of the garden. It is an evergreen, uniform in height and impenetrable. It also has the unique distinction of producing an impressive variegated effect at the end of the year as the edges of the older leaves die off, quite unlike most other species of *Sasa*.

All bamboos are really woody-stemmed grasses and some are highly ornamental, thanks to their exotic coloured stems and leaves. The genus *Sasa* has certain characteristics which identify it: usually several branches made from each stem and they are relatively low growing with fairly large leaves.

Bamboos, being grasses, do produce green panicles of flowers but this, in most cases, only happens once in the life of the plant and the branches seldom regenerate after flowering. However, it may take up to fifty years to happen and bamboos are interesting for their foliage rather than their flowers. *Sasa veitchii* is one of 200 species of *Sasa* and it grows in creeping clumps. The ends of these branches carry tight uniform clusters of leaves, each 10–15cm (4–6in) long. They are a dark shiny green on the top surface and glaucous beneath, measuring a uniform width of 5cm (2in). Both surfaces of the leaves feature rather prominent central veins. The leaves on a mature clump of *S. veitchii* are particularly spectacular when they start to brown at the edges, especially viewed from a distance.

S. veitchii should be planted thoughtfully as it can swamp smaller plants or wreak havoc on paths and bed edges. It is in its element in a very dry shaded area where nothing else will grow; in damp shade the plant might become too vigorous and invasive.

STACHYURUS CHINENSIS

Franch.

FAMILY
Stachyuraceae

ORIGIN
China

HEIGHT AND SPREAD
1.8m (6ft) × 1.5m (5ft)

FLOWERING TIME
Late winter

SPECIAL FEATURE
Weather-resistant flowers early in the year

CLIMATIC ZONE
Zone 4

Two of the most highly scented winter-flowering deciduous shrubs are wych hazel and wintersweet, followed closely by *Viburnum farreri. Stachyurus chinen-* *sis* lacks scent but surpasses most winter-flowering plants in beauty with its oriental-looking chains of yellow flowers which weigh down the branches. There are only two species of *Stachyurus* which are reliably hardy: *S. chinensis* and the similar but earlier-flowering *S. praecox.*

Stachyurus means spiked tail, a reference to the winter flowers, which are pale yellow and formed along stiff hanging branchlets. The flowers are bell shaped with a dozen or so to each branchlet, creating a packed inflorescence 7.5–15cm (3–6in) long.

At maturity, *S. chinensis* is a large, sprawling deciduous shrub with large, shiny ovate leaves, 7.5×5cm (3×2in). The leaves are similar to those of *Cornus alba*; both have a serrated edge, sometimes with a noticeable red colour, and are produced well after the plant has flowered.

One of the most remarkable features of the flowers is their ability to stand up to the worst weather winter can produce. I have seen them undaunted by blasting easterly winds day after day; where the flowers of hellebore and wych hazel have turned brown, the

Stiff flower spikes of *Stachyurus chinensis.*

Close-up of *Stachyurus chinensis* flower spikes.

off

SYRINGA MEYERI

Schneid.

FAMILY
Oleaceae

ORIGIN
North China

HEIGHT AND SPREAD
2.4m (8ft) × 2.4m (8ft)

FLOWERING TIME
Midsummer

SPECIAL FEATURES
Fragrant lilac flowers on compact growth

CLIMATIC ZONE
Zone 4

brave yellow flowers of *S. chinensis* have only been superficially affected.

Stachyurus chinensis prefers a rich acidic soil but will tolerate a neutral to slightly alkaline soil. If the soil is well drained, the plant should not be allowed to get too dry in summer. It prefers full sun but will tolerate partial shade at the expense of some vigour and restricted flowering. *S. chinensis* and *S. praecox* are hardy enough not to need protection in winter, unlike two other species of *Stachyurus* you may find in cultivation – *S. obovatus* and *S. himalaicus*, which benefit from wall protection.

Stachyurus chinensis may be propagated from semi-ripe cuttings taken in late summer; insert them in a frame in 50:50 peat and sand. Keep them fairly moist until they root some two months later.

Meyer's lilac is recognizable as a lilac, but is very different from the various forms of the ordinary *Syringa vulgaris*. *Syringa* is the correct Latin name for all the lilacs, 'syrinx' being Greek for hollow tube, in recognition of their hollow tube-like stems. (It also gives us our word syringe, incidentally.) This has led to some confusion over the lovely mock orange, *Philadelphus*, which has hollow tubular stems but is no relation.

Syringa meyeri forms a dome-shaped shrub, so thick that it becomes impenetrable even in winter and is an ideal specimen plant for a lawn or other prominent position. I am intending to try it as a low hedge which I am hoping could be pruned after it has flowered although it does not respond favourably to pruning as much of the flowering growth is inevitably lost. The plant produces an abundance of small scoop-shaped leaves, carried on short branchlets borne opposite each other in pairs. At the ends of these branchlets are panicles of fragrant pinkish purple flowers, 5–10cm (2–4in) long, and in midsummer the bush can be literally covered in blossom. *Syringa meyeri* combines a pleasing compactness of habit with a splendid fragrance capable of scenting a wide area of the garden.

It is interesting that *S. meyeri* is known only as a cultivated plant in its native China and is now widely cultivated all over the world. It is extremely hardy, and tolerant of the coldest, windiest positions. *Syringa meyeri* 'Palibin' is a dwarf clone, reaching a

182

Delicately scented *Syringa meyeri*, a dwarf lilac.

maximum height of only 1.2m (4ft). (A clone is a group of plants reproduced only vegetatively from *one* original seedling or stock plant.) It makes a good feature in a rock garden or in a tight corner exposed to harsh weather.

Syringa meyeri prefers a light soil with good drain-age and flowers best in full sun. Propagate from soft tip cuttings taken in early summer before the flower buds develop. The cuttings root quickly in a closed frame and one of the advantages of this lovely plant is that it flowers even on the very youngest plants every year.

VIBURNUM FARRERI

Stearn. 'CANDIDISSIMUM'

FAMILY
Caprifoliaceae

ORIGIN
North China

HEIGHT AND SPREAD
3m (10ft) × 1.8m (6ft)

FLOWERING TIME
Mid to late winter

SPECIAL FEATURE
White, fragrant flowers in winter

CLIMATIC ZONE
Zone 4

Viburnum farreri 'Candidissimum' in winter at Kew Gardens.

It is surprising that this lovely winter shrub, which is quite common in China, took so long to be discovered and that it is still so little known. The type species, *V. farreri*, is more widely grown and is often found commercially under the name *V. fragrans* – an appropriate name but one which sadly was given to another species before the introduction of this plant. However, it is fitting that this shrub is named after Reginald Farrer, a remarkable plantsman; apparently he used to remove the shot from his shotgun cartridges and replace it with alpine seeds to blast into an inaccessible rock face in his garden!

Viburnum farreri is a deciduous shrub with brown twigs and pale pink flowers which have an exquisite fragrance: spicy but honey sweet which lingers in the air on sunny winter days. The plant known as *V. f.* 'Candidissimum' is white-flowered; as with most white forms of an otherwise coloured plant, it has bright green twigs instead of brown and paler green foliage in summer.

Viburnum farreri 'Candidissimum' makes its flowers early in winter and is ready to burst into bloom on milder days. The small flowers are carried in clusters on the ends of the branches and in smaller clusters on the ends of the lateral branches.

It is a densely upright, branched shrub. The bottom branches often bend outwards to reach the light and curve onto the ground where they may root; this is a cheap and easy way to propagate the plant.

Occasionally showy, crimson red, lozenge-shaped fruits set. I have heard that they are edible but didn't find them very palatable myself.

V. farreri 'Candidissimum' is hardy and grows in sun or partial shade. It likes a position where it may have space to grow, but requires shelter from frost and scorching winds which can damage the flowers. If and when this does happen a second crop of flowers is usually produced which may extend the flowering period. The delicious flowers go some way to protect themselves by closing up when very cold, and emerging even daily from their huddled position when warmth encourages them to open. It will tolerate alkaline soil and flowers best if left unpruned and allowed to spread where it will.

ZONE MAP OF NORTH AMERICA

Approximate range of average annual minimum temperatures

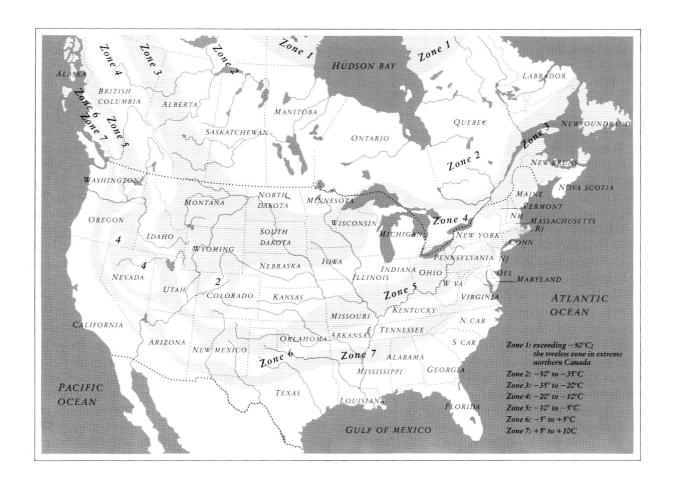

Zone 1: exceeding −50°C; the treeless zone in extreme northern Canada

Zone 2: −50° to −35°C

Zone 3: −35° to −20°C

Zone 4: −20° to −10°C

Zone 5: −10° to −5°C

Zone 6: −5° to +5°C

Zone 7: +5° to +10C

SUPPLIERS AND USEFUL ADDRESSES

Always enclose a stamped addressed envelope when asking for information.
Most nurseries charge a small sum for their catalogues.

ENGLAND

(arranged in alphabetical order
of county)

Traworth Plants,
Orchard House,
Claverton,
Bath,
Avon BA2 7BG
(Unusual herbaceous
perennials)

Terry Adnams,
Thatched Lodge,
Bury's Bank Road,
Crookham Common,
Berks RG15 8DD
Tel: 0635 42566
(Unusual plants)

Hollington Nurseries Ltd,
Woolton Hill,
Newbury,
Berks RG15 9XT
Tel: (Newbury) 0635 253 908
(Herbaceous plants & shrubs)

Savill Garden,
Windsor Great Park,
The Great Park,
Windsor,
Berks SL4 2HT
Tel: (Windsor) 075 35 60222
(Unusual plants)

J. O. Sherrard & Son,
Shaw Nursery,
Newbury,
Berks RG13 2DT
Tel: (Newbury) 0635 41097
(Shrubs)

Antony Estate Nurseries,
Antony Estate,
Torpoint,
Cornwall
Tel: (Plymouth) 0752 812364
(Shrubs & perennials)

M. Holtzhausen,
14 High Cross,
St Austell,
Cornwall PL25 4AH
Tel: (St Austell) 0726 4737
(Unusual herbaceous
perennials)

Redvale Nurseries,
St Tudy,
Bodmin,
Cornwall PL30 3PX
Tel: 0208 850378
(Geraniums)

Trelissick Garden (National
Trust),
Truro,
Cornwall
(Shrubs & perennials)

Barton Alpine Nursery,
Barton House,
Pooley Bridge,
Penrith,
Cumbria CA10 2NG
Tel: (Pooley Bridge) 085 36
260
(Alpines)

Hartside Nursery Garden,
Lowgill House,
Alston,
Cumbria CA9 3BL
(Alpines)

Ednaston Manor Gardens,
Ednaston Manor,
Brailsford,
Nr Derby,
Derbys DE6 3BA
Tel: (Brailsford) 033 528 325
(Shrubs)

Marwood Hill Gardens,
Barnstaple,
Devon EX31 4EB
Tel: (Barnstaple) 0271 2528
(Unusual plants)

Mrs M. Mottram,
Yardewell Cottages,
Yardewell Cross,
S. Molton,
Devon EX36 3HA
(Unusual herbaceous
perennials)

Rosemoor Garden Trust,
Torrington,
Devon EX38 7EG
(Rare shrubs)

Three Counties Nurseries,
Marshwood,
Bridport,
Dorset DT6 5QJ
Tel: 02977 257
(Unusual plants)

Floreat Garden,
148 Albert Road,
Upper Parkstone,
Poole,
Dorset BH12 2HA
Tel: (Parkstone) 0202 746 372
(Variegated plants)

The Knoll Gardens (Wimborne
Botanic),
Stapehill Road,
Wimborne,
Dorset BH21 7ND
Tel: (Ferndown) 0202 873931
(Half-hardy & Australasian
plants)

C. J. Marchant,
Keeper's Hill Nursery,
Nr Stapehill,
Wimborne,
Dorset BH21 7NE
Tel: (Ferndown) 0202 873140
(Unusual plants)

Great Dixter Nurseries,
Northiam,
Rye,
E. Sussex TN31 6PH
Tel: (Northiam) 079 74 3107
(Unusual plants)

The Beth Chatto Gardens,
White Barn House,
Elmstead Market,
Colchester,
Essex CO7 7DB
Tel: (Wivenhoe) 020 622 2007
(Unusual plants)

County Park Nursery,
Essex Gardens,
Hornchurch,
Essex RH11 3BU
Tel: (Hornchurch) 040 24
45205
(New Zealand plants)

Ramparts Nursery,
Baker's Lane,
Braiswick,
Colchester,
Essex CO4 5BD
Tel: (Colchester) 0206 72050
(Silver foliage plants)

Joe Elliot,
Broadwell Nursery,
Broadwell,
Moreton-in-Marsh,
Glos
Tel: (Stow-on-the-Wold) 0541
30549
(Alpines)

Kiftsgate Court Gardens,
Kiftsgate Court,
Chipping Campden,
Glos GL55 6LN
Tel: (Mickleton) 038 677 202
(Unusual plants)

The Priory Gardens,
Kemerton,
Tewkesbury,
Glos
(Unusual plants)

Green Farm Plants (John
Coke),
Bentley,
Nr Alton,

Hants
Tel: (Bentley) 0420 23202
(Unusual plants)

Hillier Nurseries (Winchester)
Ltd,
Ampfield House,
Romsey,
Hants SO5 9PA
Tel: (Braishfield) 0794 68733
(Unusual trees & shrubs)

G. Reuthe Ltd,
Foxhill Nurseries,
Jackass Lane,
Keston,
Hants BR2 6AW
Tel: (Farnborough) 0689
52249
(Unusual shrubs)

Spinners,
School Lane,
Boldne,
Lymington,
Hants SO4 8QE
Tel: (Lymington) 0590 73347
(Unusual plants)

Steven Bailey,
Silver Street,
Hordle,
Hants SO4 8ZA
Tel: 0590 682227
(Unusual plants)

Hellen Ballard,
Old Country,
Mathon,
Malvern,
Hereford & Worcs
(Helleborus & bulbs)

Michael Jefferson-Brown,
Maylite,
Martley,
Hereford & Worcs
Tel: 086 735 780
(Unusual bulbs)

Nerine Nurseries,
Brookend House,
Welland,
Hereford & Worcs WR13 6LN
Tel: 06846 2350
(Unusual bulbs)

Old Court Nurseries Ltd,
Colwall,
Nr Malvern,
Hereford & Worcs WR13 6QE
Tel: (Colwall) 0684 40315
(Unusual shrubs & perennials)

Shieldbrook Garden Nursery,
King's Caple,

Nr Hereford,
Hereford & Worcs HR1 4UB
Tel: (Carey) 043 270 670
(Unusual alpines & perennials)

Spetchley Park,
Spetchley,
Worcester,
Hereford & Worcs WR5 1RS
Tel: (Spetchley) 090 565 224
(Unusual plants)

Stone House Cottage Nurseries
(Arbuthnotts),
Stone,
Nr Kidderminster,
Hereford & Worcs DY10 4BG
Tel: (Kidderminster) 0562
69902
(Unusual climbers & shrubs)

Treasure's of Tenbury Ltd,
Burford House Gardens,
Tenbury Wells,
Hereford & Worcs WR15 8HQ
Tel: (Tenbury Wells) 0584
810777
(Clematis & unusual plants)

Growing Carpets,
The Old Farmhouse,
Steeple Morden,
Nr Royston,
Herts
Tel: 0763 852417
(Ground cover plants)

Hopleys Plants Ltd,
High Street,
Much Hadham,
Herts SG10 6BU
Tel: (Much Hadham) 027 984
2509
(Unusual plants)

Little Heath Farm Nursery,
Little Heath Lane,
Potten End,
Berkhamsted,
Herts HP4 2RY
Tel: (Berkhamsted) 04427
4951
(Unusual perennials)

Sissinghurst Castle Garden
(National Trust),
Cranbrook,
Kent TN17 2AB
Tel: (Cranbrook) 0580 712850
(Unusual plants)

Graham Trevor,
Sandwich Nurseries,
Dover Road,
Sandwich,
Kent CT13 0DG

Tel: 0304 614377
(Half-hardy & tender plants)

Washfield Nursery,
Horns Road,
Hawkhurst,
Kent TN18 4QU
Tel: (Hawkhurst) 058 05 2522
(Unusual perennials)

Holden Clough Nurseries,
Bolton by Bowland,
Clitheroe,
Lancs
Tel: (Bolton by Bowland)
02007 615
(Alpines)

Reginald Kaye Ltd,
Waithman Nurseries,
Lindetts Road,
Silverdale,
Lancs LA5 0TY
Tel: (Silverdale) 0524 701252
(Alpines & ferns)

Doris Horne Hardy Plants,
25 Station Road,
Timberland,
Lincs LN4 3SA
Tel: (Martin) 052 67 363
(Unusual foliage plants)

Potterton & Martin,
The Cottage Nursery,
Moortown Road,
Nettleton,
Caistor,
Lincs LN7 6HX
(Unusual herbaceous perennials
& bulbs)

Amands Garden Centre Ltd,
17 Beethoven Street,
London W10 7LG
Tel: 01 883 0821
(Bulbs)

D. B. Herbert,
The Nursery,
4 Old Park Road,
Palmer's Green,
London N13 4RE
Tel: 01 886 0269
(Unusual shrubs & half-hardy
perennials)

Perry's Hardy Plant Farm Ltd,
Theobald's Park Road,
Enfield,
Middx EN2 9BG
Tel: 01 363 4207
(Unusual plants)

Blooms of Bressingham Ltd,
Bressingham,

Diss,
Norfolk IP22 2AB
Tel: (Bressingham) 037 988 464
(Unusual plants)

Read's Nursery,
Hales Hall,
Loddon,
Norwich,
Norfolk NR14 6QW
Tel: (Raveningham) 050 846
395
(Unusual shrubs & rare fruit)

Mrs M. Lawley,
Herterton House Garden
Nursery,
Hartington,
Cambo,
Morpeth,
Northumberland
Tel: (Scotsgap) 067 074 278
(Unusual herbaceous
perennials)

Howard Waters & Son,
Beech Hill Nurseries,
Swanland,
North Ferriby,
N. Yorks HU14 3QY
Tel: 0482 633670
(Unusual geraniums)

V. H. Humphrey,
8 Howbeck Road,
Arnold,
Nottingham,
Notts NG5 8AD
Tel: (Nottingham) 0602
260510
(Iris specialist)

Morton Hall Gardens,
Ranby,
Retford,
Notts
(Unusual herbaceous perennials)

Eskdaleside Plants Ltd,
Hollins Farm House,
Eskdaleside,
Grosmount,
Nr Whitby,
N. Yorks
Tel: 0947 85332
(Unusual & rare herbaceous
plants; alpines)

Oland Plants,
Sawley Nursery,
Risplith,
Ripon,
N. Yorks HG4 3EW
(Unusual herbaceous
perennials; alpines)

Marten's Hall Farm,
Longworth,
Abingdon,
Oxon OX13 5EP
Tel: (Longworth) 0865 820 376
(Unusual plants)

Castle's Alpines,
Castle Road,
Wootton,
Woodstock,
Oxon OX7 1EG
Tel: (Woodstock) 0993 812162
(Alpines)

Waterpenny Horticultural
Centre,
Nr. Wheatley,
Oxon OX9 1JZ
Tel: (Ickford) 084 47 226
(Alpines & herbaceous
perennials)

Oak Cottage Herb Farm,
Nesscliffe,
Nr Shrewsbury,
Salop SY44 1DB
Tel: (Nesscliffe) 074 381 262
(Unusual plants)

Rev R. J. Blakeway-Philips,
Church Cottage,
Clun,
Craven Arms,
Salop
(Unusual bulbs)

Broadleigh Gardens,
Barr House,
Bishop's Hull,
Taunton,
Somerset TA4 1AE
Tel: (Taunton) 0823 86231
(Unusual bulbs)

Clapton Court Gardens,
Crewkerne,
Somerset
Tel: 0460 73220
(Unusual plants)

Hadspen House Garden,
Hadspen House,
Castle Cary,
Somerset
Tel: (Castle Cary) 096 35 200
(Unusual plants)

The Margery Fish Nursery,
East Lambrook Manor,
South Petherton,
Somerset TA13 5HL
Tel: (South Petherton) 0460
40328
(Unusual herbaceous perennials
& silver foliage plants)

Notcutts Garden Centre,
Woodbridge,
Suffolk IP12 4AF
Tel: (Woodbridge) 039 43
3344
(Shrubs & perennials)

Rickerts Nursery,
Yoxford,
Suffolk IP17 3LA
Tel: (Yoxford) 072 877 451
(Unusual plants)

Heady J. Stapel-Valk,
Paradise Centre,
Twinstead Road,
Lamarsh,
Bures,
Suffolk C0A 5EX
Tel: (Twinstead) 078 729
449
(Rare bulbs)

Michael Haworth-Booth,
Farall Nurseries,
Roundhurst Lane,
Blackdown Hill,
Nr Haslemere,
Surrey GU27 3BN
Tel: (Fernhurst) 042 875 224
(Shrubs)

Lye End Nursery,
Lye End Link,
St John's,
Woking,
Surrey GU21 1SW
Tel: (Woking) 048 62 69327
(Alpines & herbaceous plants)

RHS Enterprises Plant Sales
Centre,
RHS Garden,
Wisley,
Nr Woking,
Surrey GU23 6QB
Tel: (Ripley) 048 643 3524
(Unusual plants)

Cypress Nursery,
Powke Lane,
Blackheath,
Birmingham,
W. Midlands
Tel: 021 559 1495
(Pelargoniums)

A. Goatcher & Son,
The Nurseries,
Rock Road,
Washington,
Nr Pulborough,
W. Sussex RH20 3BJ
Tel: (Ashington) 0903 892 626
(Unusual plants)

Holly Gate Nurseries,
Billingshurst Lane,
Ashington,
W. Sussex RH20 3BA
Tel: (Ashington) 0903 892439
(Unusual plants & Iridaceae)

W. E. Ingwersen Ltd,
Birch Farm Nursery,
Gravetye,
East Grinstead,
W. Sussex RH19 4LE
Tel: (East Grinstead) 0342
810236
(Alpines)

Charles Kershaw,
The Nurseries & Garden
Centre,
Halifax Road,
Brighouse,
W. Yorks HD6 2QD
Tel: (Brighouse) 0484 713435
(Shrubs)

David Austin,
Bowling Green Lane,
Albrighton,
Wolverhampton WV7 3HB
Tel: 090 722 2142
(Paeonies)

IRELAND

Irish Garden Plant Society,
c/o Nat. Bot. Gardens,
Glasnevin,
Dublin 9

Carbery Nurseries,
Kilmatead,
Clondalkin,
Nr. Baldonnell,
Dublin
(Unusual shrubs)

Castletownbere Nursery,
Rodeen,
Castletownbere,
Co. Cork
(Unusual plants)

Murphy and Wood's Garden
Centre,
Hills Hire,
Johnston Road,
Cabinteely,
Co. Dublin
(Unusual plants, especially
alpines)

Orchardstown Garden Centre,
Butlerstown,
Cork Road,
Waterford
(Unusual plants)

SCOTLAND

Crarae Woodland Garden,
Cumlodden Estate Office,
Furnace,
Inveraray
Argyll & Bute PA32 8XO
Tel: (Furnace) 049 95 286
(Unusual plants)

The Garden Nursery,
Dunniglen,
Forfar,
Angus
(Unusual herbaceous
perennials)

Edrom Nurseries,
Coldingham,
Eyemouth,
Berwick TD14 5TZ
(Unusual herbaceous plants)

The Linn Nursery,
Cove,
Dumbarton
Tel: (Kelcreggan) 043 684
2242
(Less hardy shrubs & herbaceous
perennials)

King & Paton,
Barnhourie,
by Dalbeattie,
Stewartry DG5 4PU
Tel: (Southwick) 033 778 269
(Herbaceous plants)

Aberchalder Alpine Nursery,
Gorthleck,
Inverness IV1 26J
(Alpines)

Jack Drake,
Inshriach Alpine Plant
Nursery,
Aviemore,
Badenoch & Strathspey PH22
1QS
Tel: (Kincraig) 054 04 287
(Alpines)

Glendoick Garden Centre,
Glendoick,
by Perth
Perth & Kinross PH2 7NS
Tel: (Glencarse) 073 886 205
(Unusual plants)

Plus Trees,
Auchterarder House,
Auchterarder,
Perth & Kinross
Tel: (Auchterarder) 076 46
2950
(Unusual trees & shrubs)

WALES

Bodnant Garden Nursery,
Tal-y-cafn,
Colwyn Bay,
Clwyd LL28 5RE
Tel: (Tyn-y-Groes) 049 267
460
(Unusual shrubs)

P. J. & J. W. Christian,
Pentre Cottages,
Minera,
Wrexham,
Clwyd
Tel: (Wrexham) 0978 366399
(Unusual bulbs, corms &
tubers)

Rosamund's Garden Centre,
Hawarden Castle,
Deeside,
Clwyd CH5 3NY
Tel: (Hawarden) 0244 532294
(Unusual shrubs)

Powys Castle (National Trust),
Welshpool,
Powys
Tel: (Welshpool) 0938 2554
(Unusual plants)

The following addresses should
prove useful in advising you of
unusual plant suppliers in your
area:

AUSTRALIA

Association of Societies for
Growing Australian Plants Inc,
c/o Post Office,
Shenton Park,
Western Australia 6008

Canberra Horticultural Society
Inc,
GPO Box 1388,
Canberra,
ACT 2601

Horticultural Association of
South Australia,
Box 43,
P.O. Rundle Mail,
South Australia 5000

Queensland Council of Garden
Clubs,
8 Martock Street,
Camp Hill,
Queensland 4152

Royal Horticultural Society of
NSW,
55 Railway Parade,
Peakhurst,
New South Wales 2601

Royal Horticultural Society of
Victoria,
418A Station Street,
Box Hill South,
Victoria 3128

Western Australian
Horticultural Council,
P.O. Box 135,
Claremont,
Western Australia 6010

CANADA

Canadian Horticultural
Council,
3 Amberwood Crescent,
Nepean ON K2E 7L1
Tel: 631 226 4187

Canadian Society for
Horticultural Science,
Agriculture Canada,
Research Station,
Box 1000,
Agassiz BC V0M 1A0

Canadian Botanical
Association,
Dept. of Botany,
University of Alberta,
Edmonton AB T6G 2E9

NEW ZEALAND

Royal NZ Institute of
Horticulture Inc,
P.O. Box 12,
Lincoln College,
Canterbury

SOUTH AFRICA

The Botanical Society of South
Africa,
Head Office,
Kirstenbosch,
Private Bag X7,
7735 Claremont
Cape Province
Tel: 771166

Orange Free State Botanic
Garden,
P.O. Box 1536,
9300 Bloemfontein,
Orange Free State
Tel: 313530

Botanic Gardens,
Botanic Gardens Road,
4001 Durban,
Natal
Tel: 211303

The Pretoria National Botanic
Garden,
2 Cussonia Road,
Private Bag X101,
Brummeria,
0001 Pretoria (0184 for street
address)
Transvaal
Tel: 861164/5/6 861170

USA

Write to your state
horticultural society for the
addresses of local nurseries and
garden centres. The following
addresses should also prove
useful.

American Horticultural
Society,
Box 0105,
Mount Vernon, VA 22121
Tel: (703) 5700

The Garden Club of America,
598 Madison Avenue,
New York NY 10022
Tel: (212) 753 8287/88/89/90

Gardens for All,
180 Flynn Avenue,
Burlington VT 05401
Tel: (802) 863 1308

Massachusetts Horticultural
Society,
300 Massachusetts Avenue,
Boston MA 02115
Tel: (617) 536 9280

Men's Garden Clubs of America
Inc,
5560 Merle Hay Road,
Des Moines IA 50325
Tel: (515) 278 0295

National Council of State
Garden Clubs Inc,
4401 Magnolia Ave,
St Louis MO 63110
Tel: (314) 776 7574

Publishers' note: While every
effort has been made to ensure
the accuracy of the names,
addresses and telephone
numbers of suppliers and useful
organizations, readers should
remember that these are liable
to change at short notice. We
should welcome any corrections
to these pages, and advise
readers to telephone any nursery
before visiting it.

BIBLIOGRAPHY

Bean, W. J., *Trees and Shrubs Hardy in Great Britain*, John Murray, (eighth edition) 1980

Farrer, R., *The English Rock Garden* vols 1 & 2, E. C. & T. C. Jack Ltd, (third edition) 1925

Grey, C. H., *Hardy Bulbs* vols 1–3, William and Norgate, London, 1938

Grey-Wilson, C., & Mathew, B., *Bulbs*, Collins, 1981

Grey-Wilson, C., & Mathews, V., *Gardening on Walls*, Collins, 1983

Heywood, V. H., *Flowering Plants of the World*, Oxford University Press, 1978

Hortorium, L. H. B., *Hortus III*, Macmillan, New York, 1976

Mathew, B., *The Dwarf Bulbs*, Batsford, 1973

Mathew, B., *The Larger Bulbs*, Batsford, 1978

Menninger, E. H., *Flowering Vines of the World*, Hearthside Press, New York, 1970

Miller, Philip, *The Gardener's Dictionary*, The Chelsea Physic Garden, London, 1768

Perry, F., *Collins Guide to Border Plants*, Collins, 1957

Phillips, R., & Rix, M., *The Bulb Book*, Pan, 1981

Rehder, A., *Manual of Cultivated Trees & Shrubs*, Macmillan, (second edition) 1974

Stuart Thomas, G., *Perennial Garden Plants*, Dent, 1976

Willis, J. C., *Dictionary of Flowering Plants & Ferns*, Cambridge University Press, (eighth edition) 1973

Botanical Journal of the Linnaean Society vol. 87 & vol. 92, 1983 & 1986

The Botanical Register, James Ridgway & Sons, 1815–1847, London

Curtis' Botanical Magazine 1786–1987, The Royal Botanical Gardens, Kew

The European Garden Flora vols 1 & 2, Cambridge University Press

Flora Europaea vols 1–5, Cambridge University Press, 1964

Loddiges Botanical Cabinet 1818–1833, Loddiges

The R.H.S. Dictionary of Gardening vols 1–4, Oxford, (second edition) 1974

..

INDEX